Birgit Abegg, Michael Benford

Communication for Business

Satzbausteine

Zeitgemäße englische Handelskorrespondenz und Bürokommunikation

Hueber Verlag

6. 5. 4. | Die letzten Ziffern
2011 10 09 08 07 | bezeichnen Zahl und Jahr des Druckes.
Alle Drucke dieser Auflage können, da unverändert,
nebeneinander benutzt werden.
1. Auflage

Verlagsredaktion: Cornelia Dietz, München
Umschlaggestaltung, Layout und Herstellung: Christiane Gerstung, München
Druck und Bindung: Firmengruppe APPL, aprinta druck, Wemding
Printed in Germany
ISBN 978-3-19-032617-4

Vorwort

Die Benutzung elektronischer Kommunikationsmittel in allen Bereichen des heutigen Geschäftslebens führt zu einer ganzen Reihe wichtiger Veränderungen. Die Kommunikation ist vor allem schneller und infolgedessen weniger förmlich geworden. Faxe werden in Sekundenschnelle an ihren Bestimmungsort gezaubert; E-Mails finden mit ähnlicher Geschwindigkeit ihren Weg durch das Computernetz; das Internet bietet die Gelegenheit, 24 Stunden täglich an Informationen zu gelangen und diese zu übermitteln. Viele Botschaften werden einfach auf dem Bildschirm gelesen und dann zum späteren Gebrauch gespeichert, ohne dass man sie jemals ausdruckt. „Post" existiert nicht mehr nur in schriftlicher Form, weil sie um die „mündliche Post" bereichert worden ist. Dies bedeutet jedoch nicht, dass keine Briefe mehr geschrieben werden. Der traditionelle Brief spielt immer noch eine wichtige Rolle in der Geschäftswelt, teilt jedoch heute sein Dasein mit schnelleren elektronischen Möglichkeiten.

Alle diese Faktoren sind bei der Erstellung von **Communication for Business** in Betracht gezogen worden.

Das neue Merkmal des **Lehrbuchs** und der vorliegenden **Satzbausteine** ist jedoch die Vorgehensweise bei der schriftlichen Kommunikation. Lernende werden nicht, wie noch vielfach üblich, aufgefordert, vom Deutschen ins Englische zu übersetzen. Stattdessen werden sie ermutigt, ihre schriftliche Arbeit unter Benutzung des „Letter Plan" (Briefgliederung) in jeder Lehrbuch-Einheit und mit Hilfe der **Satzbausteine** zu strukturieren. Die **Satzbausteine** enthalten eine umfassende Sammlung von Ausdrücken, die so ausgerichtet sind, dass sie miteinander verbunden grammatikalisch korrekte und stilistisch einwandfreie Sätze ergeben. Dies ist eine unschätzbare Hilfe sowohl für die Arbeit mit **Communication for Business** im Unterricht als auch für die tägliche Arbeit im Büro. Ab Seite 10 zeigt der „rote Faden", wie mit Hilfe der einzelnen Bausteine ein kompletter und korrekter Brief entsteht. * bedeutet, dass dieser Teil je nach Bedarf in den Brief aufgenommen werden kann.

Selbstverständlich wird auch der traditionelleren Art der Handelskorrespondenz in den Phraseologieabschnitten der **Satzbausteine** Rechnung getragen.

Die in **Communication for Business** enthaltenen Materialien sind mit einer Vielzahl von Schülern und Schülerinnen über mehrere Jahre getestet und entsprechend geändert worden. Einige Kapitel wurden Kollegen und Kolleginnen aus der Praxis zur Prüfung und Ergänzung vorgelegt. In diesem Zusammenhang möchten wir den Schülern und Schülerinnen, Kollegen und Kolleginnen am Robert-Schuman-Berufskolleg der Stadt Essen und der Industrie- und Handelskammer zu Düsseldorf für ihre Hilfe, ihren wertvollen Rat und die konstruktive Kritik danken. Des Weiteren geht unser Dank an Herrn David Duckworth, Member of the Institute of Export, London, Frau Sparkassen-Betriebswirtin Sabine Quandt, Wuppertal, und Herrn Speditionskaufmann Thomas Dünnwald, Düsseldorf, die uns wertvolle Informationen aus ihren Fachbereichen zukommen ließen.

Birgit Abegg, Michael Benford

Contents

Unit 1

Layouts

How the inside address, salutation and complimentary close are linked:

British Forms

	Inside address	Salutation	Complimentary Close	Comments
1	The Manager	Dear Sir or Madam (Dear Sir / Madam)	Yours faithfully	The writer does not know the manager's name.
2	Mr David Brown	Dear Mr Brown	Yours sincerely	The writer knows the recipient's full name but addresses the letter to 'Mr Brown', which is more formal.
3	Mr David Brown	Dear David	Yours sincerely or: With best regards or: Best regards or: Regards	The writer is on first name terms with the recipient. 'With best regards', 'Best regards' and 'Regards' are friendly, less formal endings.
4	Ms Denise Brown Miss Denise Brown Mrs Denise Brown	Dear Ms Brown Dear Miss Brown Dear Mrs Brown	Yours sincerely	The writer knows the recipient's name so he uses it.
5	Ms Denise Brown Miss Denise Brown Mrs Denise Brown	Dear Denise	Yours sincerely	The writer is on first name terms with the recipient.
6	The Metal Box Company Ltd	Dear Sirs	Yours faithfully	The writer addresses the company using the impersonal plural form "Dear Sirs". He could also write "Dear Sir".
7	Designer Mode Ltd	Dear Designer Mode	Yours sincerely	This is a more modern and informal way of writing to a company.

American Forms

	Inside address	Salutation	Complimentary Close	Comments
1	Electronic Communications Corp.	Dear Ms. (name), or: Dear Ms. (name): or: Dear Mr. (name), or: Dear Mr. (name): or: Ladies and Gentlemen: or: Gentlemen and Ladies: or: To Whom It May Concern: or: No salutation at all (subject line instead)	Sincerely, or: Sincerely yours, or: Very truly yours, or: Yours truly, or: Yours very truly,	Try to write to a named person.
2	Electronic Communications Corp.	Dear Customer, or: Dear Supplier: or: Dear Investor, etc.	Sincerely, or: Sincerely yours,	This is used if the letter cannot be addressed to an individual person. The use of the word "customer" etc. still gives it a personal touch.
3	Mr. James Sylvester	Dear Mr. Sylvester, or: Dear Mr. Sylvester:	Sincerely, or: Sincerely yours,	Standard usage in the USA
4	Mrs. Rita Curtis:	Dear Mrs. Curtis: or: Dear Mrs. Curtis,	Sincerely, or: Sincerely yours,	Standard usage in the USA
5	Ms. Carol Kinlan	Dear Carol, or: Dear Carol:	Cordially, or: Sincerely,	The writer is on first name terms with the recipient.

Unit 2

Enquiries

1 Source of address	We have been given your company's address by We have been referred to you by	the Chamber of Commerce (the) … bank the … (country) Embassy the … (country) Consulate	in … (location)
	We have seen your company's stand at (the current) … We were most impressed by the products your company demonstrated at (the) …	… Exhibition … Trade Fair … Show	
	We saw your company's stand at (the recent) … We saw your goods demonstrated at (the recent)		
	We have seen your advertisement in	this week's/month's/quarter's/the latest edition/the current issue	of … (name of publication, e.g. Business Weekly)
	We saw your advertisement in	last week's/month's/quarter's/the last edition	
	We have seen the above-mentioned advertisement		
	We have seen your home page on the Internet		
	… and are/were (most) impressed by … … and are/were (most) interested in … … and would like to know more about … … and would be interested in receiving some information on … … and would be pleased to receive some information …	your company's products/services	
	We have obtained your company's/your name from …	The Yellow Pages The Lancashire Business Directory etc.	
	Your company has/you have been recommended to us by … Your/your company's address has been passed on to us by … Your name has been given to us by … You have been named as a reference by … We have been told that you might be prepared to provide a reference by … We have been told by … We have learned from …	… (name of person/company, e.g. Joan Thomas and Associates)	

	We have heard that you/your company …		manufacture(s) produce(s) import(s) distribute(s) wholesale(s) supply (supplies) retail(s) act(s) as an agent for	… (goods, e.g. furniture/fashion garments/packaging material etc.)		
			provide(s) a/an offer(s) a/an	comprehensive same-day on-the-spot 24-hour reliable punctual prompt	repair replacement spare parts maintenance after-sales advertising marketing advisory delivery	service
2 Description of your company	Our company is a We are a As a	major leading well-established well-known successful fast-growing	manufacturer of … producer of … importer of … distributor of … wholesaler of … supplier of … retailer of … agent for … … company … contractor	with	• excellent/well-established/extensive business contacts • an excellent reputation (for … + product/service) • a well-established/an extensive sales network • branches • offices • a factory (factories) • a plant (plants) • a distribution centre (distribution centres) • a warehouse (warehouses) • a depot (depots)	in … all over/throughout … (e.g. Germany, Europe, the EU etc.) both at home and abroad both in Europe and overseas in all major German/European cities in the EU and beyond
– reason for your enquiry	We are interested in …		… (goods/services) importing … marketing … wholesaling … retailing … supplying our customers with …			

	There is • substantial • considerable • great • growing		demand for … (goods/services) interest in … (goods/services)	among … (e.g. retailers/wholesalers, local business people etc.) on the local market in this country in the EU
	There is a • large • considerable • growing • ready		market for … (goods/services)	in … (location)
	The market for … (goods/services)		is expanding is growing	rapidly steadily at a fast rate day by day/week by week/month by month
	As goods of this nature As this type of product	are is	in demand most popular selling well	at present at the moment at this time of year as a result of … (this year's fashion trends, etc.)
		will be		in the … (e.g. summer) season in … (e.g. the (coming) spring/summer/autumn/winter) next … (e.g. month/season etc.)
	As we are now very low on … (goods/material(s)) As we are almost out of … As we have almost run out of … As our stocks/supplies of … are running low Due to the fact that our stocks/supplies of … are now almost exhausted …			
3 What you require – quotation	Please We would therefore like you to We would therefore be grateful if you would		quote us for send us a quotation for let us have your quotation for let us have your offer for quote us your lowest price(s) for let us have your most favourable quotation for give us details of your terms for	… (goods/services)

... including (details of)	all discounts discounts for an initial order quantity discounts introductory offer discounts trade discounts cash discounts early payment discounts
Is there an extra charge for Do you charge extra for	seaworthy packing? special packing?
We would require the goods to be supplied Would it be possible for the goods to be supplied Are you willing to supply goods The goods would need to be supplied	on a sale-or-return basis on approval
What quantity is required for What is the minimum quantity required for How much (...)/many (...) would you need to supply for	a trial order? a trial shipment?

We must point out that ... We would point out that ... We think it only fair to tell you that	we are only in the market for we are only interested in we will only consider our customers will only accept	top-quality top-grade high-quality first-class first-rate up-market competitively priced	goods products articles	with a/an backed by a/an	full comprehensive same-day on-the-spot 24-hour reliable punctual prompt	after-sales repair replacement spare parts maintenance advertising marketing advisory delivery	service
					six-month/one-year	• guarantee • warranty	

– information	Please let us have ... Please supply us with ... We would (therefore) be grateful if you could supply us with ...	(comprehensive) information on ... (comprehensive) details of ... a (detailed) description of ... descriptions of ...	your (entire) range of ... (e.g. furniture/fashion garments/goods/services) your (entire) product range all the goods you manufacture/produce/market/distribute/sell/export/import
		any (relevant) information you may have on ... the address(es) of .../the names and addresses of ... a profile of ... (e.g. a company) a (credit) reference on ... (e.g. a person, a company)	

4 Asking for – sales material	Please … Would you please … We would be grateful if you would … We would appreciate it if you would … Before we can place an order we would ask you to …		send us let us have supply us with provide us with post us mail us	your latest your current your most recent a recent	(illustrated colour) catalogue (illustrated colour) brochure	and your current (export) price list
				(some) sales literature on … a leaflet on … some leaflets on … a pamphlet on … some pamphlets on …		
– samples				a sample of … some samples of … a demonstration model a pattern … (some) patterns …		
– representative's/ agent's visit	Please arrange to have your representative/agent		call by visit us pay us a visit	in the near future in the next few … (e.g. days/weeks etc.) before + date (e.g. the end of the month) as soon as possible		
	Would it be possible		to have the goods demonstrated to us for your representative/agent to demonstrate the goods to us for your representative/agent to show us some samples/patterns		on our premises in our factory at our … (location) branch at our … (location) subsidiary at our Head Office in … (location)	
	Please have	your representative/agent	demonstrate the	machine machinery equipment apparatus tool(s)		
	Please ask We would be grateful if you would ask		to demonstrate the			
			to bring us some samples/patterns/a demonstration model (demonstration models)			

5	Asking about – terms (delivery and payment)	Please let us have details of your (most favourable) terms of delivery and payment Please state your terms of delivery and payment Full details of your terms of delivery and payment would be appreciated	
	– terms of delivery	Please quote us … Please let us have your quotation for delivery … We would require delivery … Are you able to deliver … Can deliveries be made …	… e.g. ex works/CIF German port/CPT Frankfurt Airport/FCA London Airport/franco … (location)/franco to our premises, carriage paid/carriage forward, etc.
	– delivery date/period	Delivery/deliveries • must • should • would need to be made We would require delivery to Could delivery/deliveries	by + date (e.g. 1 December) within + period (e.g. 3 weeks) after receipt of our order on a regular basis every … (e.g. month/2 weeks) once/twice a … (e.g. week/month) from stock
	– delivery	Are you able to deliver Are you able to supply us We would require delivery	by lorry/by rail/by air/by ship/by inland waterway vessel/by container/by special messenger/by airmail/by surface mail/by air freight
	– terms of payment	Please let us have (full) details of your terms of payment	
		Can payment be made Will you accept payment	on receipt of the goods/on receipt of your invoice/within 30 days after receipt of the goods/by cheque/by banker's draft/by bill of exchange/by bank transfer/by international money order (IMO)?
6	References*	References can be obtained from … … (name of bank/company, e.g. the Deutsche Bank in Düsseldorf/the Holzmann AG in Berlin) will be happy to provide a reference on us/on our company Should you require references please contact …, who will be pleased to supply you with any information you may desire … (name of bank/company) will be pleased to supply you with a reference on our company, if required We have excellent trade and bank references and enclose a list of our major business partners, who will be pleased to provide you with any information you may require on our company We will be happy to provide you with the usual bank and trade references	

7	Polite ending	If your/your company's goods/services	meet our requirements meet our customers' expectations correspond to our customers' wishes find our customers' approval	we will	(be able to) (be willing to) (be prepared to) (be in a position to)	place a large order (large orders) place a substantial order (substantial orders) place a sizeable order (sizeable orders) place a considerable order (considerable orders) place a large-scale order (for …) order a large amount (of …) order a large number (of …) order a large quantity (of …) place regular orders (for …) order (…) (from your company) on a regular basis order all our … (s) from your company
		Hoping to hear from you soon We hope to hear from you shortly Many thanks in advance for your attention to our enquiry Please let us have your offer as soon as possible We look forward to your reply with interest We look forward to your early reply A prompt reply to this enquiry would be most appreciated				
8	Enclosure(s)	Bank reference: Deutsche Bank, Essen, Germany Trade reference: Holzmann AG, Berlin, Germany				

Phraseology

Enquiries

1	**Source of address**	***Quelle der Anschrift***
	We have been given your company's address by the chamber of commerce in Düsseldorf	*Wir erhielten die Anschrift Ihrer Firma von der Handelskammer in Düsseldorf*
	We have seen your advertisement in this week's edition of "Business Weekly"	*Wir haben Ihre Anzeige in der Ausgabe dieser Woche des „Business Weekly" gesehen*
	We saw your advertisement in last week's edition of "Business Weekly"	*Wir sahen Ihre Anzeige in der Ausgabe des „Business Weekly" von letzter Woche*
	We have seen the above-mentioned advertisement	*Wir haben die oben erwähnte Anzeige gesehen*
	We have seen your home page on the Internet	*Wir haben Ihre Homepage im Internet gesehen*
	We have heard that your company manufactures furniture	*Wir haben gehört, dass Ihre Firma Möbel herstellt*
	We have heard that your company offers a reliable after-sales service	*Wir haben gehört, dass Ihre Firma einen verlässlichen Kundendienst anbietet*
2	**Description of your company**	***Beschreibung Ihrer Gesellschaft***
	Our company is a leading importer of fashion garments with excellent business contacts all over the EU and beyond	*Unsere Gesellschaft ist ein führender Importeur von modischer Kleidung mit exzellenten Geschäftsverbindungen innerhalb und außerhalb der EU*
	– reason for your enquiry	***– Grund für Ihre Anfrage***
	We are interested in marketing goods of this nature	*Wir sind daran interessiert, Waren dieser Art zu vertreiben*
	There is substantial demand for these articles on the local market	*Es besteht umfangreiche Nachfrage nach diesen Artikeln auf dem örtlichen Markt*
	As this type of product is in demand at present …	*Da diese Art von Produkt zur Zeit nachgefragt wird …*
	As we are now very low on raw materials …	*Da wir zur Zeit nur geringe Vorräte an Rohmaterialien haben, …*
3	**What you require:** **– quotation**	***Was Sie benötigen:*** ***– Angebot***
	We would therefore be grateful if you would quote us for 100 bales of top-grade cotton including details of all discounts	*Wir wären Ihnen daher dankbar, wenn Sie uns ein Angebot für 100 Ballen erstklassiger Baumwolle einschließlich der Einzelheiten aller Nachlässe unterbreiten würden*
	Is there an extra charge for seaworthy packing?	*Gibt es eine zusätzliche Gebühr für seemäßige Verpackung?*
	Are you willing to supply goods on approval?	*Sind Sie bereit, Waren zur Ansicht zu liefern?*
	What is the minimum quantity required for a trial shipment?	*Welche Mindestmenge wird für eine Probelieferung benötigt?*

	We must point out that our customers will only accept top-quality articles backed by a comprehensive repair service	*Wir müssen darauf hinweisen, dass unsere Kunden nur Artikel erster Qualität in Verbindung mit einem umfassenden Reparatur-Service akzeptieren*
	– information	***– Information***
	We would therefore be grateful if you could supply us with (comprehensive) details of your (entire) range of fashion garments	*Wir wären Ihnen deshalb dankbar, wenn Sie uns (umfassende) Einzelheiten Ihrer (gesamten) Palette von modischer Kleidung zukommen lassen könnten*
4	**Asking for**	***Bitte um***
	– sales material / samples	***– Verkaufsmaterial / Muster***
	We would appreciate it if you would provide us with your latest illustrated colour catalogue together with some samples of your goods	*Wir würden es begrüßen, wenn Sie uns Ihren neuesten, illustrierten Farbkatalog (zusammen) mit einigen Mustern Ihrer Waren zur Verfügung stellen würden*
	– representative's / agent's visit	***– Besuch des Vertreters / Beauftragten***
	Please arrange to have your representative call by in the next few days	*Bitte veranlassen Sie, dass Ihr Vertreter / Ihre Vertreterin in den nächsten Tagen bei uns vorbeikommt*
	Would it be possible to have the goods demonstrated to us on our premises?	*Wäre es möglich, uns die Waren in unseren Geschäftsräumen vorführen zu lassen?*
5	**Asking about**	***Fragen nach***
	– terms (delivery and payment)	***– (Liefer- und Zahlungs-)Bedingungen***
	Please let us have details of your (most favourable) terms of delivery and payment	*Bitte geben Sie uns Einzelheiten Ihrer (günstigsten) Liefer- und Zahlungsbedingungen*
	– terms of delivery	***– Lieferbedingungen***
	Please let us have your quotation for delivery franco to our premises	*Bitte lassen Sie uns Ihr Angebot für Lieferung frei unsere Geschäftsräume zukommen*
	– delivery date / period	***– Lieferdatum / Lieferzeit***
	Delivery should be made within 3 weeks after receipt of our order	*Die Lieferung sollte innerhalb von 3 Wochen nach Erhalt unserer Bestellung erfolgen*
	– delivery	***– Lieferung***
	Are you able to deliver by air?	*Können Sie per Luftfracht liefern?*
	– terms of payment	***– Zahlungsbedingungen***
	Please let us have (full) details of your terms of payment	*Bitte geben Sie uns (alle) Einzelheiten Ihrer Zahlungsbedingungen*
	Will you accept payment within 30 days after receipt of the goods?	*Akzeptieren Sie die Zahlung innerhalb von 30 Tagen nach Erhalt der Waren?*

6	**References***	***Referenzen****
	The Deutsche Bank in Düsseldorf will be happy to provide references on us	*Die Deutsche Bank in Düsseldorf wird Ihnen gern eine Referenz über uns zukommen lassen*
	References can be obtained from …	*Referenzen können eingeholt werden von …*
	Should you require references please contact the Daimler-Benz AG, who will be pleased to supply you with any information you may desire	*Sollten Sie Referenzen benötigen, wenden Sie sich bitte an die Daimler-Benz AG, die Ihnen gern jede gewünschte Information geben wird*
	We have excellent trade and bank references and enclose a list of our major business partners, who will be pleased to provide you with any information you may require on our company	*Wir haben ausgezeichnete Handels- und Bankreferenzen und fügen eine Liste unserer wichtigsten Geschäftspartner bei, die Ihnen gern jede Information geben werden, die Sie möglicherweise über unser Unternehmen benötigen*
7	**Polite ending**	***Höfliche Schlussformel***
	If your company's goods find our customers' approval we will be able to place a sizeable order	*Wenn die Dienstleistungen Ihrer Firma bei unseren Kunden Anklang finden, werden wir in der Lage sein, einen Auftrag beträchtlicher Größenordnung zu erteilen*
	Many thanks in advance for your attention to our enquiry	*Vielen Dank im Voraus für die unserer Anfrage geschenkte Aufmerksamkeit*
8	**Enclosure(s)**	***Anlage(n)***
	Bank reference: Deutsche Bank, Essen, Germany Trade reference: Holzmann AG, Berlin, Germany	*Bankreferenz:* *Deutsche Bank, Essen, Deutschland* *Handelsreferenz:* *Holzmann AG, Berlin, Deutschland*

Unit 3

Offers

1	Reference to enquiry*	Thank you for Many thanks for I refer to In reply to With reference to We were delighted to receive	your letter/fax/telex/e-mail/ communication dated/of … the phone call from your agent/ representative Mr/Ms … on … (date) the above-mentioned enquiry your telephone enquiry	enquiring about … asking for information on … requesting us to send you details of … about … regarding …	
		I am writing in connection with the pleasant/informative/interesting conversation I had with … (person) at … (e. g. company's stand at a trade fair/exhibition/at a business meeting/convention/presentation etc) in … (town, city) on … (date)			
		We are pleased to let you have the following information We take pleasure in … + ing (e. g providing you with the information requested regarding …)			
		We have obtained your company's name from We were given your company's name by Your company has been (warmly) recommended to us by We have learned from	the Chamber of Commerce and Industry in … (location) the … (e. g Canadian, American etc.) Embassy/Consulate in … (location) Mr/Ms … (name), who is a business associate of ours (the) … (name) Bank (e. g the Handelsbank in Düsseldorf/ Barclays Bank in …)		
2	Description of your company*	We are a As a	major leading well-established well-known successful fast-growing	manufacturer of … producer of … importer of … distributor of … wholesaler of … supplier of … retailer of … agent for … … company … contractor	with excellent/well-established/extensive business contacts with an excellent reputation (for … + product/ service) with a well-established/an extensive sales network with branches with offices with a factory (factories) with a plant (plants) with a distribution centre (distribution centres) with a warehouse (warehouses) with a depot (depots) | in … all over/throughout … (e. g Germany, Europe, the EU etc.) both at home and abroad both in Europe and overseas in all major German/ European cities in the EU and beyond
					with our headquarters/our Head Office in …

3 Description of goods	We • produce • manufacture • make • wholesale • retail • market • supply	a wide range of a variety of a selection of a choice selection of several types of a number of	high-quality first-rate top-grade highly successful extremely popular up-market competitively priced	goods products articles	of this nature of this type
	We have been • manufacturing • making • wholesaling • retailing • marketing • supplying		these goods high-quality goods of this nature up-market articles of this type		for the past 10 years for the last 10 years for many years since 1990 since February etc.
Description of services	We provide/offer a(n) comprehensive/same-day/ on-the-spot/24-hour/reliable/punctual/prompt	repair/replacement/spare parts/ maintenance/after-sales/ advertising/marketing/advisory/ delivery		service	at competitive prices at reasonable rates at rock-bottom prices
	… we will also be pleased to supply goods to customers' specifications … we offer a reliable service 24 hours a day				
	May we draw your attention to We would like to take this opportunity to draw your attention to	our special offer for … (product) the product/service featured on page … of our catalogue/brochure etc. the product/service featured on page … of the enclosed catalogue/ brochure etc			
	… which is selling particularly well at the moment … which is most popular at the moment … for which there is heavy demand at present				
4 Reference to information or samples etc. and/or representative's/ agent's visit	As requested For your information	we are sending you enclosed we enclose we are enclosing	our latest/illustrated/colour catalogue/brochure on (some) sales literature on … a leaflet on … some leaflets on … a pamphlet on … some pamphlets on … both our latest catalogue and a current price list of …	our latest product(s)/service(s) the article you enquire about the XYZ washing machine our DTYD mini-bar our latest software package, etc. our range of products/services	

	We will be sending you You will be receiving	a sample of … samples of our goods a demonstration model the information your require the information requested the sample(s) requested our catalogue	immediately by return in the next few days by the same post by separate post under separate cover as printed matter
	We include both our latest catalogue and a current price list with this e-mail as a file attachment Attached to this e-mail as data files you will find both written information on our products and our latest price list To obtain more information on our company's products and services please visit our web site at <http://www.germanfirm.de>		
	We will be pleased to send you We will be pleased to provide you with	a sample of … a / some sample(s) (of our goods) a demonstration model (demonstration models)	if requested on request
	We also offer advertising material free of charge		
	Our representative / agent Mr / Ms … (name) will be	contacting you visiting you / calling by calling you / (tele)phoning you pleased to contact you pleased to arrange an appointment with you	in the near future in the next few days by + date within + period of time
5 Price	Our … (goods) cost(s) … euros / £ … / US$ … each The current (wholesale) price is … euros / £ … / US$ … per article / item / unit / kilo / litre / yard / foot etc. The price per unit / kilo / litre / article / item is … FCA Essen / CIF Dover etc. The … are priced at … euros / £ / US $ … etc. per article / item / unit / kilo / litre / yard / foot etc. We are currently able to offer … (product) at … euros / £ / US$ … per article / item / unit / kilo / litre / yard / foot etc.	including excluding	packing freight and packing seaworthy packing VAT all tax(es) customs duty airport taxes
	Our prices are (quoted)	inclusive of exclusive of	
	Our prices	include exclude	

An additional charge of … is made for		special packing seaworthy packing express delivery
The … (goods) are …	packed delivered shipped transported supplied	in (special) (polystyrene) cardboard boxes in (sturdy) (reinforced) crates in (tea) chests in cases in carboys in sacks in barrels in bales on pallets

Please refer to the enclosed (export) price list/catalogue for details

Discounts

A discount of … % is granted New customers are granted a discount of … % A substantial discount is granted Substantial discounts are granted	on initial orders on orders exceeding … units on orders worth at least … euros/£/US$ … on orders for at least … (quantity) on orders for a minimum of … (quantity) on regular orders	placed by + date placed within + time

A quantity discount of An initial order discount of An introductory offer discount of A cash discount of An early payment discount of A trade discount of	… % 50 euros per unit/dozen/article/order	is granted is allowed	on substantial/bulk orders

As this would be	an initial order an order exceeding … units an order worth … euros/£/US$ … a regular order	in your case	we would be prepared to we would be willing to we would be able to we would be in a position to	grant a discount of … % reduce the price by … %

… on condition that the order is placed	by + date within + period of time

6 Terms of delivery	Our prices are quoted	EXW, FAS Hamburg, FOB Hamburg, FCA Essen, CFR Dover, CIF Dover, CPT London Airport, CIP London Airport, DES Dover, DEQ Dover, DAF Strasbourg, DDU New York, DDP New York franco domicile/free domicile carriage paid *(seller pays freight charges)* carriage forward *(buyer pays freight charges)*	
	Please refer to our catalogue/price list for details of our terms of delivery/freight charges Special quotations are available on request.		
7 Terms of payment	Our (usual) terms of payment are Our usual terms are Our terms are Our terms would be	strictly net/3 % for cash/CWO (cash with order)/COD (cash on delivery)/D/P (documents against payment/cash against documents)/D/A (documents against acceptance)/10 days 2 %, 30 days net/3 months' credit/the opening of an irrevocable and confirmed documentary letter of credit in our favour, payable at a bank in … (our city) and valid until … (date)/one third with order, one third on delivery and one third within 30 days after delivery	subject to favourable references
	We would request payment	in advance/on receipt of the goods/on receipt of our invoice/within 30 days after receipt of the goods/by cheque/by banker's draft/by bill of exchange … days (e.g 30/60/90 days) after sight (date)/by irrevocable and confirmed letter of credit/by transfer to our account no. … at … (bank)/by international money order (IMO)	
	Our terms of payment	will be reviewed will be reconsidered can be re-negotiated	in three months' time after a trial period of 2/3/4 etc. months if you place regular orders with our company if regular orders are placed with our company if you do regular business with us if substantial orders are placed
	Regular customers Long-standing customers Privileged customers Reliable customers Trusted customers Customers who have been doing business with us for a longer period of time		are granted preferential terms of payment may be eligible for credit terms may apply for open account terms may be eligible for open account terms/3 months' credit/documents against acceptance are eligible for … are granted … are allowed …

8 Delivery and shipping arrangements	Delivery/Deliveries can be made Goods are shipped The goods will be shipped The goods/article will be despatched The goods will be sent	by lorry/by rail/by air/by ship/ by inland waterway vessel/ by container/ by special messenger/by airmail/by surface mail/as (by) air freight	within ... days/weeks/ months after receipt of order from stock	subject to availability subject to (the goods) being unsold while stocks last
	The goods are	sent posted/mailed packed despatched forwarded transported	in an envelope (in envelopes)/in a cardboard box (in cardboard boxes)/in a chest (in chests)/in a crate (in crates)/in a case (in cases)/ in a sack (in sacks)/in a container (in containers) as a parcel (as parcels) on a pallet (on pallets) *(See Unit 6 "Delivery" for more details)*	
9 Validity of offer	This offer is The price(s) quoted is (are)	firm/valid for + period of time/until + date subject to confirmation without engagement subject to prior sale valid while stocks last subject to change without notice		
	As there has been heavy demand for these goods/products/ articles/items As demand for these goods/products/articles/items has been considerable As there has been a great amount of interest in these goods/ products/articles/items	we recommend (that) we suggest (that)	you order now while stocks last you place your order now you place your order as soon as possible	
10 Instructions*	We would ask you to let us know by fax/e-mail/telephone if you wish to place an order/a trial order Please use the enclosed order form when placing an order			
	Please quote the article/catalogue/model number when placing your order Please indicate the size/colour/model/style/quality/design required when placing your order	so we can process it to enable us to process it so it can be • processed • dealt with • attended to • completed • carried out • executed • filled	as quickly as possible as efficiently as possible more quickly more easily	

11 Offer of agency/ exclusive right of sale*	We are also looking for a suitable company in … (location) for the sole agency for our products We would also be prepared to grant you the exclusive right of sale for our products should your company be interested
12 Polite ending	We hope our offer/quotation meets your expectations We look forward to receiving your order We recommend you place a trial order You may rest assured that any order placed will be dealt with promptly and carefully We feel sure that a trial order will convince you of the quality of our goods/service(s) We hope to receive your order in the near future We hope that our offer is to your liking We hope that our offer/quotation/tender will prove acceptable to you Please do not hesitate to contact us if you require further details/if you have any queries regarding … We look forward to doing business with you (in the near future)
13 Enclosure(s)	Catalogue(s), brochure(s), leaflet(s), pamphlet(s), order form(s), (export) price list, sample(s), pattern(s)

1	Reference to enquiry*	*Bezugnahme auf Anfrage**
	Thank you for … Many thanks for … In reply to … With reference to …	*Vielen Dank für…* *Besten Dank für…* *In Beantwortung …* *Unter Bezugnahme auf …*
	… the above-mentioned enquiry … your telephone enquiry	*… die oben erwähnte Anfrage* *… Ihre telefonische Anfrage*
	I refer to …	*Ich beziehe mich auf …*
	… the phone call from your agent / representative Mr/Ms … on … (date)	*… den Anruf Ihres Vertreters / Beauftragten Herrn / Ihrer Vertreterin / Beauftragten Frau … am … (Datum)*
	… the pleasant / informative / interesting conversation I had with … (person) at … (e.g. company's stand at a trade fair / exhibition / at a business meeting / convention / presentation etc) in … (town, city) on … (date) …	*… die angenehme / informative / interessante Unterhaltung, die ich mit … (Person) auf … (z.B. dem Firmenstand einer Fachmesse / einer Ausstellung) / bei … einem geschäftlichen Treffen / … einer Tagung / Präsentation usw.) in … (Stadt) am … (Datum) führte …*
	… about … … regarding … …, in which you enquire about … …, in which you request us to send you details of …	*… über …* *… hinsichtlich …* *…, in welcher Sie bezüglich … anfragten,* *…, in welcher Sie uns bitten, Ihnen Einzelheiten von … zu schicken …*
	… we are pleased to let you have the following information	*… freuen wir uns, Ihnen folgende Informationen zukommen zu lassen*
	… we take pleasure in … + ing (e.g. providing you with the information requested regarding …)	*… freuen wir uns, … (z.B. Ihnen die erbetene Infomation bezüglich … zur Verfügung zu stellen)*
	We have obtained your company's name from …	*Wir haben den Namen Ihrer Firma von … erhalten*
	We were given your company's name by …	*Wir erhielten den Namen Ihres Unternehmens von …*
	Your company has been (warmly) recommended to us by …	*Ihr Unternehmen wurde uns von … (wärmstens) empfohlen*
	We have learned from …	*Wir haben von … erfahren*
	the Chamber of Commerce and Industry in … (location)	*die Industrie- und Handelskammer in … (Ort)*
	the … (e.g. Canadian, American etc.) Embassy / Consulate in … (location)	*die / das … (z.B. Kanadische, Amerikanische usw.) Botschaft / Konsulat in … (Ort)*
	Mr/Ms … (name), who is a business associate of ours	*Herr / Frau … (Name), der (die) ein(e) Geschäftspartner(in) von uns ist*
	(the) … (name) Bank (e.g. the Handelsbank in Düsseldorf / Barclays Bank in …)	*die … (Name) Bank (z.B. die Handelsbank in Düsseldorf / Barclays Bank in …)*

2	**Description of your company***	***Beschreibung Ihrer Gesellschaft / Firma****
	We are a / As a major / leading / well-established / well-known / successful / fast-growing …	*Wir sind ein / Als größerer / führender / gut eingeführter / bekannter / erfolgreicher / schnell wachsender …*
	manufacturer of … producer of … importer of … distributor of … wholesaler of … supplier of … retailer of … agent for … … company (e.g. freight forwarding company) … contractor (e.g. building contractor)	*Hersteller von …* *Produzent von …* *Importeur von …* *Vertriebshändler von …* *Großhändler von …* *Lieferant von …* *Einzelhändler von …* *Vertreter für …* *… Gesellschaft (z. B. Frachtspeditionsfirma)* *… Unternehmer (z. B. Bauunternehmen)*
	… with excellent / well-established / extensive business contacts …	*… mit ausgezeichneten / gut eingeführten / ausgedehnten Geschäftskontakten …*
	… with an excellent reputation (for … + product/service) …	*mit ausgezeichnetem Ruf für … (ein Produkt / eine Dienstleistung)*
	… with a well-established / an extensive sales network …	*mit einem gut eingeführten / einem ausgedehnten Verkaufsnetz …*
	… with branches / offices / a factory (factories) / a plant (plants) / a distribution centre (distribution centres) / a warehouse (warehouses) / a depot (depots) in …	*mit Filialen / Büros / einer Fabrik (Fabriken) / einer Produktionsstätte (Produktionsstätten) / einem Vertriebszentrum (Vertriebszentren) / einem Lager (Lagern) / einem Warendepot (Warendepots) in …*
	… all over / throughout … (e.g. Germany, Europe, the EU etc.)	*… in ganz / überall in … (z. B. Deutschland, Europa, der EU usw.)*
	… both at home and abroad … both in Europe and overseas … in all major German / European cities … in the EU and beyond	*… im In- und Ausland* *… sowohl in Europa als auch in Übersee* *… in allen größeren deutschen / europäischen Städten* *… in der EU und darüber hinaus*
	… with our headquarters / our Head Office in …	*… mit unserer Zentrale / unserer Hauptverwaltung in …*
3	**Description of goods**	***Beschreibung der Waren***
	We produce / manufacture / make / wholesale / retail / market / supply	*Wir produzieren / fertigen / stellen … her / sind Großhändler / Einzelhändler für … / vertreiben / liefern*
	… a wide range / variety / selection of …	*… eine große Palette / Vielfalt / Auswahl von …*
	… a choice selection of … (e.g. wines, continental food products)	*… ein auserlesenes Sortiment von … (z. B. Weinen, Lebensmittelprodukten aus Kontinentaleuropa)*
	… several types of …	*… verschiedene Arten von …*

… a number of …	*… eine Anzahl von…*
… high-quality / first-rate / top-grade / highly successful / extremely popular / up-market / competitively priced … (goods)	*hochwertigen / ausgezeichneten / erstklassigen / höchst erfolgreichen / außergewöhnlich beliebten / exklusiven / wettbewerbsmäßig günstigen … (Waren)*
We have been manufacturing / making / wholesaling / retailing / marketing / supplying … (goods) for the past 10 years / for the last 10 years / for many years / since 1990 / since February etc.	*Seit den letzten / vergangenen 10 Jahren / seit vielen Jahren / seit 1990 / seit Februar usw. … stellen wir … her / fertigen wir / verkaufen wir als Großhändler / als Einzelhändler / vertreiben wir / liefern wir… (Waren)*
… of this nature … of this type	*dieser Art* *dieses Typs*

Description of services | *Beschreibung der Dienstleistungen*

We provide / offer a(n) comprehensive / same-day / on-the-spot / 24-hour / reliable / punctual / prompt … (service)	*Wir stellen / bieten einen umfassenden … Service, der am gleichen Tag / sofort / innerhalb 24 Stunden / zuverlässig / pünktlich / prompt erfolgt*
We offer a reliable service 24 hours a day	*Wir bieten einen zuverlässigen Service rund um die Uhr*

Types of services | *Arten der Dienstleistungen*

a(n) repair service / replacement service / spare parts service / maintenance service / after-sales service / advertising service / marketing service / advisory service / delivery service	*einen Reparatur-Service / Ersatz-Service / Ersatzteil-Service / Wartungs-Service / Kundendienst-Service / Werbe-Service / Marketing-Service / Beratungs-Service / Liefer-Service*
… at competitive prices … at reasonable rates … at rock-bottom prices	*… zu konkurrenzfähigen Preisen* *… zu angemessenen Preisen* *… zu Tiefstpreisen*
… we will also be pleased to supply goods to customers' specifications	*… sind auch gern bereit, Spezialanfertigungen zu übernehmen*
May we draw your attention to …	*Dürfen wir Sie aufmerksam machen auf …*
We would like to take this opportunity to draw your attention to …	*Wir möchten diese Gelegenheit wahrnehmen, um Ihre Aufmerksamkeit auf … zu lenken*
… which is selling particularly well at the moment	*… der (die, das) sich im Augenblick besonders gut verkauft (verkaufen)*
… which is most popular at the moment	*… der (die, das) im Augenblick ausgesprochen beliebt ist (sind)*
… for which there is heavy demand at present	*… für den (die, das) zur Zeit eine rege Nachfrage besteht (bestehen)*
… our special offer for … (product)	*… unser Sonderangebot für … (Produkt)*

… the product / service featured on page … of our catalogue / brochure etc.	*… das Produkt / die Dienstleistung, das / die auf Seite … unseres Katalogs / unserer Broschüre etc. gezeigt wird,*
… the product / service featured on page … of the enclosed catalogue / brochure	*… das Produkt / die Dienstleistung, das / die auf Seite … des beigefügten Katalogs / der beigefügten Broschüre dargestellt ist*

4 Reference to information or samples etc. and/or representative's / agent's visit — *Bezugnahme auf Informationen oder Muster usw. sowie / oder auf den Besuch des Beauftragten/Vertreters*

As requested	*Wie gewünscht*
We are sending you enclosed …	*Wir senden Ihnen anbei …*
We enclose …	*Wir fügen … bei*
For your information we enclose …	*Zu Ihrer Information fügen wir … bei*
… our latest / illustrated / colour catalogue / brochure on	*… unsere(n) jüngste(n) / bebilderte(n) / farbige(n) Katalog / Broschüre für*
… (some) sales literature on …	*… (etwas) Verkaufsmaterial (+ Genitiv)*
… a leaflet on …	*… einen Prospekt (+ Genitiv) …*
… some leaflets on …	*… einige Prospekte (+ Genitiv) …*
… a pamphlet on …	*… ein Faltblatt (+ Genitiv) …*
… some pamphlets on …	*… einige Faltblätter (+ Genitiv) …*
… both our latest catalogue and a current price list of …	*… unseren neuesten Katalog sowie eine aktuelle Preisliste des / der …*
… our latest product(s) / service(s)	*… unser(e) jüngstes(n,e) Produkt(e) / Dienstleistung(en)*
… the article you enquire about	*… den von Ihnen angefragten Artikel*
… the XYZ washing machine	*… die XYZ Waschmaschine*
… our DTYD mini-bar	*… unsere DTYD Minibar*
… our latest software package	*… unser jüngstes Software-Paket*
… our range of products / service(s)	*… unsere Produkt- / Dienstleistungs-palette*
We will be sending you …	*Wir werden Ihnen … schicken*
You will be receiving …	*Sie erhalten …*
… a sample of …	*… ein Muster von …*
… samples of our goods	*… Muster unserer Waren*
… a demonstration model	*… ein Vorführmodell*
… the information your require	*… die von Ihnen benötigte Information*
… the information requested	*… die gewünschten Informationen*
… the sample(s) requested	*… das (die) gewünschte(n) Muster*
… our catalogue	*… unseren Katalog*
… immediately	*… sofort*
… by return	*… umgehend*
… in the next few days	*… in den nächsten Tagen*
… by the same post	*… mit gleicher Post*
… by separate post	*… mit getrennter Post*
… under separate cover	*… mit separater Post*
… as printed matter	*… als Drucksache*

We will be pleased to send you …	*Wir freuen uns, Ihnen … zuzusenden*
We will be pleased to provide you with …	*Wir freuen uns, Ihnen … zukommen zu lassen*
… a sample (of)… … (some) samples (of) … (goods) … a demonstration model … … (some) demonstration models …	*… ein Muster (von) …* *… (einige) Muster (der) … (Waren)* *… ein Vorführmodell …* *… (einige) Vorführmodelle …*
… if requested	*… auf Wunsch*
We also offer advertising material free of charge	*Wir bieten (Ihnen) ebenfalls kostenloses Werbematerial an*
Our representative / agent Mr / Ms … (name) will be contacting you / visiting you / calling by / calling you / (tele)phoning you / pleased to contact you / arrange an appointment with you …	*Unser Beauftragter / Vertreter Herr … (Name) / Unsere Beauftragte / Vertreterin Frau … (Name) wird mit Ihnen Kontakt aufnehmen / Sie besuchen / bei Ihnen vorbeikommen / Sie anrufen / telefonisch mit Ihnen in Verbindung treten / erfreut sein, Kontakt mit Ihnen aufzunehmen / einen Termin mit Ihnen vereinbaren*
… in the near future … in the next few days … by + date … within + period of time	*… in Kürze* *… in den nächsten Tagen* *… bis (Datum)* *… innerhalb … (Zeitraum)*
5 Price	***Preis***
Our … (goods) cost(s) … euros / £ … / US$ … each	*Unser(e) … (Ware(n)) kostet(n) je … Euro / … Pfund /… US$*
The current (wholesale) price is … euros (e.g. 50 euros) / £ … (e.g. £100.00) / US$ … (e.g. US$35.50) per article / item / unit / kilo / litre / yard / foot etc.	*Der gegenwärtige (Großhandels-)Preis beträgt … Euro (z. B. 50 Euro) / … £ (100,00 £) / … US$ (z. B. 35,50 US$), pro Artikel / Position / Stück / Kilo / Liter / Yard / Fuß usw.*
The price per unit / kilo / litre / article / item is … FCA Essen / CIF Dover etc.	*Der Preis pro Stück / Kilo / Liter / Artikel / Position beträgt … FCA Essen / CIF Dover usw.*
The … (article/s) is / are priced at … euros / £ / US$ … etc. per article / item / unit / kilo / litre / yard / foot etc.	*Der (die) … Artikel kostet(n) … Euro / £ / US$ usw. pro Artikel / Position / Stück / Kilo / Liter / Yard / Fuß usw.*
We are currently able to offer … (product) at … euros / £ / US$ … per article / item / unit / kilo / litre / yard / foot etc.	*Im Augenblick sind wir in der Lage, … (Produkt) zu … Euro / £ / US$ pro Artikel / Position / Stück / Kilo / Liter / Yard / Fuß usw. anzubieten.*
including … excluding …	*einschließlich …* *ausschließlich …*
Our prices are quoted … (Incoterm + destination)	*Wir bieten unsere Preise … (Incoterm + Bestimmungsort) an*
… inclusive of … / … exclusive of …	*… einschließlich … / ausschließlich …*

Our prices include / exclude packing	*In unseren Preisen ist die Verpackung enthalten / nicht enthalten…*
An additional charge of … is made for …	*Es werden … für … zusätzlich berechnet*
… packing / seaworthy packing / special delivery / express delivery / freight and packing / VAT / tax / taxes / all taxes / customs duty / airport taxes …	*… Verpackung / seemäßige Verpackung / Sonderzustellung / Eilzustellung / Fracht und Verpackung / MWSt / Steuer / Steuern / alle Steuern / Zollgebühren / Flughafengebühren …*
Please refer to the enclosed (export) price list / catalogue for details	*Bitte sehen Sie in der beigefügten (Export-)Preisliste / im Katalog bezüglich der Einzelheiten nach*
The … (goods) are packed / delivered / shipped / transported / supplied …	*Die … (Waren) werden … versandt / geliefert / verschifft / transportiert / geliefert*
… in (special) cardboard boxes (polystyrene boxes)	*… in (speziellen) Pappkartons (Styroporkartons)*
… in (sturdy) (reinforced) crates	*… in (stabilen) (verstärkten) Kisten*
… in (tea) chests	*… in (Tee) Kisten*
… in cases	*… in Kisten*
… in carboys	*… in Glasballons*
… in sacks	*… in Säcken*
… in barrels	*… in Fässern*
… in bales	*… in Ballen*
… on pallets	*… auf Paletten*
Discounts	***Nachlässe***
A discount of … % is granted	*Es wird ein Nachlass von … % gewährt*
New customers are granted a discount of … %	*Neue Kunden erhalten einen Nachlass von … %*
A substantial discount is granted …	*Ein erheblicher Nachlass wird … gewährt*
Substantial discounts are granted …	*Wir gewähren große Nachlässe …*
… on initial orders	*… auf Erstaufträge*
… on orders exceeding … units	*… auf Aufträge, die … Stück übersteigen*
… on orders worth at least … euros / £ / US$ …	*… auf Aufträge im Wert von mindestens … Euro / £ / US$*
… on orders for at least … (quantity) / … on orders for a minimum of … (quantity)	*… auf Aufträge für mindestens … (Menge)*
… on regular orders	*… für Daueraufträge*
… placed by + date … placed within + time	*… die bis … (+ Datum) erteilt werden* *… die innerhalb … (+ Zeit) erteilt werden*
A quantity discount of … % is granted on substantial / bulk orders	*Ein Mengenrabatt von … % wird auf größere / Großaufträge gewährt*

An initial order discount of …	*Ein Nachlass von … wird für Erstaufträge*
An introductory offer discount of …	*Ein Nachlass von … wird für einen Einführungsauftrag*
A cash discount of …	*Ein Nachlass von … wird für Barzahlung*
An early payment discount of …	*Ein Nachlass von … wird für sofortige Bezahlung*
A trade discount of 50 euros per unit / dozen / article / order … is allowed / is granted	*Ein Großhandelsrabatt von 50 Euro pro Stück / Dutzend / Artikel / Auftrag wird gewährt*
As this would be an initial order / an order exceeding … units / an order worth … euros / £ / US$ … / a regular order in your case	*Da es sich hierbei um einen Erstauftrag / einen Auftrag, der … Stück übersteigt / einen Auftrag im Werte von … Euro / £ / US$ / einen Dauerauftrag handeln würde*
we would be prepared to we would be willing to we would be able to we would be in a position to	*wären wir bereit* *wären wir gewillt* *könnten wir* *wären wir in der Lage*
grant a discount of … % reduce the price by … %	*einen Nachlass von … % zu gewähren* *den Preis um … % zu reduzieren*
… on condition that the order is placed by + date / within + period of time	*unter der Bedingung, dass der Auftrag bis … (Datum) / innerhalb … (Zeitraum) erteilt wird*

6 Terms of delivery — *Lieferbedingungen*

Our prices are quoted …	*Unsere Preise verstehen sich …*
EXW, FAS Hamburg, FOB Hamburg, FCA Essen, CFR Dover, CIF Dover, CPT London Airport, CIP London Airport, DES Dover, DEQ Dover, DAF Strasbourg, DDU New York, DDP New York	*EXW, FAS Hamburg, FOB Hamburg, FCA Essen, CFR Dover, CIF Dover, CPT Flughafen London, CIP Flughafen London, DES Dover, DEQ Dover, DAF Straßburg, DDU New York, DDP New York*
franco domicile / free domicile	*frei Haus*
carriage paid (seller pays freight charges)	*Fracht bezahlt (Verkäufer zahlt Frachtgebühren)*
carriage forward (buyer pays freight charges)	*unfrei (Käufer zahlt Frachtgebühren)*
Please refer to our catalogue / price list for details of our terms of delivery / freight charges	*Bitte informieren Sie sich über unsere Lieferbedingungen / Frachtgebühren in unserem Katalog / in unserer Preisliste*
Special quotations are available on request	*Spezielle Preisangebote sind auf Wunsch erhältlich*

7 Terms of payment — *Zahlungsbedingungen*

Our (usual) terms of payment are …	*Unsere (üblichen) Zahlungsbedingungen sind …*
Our usual terms are …	*Unsere üblichen Bedingungen sind …*

Our terms are … Our terms would be …	*Unsere Bedingungen sind …* *Unsere Bedingungen wären …*
strictly net	*ausschließlich netto*
3 % for cash	*bei Barzahlung 3 %*
CWO (cash with order)	*Barzahlung bei Auftragserteilung*
COD (cash on delivery)	*per Nachnahme*
D/P (documents against payment / cash against documents)	*Kasse gegen Dokumente*
D/A (documents against acceptance)	*Dokumente gegen Akzept*
10 days 2 %, 30 days net	*bei Zahlung innerhalb von 10 Tagen 2 %, netto bei Zahlung innerhalb von 30 Tagen*
3 months' credit	*ein 3-monatiger Kredit* *3 Monate Ziel*
the opening of an irrevocable and confirmed documentary letter of credit in our favour, payable at a bank in … (city) and valid until … (date)	*die Eröffnung eines unwiderruflichen und bestätigten Dokumenten-akkreditivs zu unseren Gunsten, zahlbar bei einer Bank in … (Stadt) und gültig bis … (Datum)*
one third with order, one third on delivery and one third within 30 days after delivery	*ein Drittel bei Auftragserteilung, ein Drittel bei Lieferung und ein Drittel innerhalb von 30 Tagen nach Lieferung*
subject to favourable references	*abhängig von positiven Referenzen* *gute Referenzen vorausgesetzt*
We would request payment …	*Wir bitten um Zahlung …*
in advance	*im Voraus*
on receipt of the goods	*bei Erhalt der Waren*
on receipt of our invoice	*bei Erhalt unserer Rechnung*
within 30 days after receipt of the goods	*innerhalb von 30 Tagen nach Erhalt der Waren*
by cheque	*per Scheck*
by banker's draft	*per Bankscheck*
by bill of exchange … days (e.g. 30/60/90 days) after sight(date)	*durch … Tage-Wechsel (z. B. 30/60/90 Tage) nach Sicht (Datum)*
by irrevocable and confirmed letter of credit	*durch unwiderrufliches und bestätigtes Akkreditiv*
by transfer to our account no. … at … (bank)	*durch Überweisung auf unser Konto Nr. … bei der … (Bank)*
Our terms of payment … will be reviewed … will be reconsidered … can be re-negotiated …	*Unsere Zahlungsbedingungen …* *werden erneut geprüft …* *werden überarbeitet …* *können neu verhandelt werden …*
… in three months' time … after a trial period of 2/3/4 etc. months	*… nach einer Frist von 3 Monaten* *… nach einer Probezeit von 2/3/4 usw. Monaten*

… if you place regular orders with our company	*… wenn Sie unserer Firma regelmäßige Aufträge erteilen*
… if regular orders are placed with our company	*… wenn unserer Firma Daueraufträge erteilt werden*
… if you do regular business with us	*… wenn Sie regelmäßige Geschäfte mit uns tätigen*
… if substantial orders are placed	*… wenn größere Bestellungen erfolgen*
Regular customers … Long-standing customers … Privileged customers … Reliable customers … Trusted customers …	*Regelmäßige Kunden …* *Dauerkunden …* *Bevorzugte Kunden …* *Zuverlässige Kunden …* *Vertrauenswürdige Kunden …*
Customers who have been doing business with us for a longer period of time …	*Kunden, die seit längerer Zeit mit uns Geschäfte machen …*
… are granted … … may be eligible for … … may apply for … … are allowed …	*… erhalten …* *… können für … ausgewählt werden …* *… können … beantragen* *… bekommen …*
… preferential terms of payment … credit terms … open account terms … 3 months' credit … documents against acceptance	*… bevorzugte Zahlungsbedingungen* *… Kreditbedingungen* *… ein offenes Zahlungsziel* *… einen 3-monatigen Kredit* *… Dokumente gegen Akzept*
8 Delivery and shipping arrangements	***Lieferungs- und Versandvereinbarungen***
Delivery / Deliveries can be made …	*Die Lieferung(en) kann (können) erfolgen …*
Goods are shipped …	*Die Waren werden versandt (verschifft) …*
The goods will be shipped …	*Die Waren werden versandt (verschifft) werden …*
The goods / article(s) will be despatched …	*Die Waren / Artikel werden versandt …*
The goods will be sent …	*Die Waren werden geschickt (werden) …*
The goods are sent posted / mailed packed despatched forwarded transported	*Die Waren werden geschickt* *per Post zugestellt* *verpackt* *versandt* *geliefert* *transportiert*
in an envelope (in envelopes) / in a cardboard box (in cardboard boxes) / in a chest (in chests) / in a crate (in crates) / in a case (in cases) / in a sack (in sacks) / in a container (in containers)	*in einem Umschlag (in Umschlägen) / in einem Pappkarton (in Pappkartons) / in einem Kasten (in Kästen) / in einem Verschlag (in Verschlägen) / in einer Kiste (in Kisten) / in einem Sack (in Säcken) / in einem Container (in Containern)*

	as a parcel (as parcels)	*als Paket (als Pakete)*
	on a pallet (on pallets)	*auf einer Palette (auf Paletten)*
	(See Unit 6 "Delivery" for more details)	*(Siehe Unit 6 „Delivery" für weitere Einzelheiten)*
	... within ... days / weeks / months after ... receipt of order	*... innerhalb ... Tagen / Wochen / Monaten nach ... Auftragserhalt*
	... from stock	*... ab Lager*
	... by lorry / by rail / by air / by ship / by inland waterway vessel / by container / by special messenger / by airmail / by surface mail / as (by) air freight	*... per Lkw / per Schiene / durch Luftfracht / per Schiff / per Binnenschiff / per Container / durch Sonderkurier / mit Luftpost / mit gewöhnlicher Post / als Luftfracht*
9	**Validity of offer**	***Gültigkeit des Angebots***
	This offer is ...	*Dieses Angebot ist ...*
	The price quoted is ...	*Der angebotene Preis ist...*
	The prices quoted are ...	*Die angebotenen Preise sind...*
	... firm / valid for ... + period of time / until + date	*... fest / gültig für...+ Zeitraum / bis + Datum*
	... subject to confirmation	*... vorbehaltlich Ihrer Bestätigung*
	... without engagement	*... unverbindlich*
	... valid while stocks last	*... gültig, solange der Vorrat reicht*
	... subject to change without notice	*... können / kann ohne Benachrichtigung geändert werden*
	... subject to prior sale	*... Zwischenverkauf vorbehalten*
	As there has been heavy demand for these goods / products / articles / items ...	*Da große Nachfrage nach diesen Waren / Produkten / Artikeln / Posten besteht ...*
	As demand for these goods / products / articles / items has been heavy ...	*Da die Nachfrage nach diesen Waren / Produkten / Artikeln / Positionen groß war ...*
	As there has been a great amount of interest in ... (goods)	*Da großes Interesse nach ... (Waren) besteht*
	we recommend (that) ...	*empfehlen wir, (dass) ...*
	we suggest (that) ...	*schlagen wir vor, (dass) ...*
	... you order now while stocks last	*... Sie jetzt bestellen, solange der Vorrat reicht*
	... you place your order now	*... Sie Ihre Bestellung jetzt aufgeben*
	... you place your order as soon as possible	*... Sie Ihren Auftrag so bald wie möglich erteilen*
10	**Instructions***	***Anweisungen****
	We would ask you to let us know by fax / e-mail / telephone if you wish to place an order / a trial order	*Wir möchten Sie bitten, uns per Fax / E-Mail / Telefon mitzuteilen, ob Sie einen Auftrag / einen Probeauftrag erteilen wollen*
	Please use the enclosed order form when placing an order	*Bitte benutzen Sie das beigefügte Auftragsformular, wenn Sie Ihren Auftrag erteilen*

	Please quote the article / catalogue / model number when placing your order	*Bitte nennen Sie den Artikel / die Katalog- / die Modell-Nummer, wenn Sie Ihre Bestellung aufgeben*
	Please indicate the size / colour / model / style / quality / design required when placing your order	*Bitte geben Sie die gewünschte Größe / Farbe / das Modell / den Stil / die Qualität / das Design an, wenn Sie Ihren Auftrag erteilen*
	… so we can process it	*… damit wir ihn bearbeiten können*
	… to enable us to process it	*… um uns in die Lage zu versetzen, ihn zu bearbeiten*
	… so it can be processed …	*… damit er … bearbeitet werden kann*
	dealt with …	*… damit wir uns … um ihn kümmern können*
	attended to …	*… damit er … durchgeführt werden kann*
	completed …	*… damit er … vervollständigt werden kann*
	carried out … / executed …	*… damit er … ausgeführt werden kann*
	filled …	*… damit er … erfüllt werden kann*
	… as quickly as possible … as efficiently as possible … more quickly … more easily	*… so schnell wie möglich* *… so effizient wie möglich* *… schneller* *… leichter*
11	**Offer of agency / exclusive right of sale***	***Vertretungsangebot / Alleinverkaufsrecht****
	We would also be prepared to grant you the exclusive right of sale for our products should your company be interested	*Wir wären auch bereit, Ihnen, falls Ihre Gesellschaft daran interessiert ist, das Alleinverkaufsrecht für unsere Produkte einzuräumen*
	We are also looking for a suitable company in … (location) for the sole agency for our products	*Wir suchen in … (Ort) ebenfalls nach einem geeigneten Unternehmen für die Alleinvertretung unserer Produkte*
12	**Polite ending**	***Höflicher Schluss***
	We hope our offer / quotation meets your expectations	*Wir hoffen, dass unser Angebot / Preisangebot Ihren Erwartungen entspricht*
	We look forward to receiving your order	*Wir freuen uns, Ihre Bestellung zu erhalten*
	We recommend you place a trial order	*Wir empfehlen Ihnen, einen Probeauftrag zu erteilen*
	You may rest assured that any order placed will be dealt with promptly and carefully	*Sie können versichert sein, dass jeder erteilte Auftrag prompt und sorgfältig ausgeführt wird*
	We feel sure that a trial order will convince you of the quality of our goods / service(s)	*Wir sind sicher, dass ein Probeauftrag Sie von der Qualität unserer Waren / Dienstleistung(en) überzeugen wird*

We hope to receive your order in the near future	*Wir hoffen, in nächster Zeit Ihren Auftrag zu erhalten*
We hope that our offer is to your liking	*Wir hoffen, dass unser Angebot Ihnen zusagt*
We hope that our offer / quotation / tender will prove acceptable to you	*Wir hoffen, dass unser Angebot / Preisangebot / unsere Offerte für Sie akzeptabel ist*
Please do not hesitate to contact us if you require further details / if you have any queries regarding …	*Bitte zögern Sie nicht, mit uns Kontakt aufzunehmen, wenn Sie weitere Einzelheiten benötigen / wenn Sie irgendwelche Fragen bezüglich … haben*
We look forward to doing business with you in the near future	*Wir freuen uns, mit Ihnen in Kürze Geschäfte zu tätigen*

13 Enclosure(s) — *Anlage(n)*

Catalogue(s), brochure(s), leaflet(s), pamphlet(s), order form(s), (export) price list, sample(s), pattern(s)	*Katalog(e), Broschüre(n) / Prospekt(e), Faltblatt (Faltblätter), Auftragsformular(e), (Export)Preisliste, Probe(n) / Muster (Modelle), (Stoff-) Muster*

Unit 4

Orders

Standard Expressions

Orders

1 Reference to offer*	Thank you for Many thanks for I refer to We have received With reference to	your offer for your quotation for the above-mentioned offer for		goods/services	dated/of …
	We have • examined • studied • checked • tested	the sample(s) of … (product/material(s))			
	The sample(s) of … (product/material(s))	delivered supplied despatched sent forwarded shipped	to us	on … (date)	meet(s) our requirements meet(s) our specifications has/have been (thoroughly) tested is/are to our liking correspond(s) to our expectations conform(s) to … (e. g. EU regulations)
	The … (product(s))	demonstrated shown delivered supplied		by your representative … (Mr/Ms etc. …) by your agent (Mr/Ms etc. …)	complies/comply with … (e. g. EU regulations) is/are as promised … is/are as described …
	We have • studied • examined On the basis of the terms stated in	the catalogue the brochure the sales literature	sent to us given to us provided	by your • representative … (Mr/Ms etc. …) • agent, … (Mr/Ms etc. …) • Sales Department/Section • Marketing Department/Section	in … (location) on … (date) last week/month etc.
	On the basis of • your offer … • the terms stated in your offer … • the conditions in your offer …			dated/of …	as submitted to us by your agent/representative … (Mr/Ms etc.)
2 Details of goods/services required	Please find enclosed our (purchasing) order no. 234 We thank you for your offer dated/of … and enclose our order no. 234 We enclose our order no. 234			for … (goods/services)	
	We wish to … We would like to … … and now wish to … … we would therefore like to …	order … place an order (for …)		at … (price) priced at … list price …	each per unit/article/crate/item/bale/bag/case/sack/bottle per dozen/gross per kilo/litre/yard/foot etc.
				as follows: (list)	

	We would therefore request you to We would therefore ask you to We would therefore like you to	send us … supply us with … provide us with …	goods/ services	immediately as soon as possible by return without delay within + period of time (e. g. 3 weeks) by + date (e. g. 30 June)	
	Please arrange to have … (goods) Please have … (goods)	sent to us despatched to us forwarded to us shipped to us		within the period stated on the next flight from … (city) to … (city) on the next available flight on the next available ship to … (destination)	
	We (now) wish to place	an initial order for … a trial order for … a standing order for … a repeat order for …		subject to on the basis of	the conditions stated in your offer dated/of … our General Terms and Conditions (see reverse of our Order Form)
				on a sale-or-return basis	
	Having studied your offer we would request you to / reconsider review your	prices … terms … discounts …	as/since	this would be our first order competition is stiff our competitors have reduced their prices by … %	
3 Prices and discount(s)	We confirm that the prices and discounts are … … prices and discounts …			as per as stated in in accordance with	your offer dated/of … your quotation dated/of … your (export) price list (of/dated …/no. …) your catalogue (of/dated …/no. …)
				as follows: as indicated below: as listed below: as detailed in the following list: as below:	
	We are pleased to note that	you grant you will grant you have granted you have allowed us your prices include your quotation includes		a quantity discount … an initial order discount … an introductory offer discount … a cash discount … an early payment discount … a trade discount …	of 10 %
	We note with regret that … We were disappointed to note that … We were disappointed to discover that …			your quotation only includes you have only granted us you have only allowed us	

4 Terms of delivery	... delivery to be made ... Please arrange for the goods to be delivered ... Please arrange to have the goods delivered ... We (would also) confirm that delivery is to be made ...		(Incoterm + destination, e.g. CFR Bremen – *see Unit 3 "Offers" for more details*) carriage forward carriage paid franco domicile/free domicile franco (to) our premises franco (to) our warehouse
5 Terms of payment	Payment will be made/effected We will make/effect payment Our company will make/effect payment	as agreed as stipulated as requested	in advance CWO (cash with order) COD (cash on delivery) D/A (documents against acceptance) D/P (documents against payment/cash against documents) by opening an irrevocable and confirmed documentary letter of credit in your favour, payable at a bank in ... (your city) and valid until ... (date) one third with order, one third on delivery and one third within 30 days after delivery on receipt of the goods on receipt of your invoice within 30 days after receipt of the goods by cheque by banker's draft by bill of exchange ... days (e.g. 30/60/90 days) after sight (date) by transfer to your account no. ... at ... (bank) by international money order (IMO)
	The invoice amount will be remitted ...		in advance on receipt of the goods on receipt of your invoice within 30 days after receipt of the goods by cheque by banker's draft by bill of exchange ... days (e.g. 30/60/90 days) after sight(date) by transfer to your account no. ... at ... (bank) by international money order (IMO)

6 Delivery	... the goods are to be delivered ... ... delivery (is) to be made ... ... delivery (is) to be effected ...	by + date by the end of ... (e. g. by the end of the month) within + period of time immediately as soon as possible			
		by the date stated within the period stated in the time stated	in your offer (dated/of ...) in your quotation (dated/of ...) in your letter (dated/of ...) in your sales literature by your representative, Mr/Ms ... (name) by your agent, Mr/Ms ... (name)		
	Please deliver ... Please make delivery ... ... deliveries to be made ... Deliveries are to be made ...	on a weekly/monthly/quarterly/6-monthly basis every two weeks/month/3 months etc. at the end of each month/quarter on the ... (e. g. 1st/15th) of each month as per our advice by telephone/fax/e-mail as instructed as per our written instructions			
7 Instructions*	Please acknowledge this order and indicate the delivery date for the goods We would be grateful if you would send us your acknowledgement and state the date of delivery Please confirm receipt of this order and let us know when we can expect delivery Please let us know when we can take delivery of the goods Please sign the copy of the enclosed order form and return it to us by way of confirmation				
	Please send/pack the goods/articles Please arrange for the goods/articles to be packed/sent Please ensure that the goods/articles are packed/sent	in	an envelope (envelopes) a parcel (parcels) a cardboard box (boxes) a chest (chests) a crate (crates) a case (cases) a sack (s) a container (containers) *(See Unit 6 "Delivery" for more details)*	marked ...	"to be collected" "TWE/4035/JED/1-6/6" (for 6 containers) "fragile" "caution" etc.

	Please arrange for the goods/articles to be Please ensure that the goods /articles are	sent despatched transported shipped forwarded	by	road (van/lorry/truck) rail ship air special messenger special courier motor-cycle despatch rider	with the usual marks
	Please ensure that the goods are packed We would point out that the goods must be packed		carefully with care with the utmost care with the utmost care and attention		
	Our packing instructions are enclosed Please refer to the instructions enclosed for details of how the goods should be packed				
	Please arrange for the information/data to be	sent transferred communicated	to us to our company to Mr/Ms …	by	fax e-mail file transfer satellite link special messenger special courier motor-cycle despatch rider
	Please advise us Please notify us Please let us know	as soon as the goods have been	shipped loaded loaded on board ship despatched collected by … (name of carrier) delivered to … (name of carrier)		
	The goods will be collected at … (location) on our behalf by … (name of carrier)				
Special arrangements*	We confirm that	insurance is to be insurance will be	effected obtained	by us by you	
	… insurance to be …				
	Please arrange for the goods to be insured … Please arrange for insurance cover for the goods …		from warehouse to warehouse in transit against all risks, including particular average and force majeure in accordance with Institute Cargo Clauses A (B,C) with general but excluding particular average		
	Please arrange for the goods to be insured		by … (name of insurance company)		

	Please send us the insurance certificate We will send you the insurance certificate as soon as it has been issued					
	If … (description, article no. etc.) is not Should … (description, article no. etc.) not be	available available in sufficient quantities in stock	please substitute … (different item(s)) please supply a product/goods of a comparable nature please supply (a) suitable substitute(s) please supply the nearest you have to the sample enclosed/provided			
	If … (description, article no. etc.) is Should … (description, article no. etc.) be	unavailable unavailable in sufficient quantities in short supply out of stock sold out				
Qualifications*	We reserve the right to We will (unfortunately) have no alternative but to We will (unfortunately) have no choice but to We will (unfortunately) be obliged to We regret we will have to	return the goods carriage forward cancel our order hold you liable (for loss of custom/business)	if the goods	are not up to sample do not correspond to the samples provided are not as stipulated fail to meet our specifications do not match the pattern are delivered late are not delivered by + date are not delivered within + period of time		
		cancel our order hold you liable (for loss of custom/business)	if your service	is not prompt is not as stated in your offer is not satisfactory		
			if you are unable to	repair maintain service replace overhaul install re-install	the article(s) the goods the machine(s) the machinery the equipment the apparatus	promptly punctually in good time within + period of time by + date as promised as agreed
	This order is placed on condition that	delivery can be made delivery is made without fail the goods are supplied	by + date by the date specified within + period of time			

	This order is placed on condition that	our instructions are strictly observed the material supplied corresponds exactly to that of the sample provided there are no extra charges whatsoever in addition to those quoted	
		a six-month/a year's/a 2-year etc. guarantee is given on … (goods, equipment etc.) the goods come with a six-month/a year's/a 2-year etc. guarantee there is a six-month/a year's/a two-year etc. guarantee on … (goods, equipment) there is a six-month/a year's/a two-year warranty on … (goods, equipment)	
	Payment will be made	as soon as	the goods have been • examined • inspected • checked • counted • weighed • tested • sampled samples have been taken the goods have been passed by our Quality Control Department the usual checks have been carried out
8 Polite ending	We expect to be receiving your	• advice of despatch • sales invoice	in the near future in the (course of the) next few days/weeks as agreed
	We trust our order will arrive punctually and in good condition We look forward to taking delivery of our order in the near future Thank you for your prompt attention to this matter We feel sure our order will be dealt with with your usual care and attention We hope that this will be the beginning of a long and pleasant business relationship		
	We look forward to placing further orders with your company We will be in a position to place regular orders		if the goods correspond to our customer's/customers' expectations if the goods sell well on the local market if the goods meet our customer's/customers' requirements if our trial order is well received if you are able to offer the goods on the same terms in future
9 Enclosure(s)	Order No. 234 Order Form Our General Terms and Conditions Our Packing Instructions Sample(s)		

1	Reference to offer*	*Bezugnahme auf Angebot**
	Many thanks for your quotation for camping equipment dated …	*Vielen Dank für Ihr Angebot für Camping-Ausrüstung vom …*
	We have examined the samples of roofing tiles supplied to us	*Wir haben die Muster der uns gelieferten Dachziegel geprüft*
	The samples of summer fabrics forwarded to us on 15 April meet our requirements	*Die Muster der uns am 15. April zugesandten Sommerstoffe entsprechen unseren Anforderungen*
	As the samples of packing materials shown to us by your agent, Ms Anita Clooney, are as described in your brochure …	*Da die Muster der uns von Ihrer Vertreterin, Frau Anita Clooney, gezeigten Verpackungsmaterialien der Beschreibung in Ihrer Broschüre entsprechen, …*
	On the basis of the terms stated in the sales literature sent to us by your Marketing Department in Boston last week …	*Aufgrund der Bedingungen, welche in dem uns von Ihrer Marketing-Abteilung in Boston in der letzten Woche zugesandten Werbematerial aufgeführt sind, …*
2	Details of goods / services required*	*Einzelheiten der benötigten Waren / Dienstleistungen**
	We thank you for your offer dated 5 April and enclose our order no. 234 for hiking boots	*Wir danken Ihnen für Ihr Angebot vom 5. April und fügen unseren Auftrag Nr. 234 für Wanderstiefel bei*
	We would like to place an order for 100 air conditioning units at $350 each	*Wir möchten gern einen Auftrag für 100 Klimaanlagengeräte zum Stückpreis von 350 $ erteilen*
	We would therefore ask you to supply us with these materials by 30 June	*Wir möchten Sie deshalb bitten, uns bis zum 30. Juni mit diesem Material zu beliefern*
	Please arrange to have the furniture shipped to us on the next available flight	*Bitte veranlassen Sie, dass die Möbel mit dem nächsten verfügbaren Flug an uns geschickt werden*
	We now wish to place a trial order for the wines listed, on the basis of the conditions stated in your offer of 1 May, i. e. on a sale-or-return basis	*Wir möchten nunmehr aufgrund der in unserem Angebot vom 1. Mai genannten Bedingungen einen Probeauftrag für die aufgelisteten Weine auf der Basis eines Rückgaberechts erteilen*
	Having studied your offer we would request you to reconsider your terms, since competition is stiff here	*Nachdem wir Ihr Angebot geprüft haben, möchten wir Sie bitten, Ihre Bedingungen noch einmal zu überdenken, da die Konkurrenz hier sehr hart ist*
3	Prices and discount(s)*	*Preise und Nachlass (Nachlässe)**
	… prices and discounts as stated in your export price list no. 99EX dated 1 January	*… Die Preise und Nachlässe entsprechen Ihrer Exportpreisliste Nr. 99EX vom 1. Januar*

	We are pleased to note that you grant a quantity discount of 10 %	*Wir freuen uns festzustellen, dass Sie einen Mengenrabatt von 10 % gewähren*
	We were disappointed to note that your quotation only includes an introductory offer discount of 10 %	*Wir waren enttäuscht festzustellen, dass Ihr (Preis-)Angebot nur einen Einführungsrabatt von 10 % vorsieht*
4	**Terms of delivery**	***Lieferbedingungen***
	Please arrange to have the goods delivered CFR Bremen	*Bitte veranlassen Sie die Lieferung der Güter CFR Bremen*
	We confirm that delivery is to be made FOB Dover	*Wir bestätigen, dass die Lieferung FOB Dover zu erfolgen hat*
5	**Terms of payment**	***Zahlungsbedingungen***
	Payment will be made as stipulated by opening an irrevocable and confirmed documentary letter of credit in your favour, payable at a bank in London and valid until 30 June	*Die Zahlung erfolgt wie festgelegt durch die Eröffnung eines unwiderruflichen und bestätigten Akkreditivs zu Ihren Gunsten, zahlbar bei einer Bank in London und gültig bis zum 30. Juni*
	As requested we will make payment one third with order, one third on delivery and one third within 30 days after delivery	*Wie gewünscht, wird von uns die Zahlung mit einem Drittel bei Auftragserteilung, einem Drittel bei Lieferung und einem Drittel innerhalb von 30 Tagen nach Lieferung geleistet*
	Our company will make payment by bill of exchange payable 60 days after sight	*Unsere Firma wird die Zahlung durch einen 60 Tage nach Sicht fälligen Wechsel leisten*
	The invoice amount will be remitted as agreed on receipt of the goods / on receipt of your invoice	*Der Rechnungsbetrag wird, wie vereinbart, bei Erhalt der Waren / bei Erhalt Ihrer Rechnung überwiesen*
6	**Delivery**	***Lieferung***
	Delivery is to be made within 6 weeks	*Die Lieferung hat innerhalb von 6 Wochen zu erfolgen*
	The goods are to be delivered by the date stated by your representative, Mr Higgins	*Die Güter sind bis zu dem von Ihrem Vertreter, Herrn Higgins, festgesetzten Datum zu liefern*
	Please deliver every two weeks	*Bitte liefern Sie alle zwei Wochen*
	… deliveries to be made as instructed	*Die Lieferungen sollen gemäß Anweisung erfolgen*
7	**Instructions***	***Anweisungen****
	Please acknowledge this order and indicate the delivery date for the goods	*Bitte bestätigen Sie diesen Auftrag und geben Sie das Lieferdatum für die Güter an*
	Please confirm receipt of this order and let us know when we can expect delivery	*Bitte bestätigen Sie den Erhalt dieser Bestellung und lassen Sie uns wissen, wann wir mit der Lieferung rechnen können*

Please arrange for the goods to be packed in cases marked "TWE/4035/JED/1-6/6"	*Bitte veranlassen Sie, dass die Waren in Kisten mit der Markierung „TWE/4035/JED/1-6/6" verpackt werden*
Please ensure that the goods are sent by air	*Bitte stellen Sie sicher, dass die Waren auf dem Luftwege versandt werden*
Please arrange for the articles to be shipped by road with the usual marks	*Bitte sorgen Sie dafür, dass die Artikel mit den üblichen Markierungen per Lkw versandt werden*
We would point out that the goods must be packed with the utmost care and attention	*Wir möchten darauf hinweisen, dass die Güter mit der größten Sorgfalt und Aufmerksamkeit verpackt werden müssen*
Our packing instructions are enclosed	*Unsere Verpackungsanweisungen sind beigefügt*
Please arrange for the data to be transferred to our company by e-mail	*Bitte veranlassen Sie, dass die Daten unserer Gesellschaft per E-Mail übermittelt werden*
Please advise us as soon as the goods have been loaded on board ship	*Bitte informieren Sie uns, sobald sich die Waren an Bord des Schiffes befinden*
The goods will be collected at Hamburg on our behalf by Intertrans GmbH	*Die Güter werden in Hamburg in unserem Auftrag von der Intertrans GmbH abgeholt*
Special arrangements*	***Besondere Vereinbarungen****
Please arrange for the goods to be insured	*Bitte veranlassen Sie, dass die Güter versichert werden*
We confirm that insurance will be obtained by us	*Wir bestätigen, dass die Versicherung durch uns abgeschlossen wird*
… insurance to be obtained by you	*Die Versicherung ist durch Sie abzuschließen*
Please arrange for the goods to be insured from warehouse to warehouse	*Bitte veranlassen Sie, dass die Waren von Lager bis Lager versichert werden*
Please arrange for insurance cover for the goods against all risks, including particular average and force majeure	*Bitte sorgen Sie für eine Versicherungsdeckung für die Waren gegen alle Risiken, einschließlich besonderer Havarie und höherer Gewalt*
Please arrange for insurance cover for the goods with general but excluding particular average	*Bitte veranlassen Sie die Versicherungsdeckung für die Güter mit allgemeiner, aber ausschließlich besonderer Havarie*
We will send you the insurance certificate as soon as it has been issued	*Wir werden Ihnen das Versicherungszertifikat schicken, sobald es ausgestellt worden ist*
If Rockfield insulating material is not available in sufficient quantities please substitute Foamtek 99	*Wenn das Rockfield Isoliermaterial nicht in ausreichender Menge verfügbar ist, ersetzen Sie es bitte durch Foamtek 99*

	Should terra cotta floor tiles be out of stock please supply suitable substitutes	*Sollten Terracotta-Bodenfliesen nicht mehr auf Lager sein, so liefern Sie bitte geeigneten Ersatz*
	Qualifications*	***Bedingungen****
	We reserve the right to return the goods carriage forward if they are not up to sample	*Wir behalten uns das Recht vor, die Waren unfrei zurückzuschicken, wenn sie nicht dem Muster entsprechen*
	We will unfortunately have no choice but to cancel our order if the goods are not delivered by 30 June	*Wir werden leider keine andere Wahl haben, als unseren Auftrag zu stornieren, wenn die Güter nicht bis zum 30. Juni geliefert werden*
	We regret we will have to hold you liable for loss of custom if your service is not satisfactory	*Wir bedauern, Sie wegen Verlust von Kundschaft haftbar machen zu müssen, wenn Ihr Service nicht zufriedenstellend ist*
	This order is placed on condition that there are no extra charges whatsoever in addition to those quoted	*Dieser Auftrag wird unter der Bedingung erteilt, dass keinerlei zusätzliche Gebühren außer den angegebenen entstehen*
	This order is placed on condition that a six-month guarantee is given on all equipment	*Dieser Auftrag wird unter der Bedingung erteilt, dass eine sechsmonatige Garantie auf die gesamte Ausrüstung gegeben wird*
	Payment will be made as soon as the goods have been passed by our Quality Control Department	*Die Zahlung erfolgt, sobald die Güter unsere Qualitätskontrolle passiert haben*
8	**Polite ending**	***Höflicher Schluss***
	We expect to be receiving your advice of despatch in the course of the next few days	*Wir erwarten den Erhalt Ihres Versandavis (Ihrer Versandanzeige) im Laufe der nächsten Tage*
	We trust our order will arrive punctually and in good condition	*Wir vertrauen darauf, dass unser Auftrag pünktlich und in gutem Zustand ankommen wird*
	Thank you for your prompt attention to this matter	*Wir wären Ihnen dankbar, wenn Sie sich sofort um diese Angelegenheit kümmern würden.*
	We look forward to placing further orders with your company if our trial order is well received	*Wir freuen uns darauf, Ihrer Firma weitere Aufträge zu erteilen, wenn unser Probeauftrag gut ankommt*
9	**Enclosure(s)**	***Anlage(n)***
	Order No. 234	*Auftrag / Bestellung Nr. 234*
	Order Form	*Auftragsformular*
	Our General Terms and Conditions	*Unsere Allgemeinen (Geschäfts) Bedingungen*
	Our Packing Instructions	*Unsere Verpackungsanweisungen*
	Sample(s)	*Muster*

Unit 5

Acknowledgements

1 Reference to order	Thanks for Many thanks for Thank you for Thank you very much for We thank you for We have received We were pleased to receive We were delighted to receive We refer to With reference to	your order for … (goods/services) dated/of … the above-mentioned order dated/of …	which arrived today/yesterday etc.		
	Your order for … (goods/services) The above-mentioned order	has been received has been noted has been passed on to our Despatch Department has been put in hand is receiving attention is (now) being • dealt with • attended to • made up • put together • processed			
	… we … our representative/agent … our Mr/Ms … (name)	will be contacting you will be getting in touch with you will be writing to you	shortly soon in the near future in the next few days in due course		
2 Confirmation of order	We are pleased to confirm that … We are pleased to advise you that … This is to advise you that …	the goods ordered as per your letter/fax/e-mail/telex dated/of …	will be have (now) been	delivered shipped (to you) sent (to you) forwarded (to you) supplied (to you)	as requested as stipulated
			can (now) be	collected	
	We enclose our confirmation of order Our confirmation of order is enclosed/attached				

Repetition of order	… the details of which are (once again)	as follows: listed below: as listed below: listed in the following:		
	Your order, as listed below, is being attended to: (list) We are pleased to advise you that your order dated/of … is now being made up	• as follows: • as listed below:		
Modification of order	We're sorry we won't be able to We are unfortunately unable to We unfortunately cannot We regret that it is impossible for us to	supply the goods provide the service(s) manufacture goods to the specifications	you require you enquire about mentioned	at present at the moment for the time being on this occasion this time for the next two months for approx. two months
		help you assist you give you any assistance		
	It/they — will not be available will be unavailable cannot be supplied will be in short supply	until + date (e.g. 1 January) for another + period of time (e.g. for another 3 weeks) for some time to come		
	The goods are This product/article/item is	out of stock no longer in stock unavailable no longer (being) manufactured		
	Production of this article/item etc.	has been discontinued		
	This product/article/item/machine/ machinery/equipment	is now — serviced maintained repaired installed	by … (name of company)	at … (address)
	The service you require is now provided			
	(May) we suggest you contact this company			

– substitutes	May we recommend We suggest you purchase	… (new article) instead of … (old article)	The new • version • model	is	faster better quieter more reliable more economical more stylishly designed etc.	than	the old one its predecessor the previous model
					similar (in style/appearance)	to	
	… and also competitively/favourably priced … and sells at (almost) the same price						
	Might we (therefore) suggest substituting … we would suggest substituting	… (new article) for … (old article)					
	The article you mention	has now been replaced by	… (product) a more modern version an entirely new model/machine	with (many) new features incorporating … incorporating many of the other model's (major) features			
	We enclose We are enclosing We are sending you	a brochure some sales literature	for your information				
– delay	Production of … (goods)	is delayed cannot start	until + date (e.g. the end of the month) for + period of time (e.g. for the next three weeks)				
		will take longer (than anticipated)					
	We are still waiting for	further supplies of … another delivery of … a consignment of …	goods material(s) equipment machinery apparatus				
	… and expect	delivery the goods to arrive them/it to be available	by + date within + period of time				
	This is because This is due to the fact that This has come about because	there has been very high / unexpected demand for there has been a rush of orders for	these goods/articles/ products/items this product/article/item/ equipment/machinery etc.	which has delayed	• production • manufacture • distribution • deliveries		
		there has been a strike by … (workers/employees) there has been flooding/an earthquake/a hurricane/a tornado/a forest fire etc. in … (place)					

– order is noted for later delivery	We have noted your requirements and will We have made a record of your request and will We have made a note of your requirements and will Your request has been registered and we will A record has been made of your requirements and we will	get in touch (with you) contact you let you know	as soon as	your order can be processed your order can be attended to your order can be dealt with we have received further supplies the goods become available we have filled all our outstanding orders we have reduced the backlog of outstanding orders	
Refusal of order	Owing to As a result of	massive demand for this product … an unexpected number of advance orders … a lack of raw material(s) … production difficulties … political problems (in …) … a strike on the part of (e. g. our suppliers) a strike in the … (e. g. steel, road haulage etc.) industry a lack of demand for articles / goods of this nature … the small quantity ordered … the fact that • you are not an authorised dealer … • you are not in our sales territory … • we are unable to give a definite date for delivery … • we have had no previous dealings with your company …			
	As Since Owing to the fact that	Article No. DTYD 89 is no longer available we are completely out of … (article / goods / material(s)) we have run out of … (article / goods / material(s)) we have no further stocks of … (article / goods / material(s)) our stocks of … (article / goods / material(s)) are low / depleted / exhausted			
	… we are sorry that we / our company … we regret that we / our company	will be unable to will not be in a position to would be unable to would not be prepared to would not be willing to	supply the goods ordered provide the services required	on the terms / conditions	requested mentioned outlined stated desired

	As we would only be prepared to supply	if payment is made	in advance … with order …		
		on a cash basis … subject to favourable references … if you are able to supply good references …			
	Since our terms would (have to) be	strictly cash cash with order (CWO) payment in advance			
	… we're sorry to have to … we regret to inform you that we must … we have no alternative but to … we are unfortunately obliged to	decline your order refuse your order			
	… we're sorry we can't … we unfortunately cannot … we regret we will be unable to	accept your order carry out your order execute your order			
	We're sorry but We are sorry that We regret that We regret having to inform you that	it will not (won't) be possible for • us • our company	to make to manufacture to supply	(the) goods	to the specifications • supplied • outlined • stated • desired
3 (Repetition of) prices and discounts*	This is to confirm We are glad to confirm We hereby confirm	our prices and discounts our charges our commission/fees for the services requested		as follows: (list)	
	We are pleased to confirm that, as stated in our offer, we/our company	will be pleased to will be able to will be in a position to are willing to are prepared to	grant allow	a … % (e.g. 10 %) • discount • reduction	on the • list price • trade price • catalogue price • export price • price(s) quoted

Modification of prices	We must unfortunately point out that We regret to inform you that Owing to an increase in • production costs • in the price of raw materials • labour costs • freight rates • shipping charges	the prices stated the prices quoted in your order the prices you quote	are no longer applicable no longer apply are no longer valid are out of date are subject to a 10 % increase have been increased by 10 % are based upon an out-of-date price list	
	We are unable to supply the goods at • the price requested because • the price originally quoted because	the new (improved) model sells at a higher price we only use materials of the best quality we employ expert craftsmen our goods are manufactured using highly skilled labour		
	We must point out that We must draw your attention to the fact that As a result of the (general) increase in • the cost of raw materials • transport costs • freight rates • insurance rates	there will be an additional charge of … (e. g. $10 per unit) there has been a price increase of … % we are compelled/forced/obliged to make an additional charge of … the price of this article has now been increased by … % resulting in a final price of … (price, e. g. $1,100.00)		
Modification of discounts	You are no longer eligible for the discount claimed because We are unfortunately not able to grant you the discount(s) claimed because The discounts you mention no longer apply because	this is not an initial order the quantity ordered is insufficient a minimum of … units/kg etc. must be ordered the special offer has now expired our introductory offer expired on … (date) you have placed your order too late		
	We are (unfortunately) unable to grant/allow you We will unfortunately not be in a position to grant you	a discount of … % because the discount requested because the reduction in price you ask for because	our goods are already being sold at rock-bottom prices our profit-margin is already minimal on this item our prices have been cut to the bone we would be selling the goods at a loss	
	We are pleased to tell you that	our … discount has been all discounts have been	increased raised	by … % to … % (e. g. by 2 % to 15 %) from … % to … % (e. g. from 13 % to 15 %)
	Since/as this is an order exceeding … (units/ kg etc.) Since/as this is a repeat order Since/as this is your/the … (e. g. 4th, 5th etc.) order As this is not the article originally ordered As we are offering (a) substitute(s)	you now qualify for a discount of … % you are now entitled to a discount of … % we are willing to grant you a discount of … % we are willing to grant you a reduction in price of … %	on the trade price on the list price on the catalogue price	

4 (Repetition of) terms of delivery	As previously stated As stated in previous correspondence As stated in our offer As agreed As per our offer dated/of …		our prices include delivery our prices cover delivery all prices are	… (Incoterm + location, e.g. CPT Newcastle)
	Delivery will be made The goods will be delivered	as agreed as requested as stated as arranged	… (Incoterm + location)	on … (date) by + date within + period of time in good time for … (e.g. The Motor Show etc.) 2 days before … (e.g. the International Trade Fair)
	The • goods • consignment • articles • machine • machinery • equipment • apparatus • tool(s)	will be will in all probability be will most probably be	ready for despatch ready for collection available completed	
	The goods will be We expect the goods to be We guarantee that the goods will be We undertake to have the goods			
(Modification of) terms of delivery	We will (unfortunately) only be able to deliver the(se) goods … (delivery term) and not … (delivery term) as requested We must point out that delivery can only be made … (delivery term) Consignments of this nature can only be delivered … (delivery term) at the price quoted Please note that delivery can only be made … (delivery term)			
	If delivery is to be made … (delivery terms) If delivery is required … Should you require delivery …	there will be an extra charge of we will be obliged to charge you a further we will have no alternative but to charge you a further		£/$ …/… euros etc. per unit/kg etc.
	We will assume that you accept these terms if	we are not informed to the contrary we are not notified we do not hear from you		within the next … days/weeks by + date
(Repetition of) terms of payment	As stated in our As already indicated in our As previously stated in our	offer quotation letter dated/of …		our terms of payment are …
	Our terms of payment are … *(see Unit 3 "Offers")*			

Please remit the invoice amount		by bank transfer to our account no. …	at (the) … Bank in …
As arranged As agreed	we enclose our we are enclosing our	(sight) draft 30/60/90-day draft	for your acceptance which we would ask you to accept and return to us
		statement of account	covering the period up to … (date, e.g. March 31st) for January, February etc. for the first/second quarter etc.
… together with		our pro-forma invoice a copy of our General Conditions of Sale the Sales Agreement a duplicate Sales Agreement a Contract of Sale	

5 (Repetition/ modification of) date and mode of delivery	We confirm that delivery will be made … delivery to be made	by … (mode of delivery, e.g. by road/rail/air/ship etc.) using … (name of carrier, e.g. by Intertrans Inc.)	by + date within + period of time	at the latest without fail
	We must point out that We regret that Please accept our apologies for the fact that	we are unfortunately unable to we will unfortunately not be able to we unfortunately cannot it is impossible for us to it will not be possible for us to we will not be in a position to we doubt if we will be able to	deliver supply the goods make delivery arrange for delivery guarantee delivery promise delivery	by + date by the date specified before + date within + period of time on the date/day requested within the period of time stated /requested
	Delivery cannot be made	for the next + period of time (e.g. 3 weeks) until + date (e.g. 30 June) before + date by the time requested/stated		
– reason	… as … … since … … because … … owing to … … as a result of … … as a consequence of … This is due to the fact that … This is because The reason for this is that …	(reasons – see "2, Refusal of order")		

6 Technicalities – marks	The (cardboard)	• boxes • packages • crates • cases • chests • bags • sacks • containers	have been will be	numbered labelled marked	… (e. g. EPD/40920A/Dover/1-25/EU, To be collected)	
	The boxes etc.			marked labelled	"This side up" "Use no hooks" "Fragile" "Inflammable liquid" "Poison" "With care"	as per your letter dated/ of … in accordance with your instructions as instructed as requested
	The usual marks have been used					
	Please use our order form(s) We would request you to use the order form(s) enclosed For your convenience we have enclosed an order form (order forms) for you to use				for all future orders when placing your next order the next time you order	
	Please remember to We would kindly request you Please make sure you			quote state include indicate give details of	the article number(s) the sizes the colours the weights the dimensions etc.	when ordering when placing your (next) order
– packing	As per your instructions In accordance with your instructions As instructed As per your letter dated/of …			the goods have been	packed sent despatched shipped forwarded transported	in … (packing, *see Unit 6, "Delivery"*)
	Please send us your packing instructions Your packing instructions will be strictly observed					

– shipping	As per your instructions In accordance with your instructions As instructed As per your letter dated/of …	the goods	will be shipped have been shipped were shipped	by … (mode of shipment, e.g. rail, road, air, sea, (cross-channel) ferry) on board "MS Anastasia", which sets sail on … (date) and docks in … (name of port) on … (date) via the Channel Tunnel by British Rail to … (location)
	… the goods can only be shipped	… (mode of transport) and not … (mode of transport) since … (see "– reason" above)		
	We must point out that We regret that Unfortunately,	it will only be possible for us to ship the goods by … (mode of shipment)		
	Please let us know whether the goods are to be shipped … (e.g. by rail) or … (e.g. by road)			
	The goods will be shipped as soon as we have received your shipping instructions Unless otherwise instructed we will ship the goods … (mode of shipment) Please let us know • by … (+ date) • within … (+ period of time) if you wish us to ship the goods other than by … (mode of shipment) Goods of this nature are shipped by … (mode of shipment) It is standard practice to ship goods of this nature by … (mode of shipment) Please send us your shipping instructions Please let us know how you wish the goods to be shipped			
	We will • advise your freight forwarders/shipping agent/shipping company • notify • inform • contact			as soon as the goods are ready for collection as soon as the goods can be collected
7 Conditions to be fulfilled	Please note that We would point out that We wish to draw your attention to the fact that	this order is subject to	our General Conditions of Sale, a copy of which	is enclosed is printed on the back of our Order Form has been sent to you was sent to you with our offer dated/of …
		your order can only be your order will be	processed dealt with attended to carried out executed	subject to favourable references if … on the terms requested

	if … provided that … on condition that … as long as …	payment is made … your remittance has been received … the invoice amount has been • received • transferred to our account		by + date within + period of time in advance as agreed as stated in our General Conditions of Sale	
		you send us written confirmation that …		payment will be made by … (means of payment, e.g. documentary credit)	
	Please arrange	to have the documentary credit opened for payment to be made for the sum of … to be transferred to our account at the … (bank) for your freight forwarders to contact us for this information (e.g. shipping instructions etc.) to be sent to us	to enable us to start	processing dealing with making up	your order the consignment the shipment the load
	Please advise us Please send us instructions	as regards … (e.g. shipping routes, shipping arrangements, customs regulations, import regulations etc.)			
	… our … (e.g. pro-forma invoice, order form, sales agreement in duplicate)		is enclosed		
– delivery	Delivery will be made The goods will arrive We expect the goods to be delivered The goods will reach you		by + date before + date within + period of time		
	Please arrange for the goods to be collected		by + carrier/freight forwarder (e.g. by your freight forwarder(s))		
8 Request for confirmation	We look forward to We trust we will be	receiving your instructions hearing from you	on this matter as regards … with respect to …		
	Please advise us Please let us know Please confirm Please let us have your confirmation	by fax by e-mail by telex in writing	if you • accept • wish to accept • are willing to accept • are able to accept • agree to • have no objections to	our new offer the goods we recommend these terms this arrangement our suggestion the mode of transport suggested	

	Please advise us Please send us written confirmation Please call us Please (tele)phone us	if our new offer is (not) acceptable to you if our new offer is (not) to your liking if our new offer meets/does not meet your approval			
	We will start processing Work will begin on	your order	as soon as you have	sent us your written confirmation of confirmed consented to agreed to	these arrangements this suggestion the(se) (new) terms
	Your order will be attended to Your order will be dealt with Your order will be made up Your order will be put in hand				
9 Polite ending	We feel sure that the goods	will be to your liking will meet your expectations			
	Please do not hesitate to	contact us get in touch with us let us know tell us	should you have any queries if you require further information		
	You will be receiving	our advice of despatch	in the next few days/weeks etc. in the course of the next few days/weeks etc. in due course in the near future as soon as possible		
	We will be • sending you • faxing • posting • mailing				
	We look forward to hearing from you soon We look forward to doing further business with you Thank you for your custom Thank you for choosing to place your order with us/… (name of your company, e.g. Easifit Ltd.) Thank you for giving us the opportunity to convince you of the quality of our goods/services				
10 Enclosure(s)	Confirmation of Order General Conditions of Sale Pro-forma invoice (Duplicate) Sales Agreement Contract of Sale Draft(s) Bill(s) of exchange Statement of account etc.				

Phraseology
Acknowledgement

1	**Reference to order**	***Bezugnahme auf Auftrag***
	Many thanks for your order for … (goods / services) dated / of …	*Vielen Dank für Ihren Auftrag für … (Waren / Dienstleistungen) vom …*
	We were delighted to receive the above-mentioned order dated / of …	*Wir haben uns gefreut, Ihren obengenannten Auftrag vom … zu erhalten*
	The above-mentioned order has been noted	*Wir haben den obengenannten Auftrag zur Kenntnis genommen*
	Your order has been put in hand	*Ihr Auftrag ist zur Bearbeitung weitergeleitet worden*
	Your order is now being attended to	*Ihr Auftrag wird jetzt bearbeitet*
	Our representative / agent will be getting in touch with you in the next few days	*Unsere Repräsentantin / Unser Vertreter wird in den nächsten Tagen mit Ihnen in Verbindung treten*
2	**Confirmation of order**	***Auftragsbestätigung***
	We are pleased to advise you that the goods ordered as per your letter / fax / e-mail / telex dated / of … have (now) been shipped as requested	*Wir freuen uns Ihnen mitzuteilen, dass die mit Ihrem Brief / Fax / Telex / Ihrer E-Mail vom … bestellten Waren (jetzt) wie gewünscht versandt / verschifft worden sind*
	Our confirmation of order is enclosed / attached	*Unsere Auftragsbestätigung ist beigefügt*
	Repetition of order	***Wiederholung des Auftrags***
	Your order, as listed below, is being attended to: (list)	*Ihr nachstehend aufgelisteter Auftrag wird zur Zeit bearbeitet: (Liste)*
	Modification of order	***Änderung des Auftrags***
	We regret that it is impossible for us to supply the goods you require for the time being	*Wir bedauern, dass es uns zur Zeit nicht möglich ist, die von Ihnen gewünschten Waren zu liefern*
	They will be in short supply for another 3 weeks	*Sie werden weitere 3 Wochen lang schwer lieferbar sein*
	This article is out of stock	*Dieser Artikel ist nicht auf Lager*
	Production of this item has been discontinued	*Die Herstellung dieses Postens ist eingestellt worden*
	This machine is now maintained by … (name of company) at … (address)	*Diese Maschine wird nunmehr von … (Name der Firma) in … (Adresse) gewartet*
	Substitutes	***Ersatz***
	We suggest you purchase our new A45 photocopier instead of the older A40 model	*Wir schlagen vor, dass Sie statt des älteren A40-Modells unseren neuen Fotokopierer A45 kaufen*
	The new version is more economical than its predecessor and also competitively priced	*Die neue Version ist sparsamer als ihr Vorgänger und preislich ebenfalls wettbewerbsfähig*

Might we (therefore) suggest substituting … (new article) for … (old article)	*Dürfen wir (daher) vorschlagen, dass wir den … (alten Artikel) durch den … (neuen Artikel) ersetzen*
The article you mention has now been replaced by an entirely new model incorporating many of the other model's major features	*Der von Ihnen erwähnte Artikel ist jetzt von einem völlig neuen Modell ersetzt worden, das viele der Hauptmerkmale des anderen Modells beinhaltet*
Delay	***Verzögerung***
Production of … (goods) will take longer than anticipated	*Die Herstellung der … (Waren) wird länger als vorgesehen dauern*
This is due to the fact that there has been flooding in … (place)	*Dies ist auf die Tatsache zurückzuführen, dass es in … (Ort) eine Überschwemmung gab*
This has come about because there has been very high demand for these articles, which has delayed distribution	*Dies ist dadurch zustande gekommen, dass diese Artikel sehr stark nachgefragt wurden, wodurch sich der Vertrieb verzögert hat*
Order is noted for later delivery	*Der Auftrag wird für spätere Lieferung vorgemerkt*
A record has been made of your requirements and we will get in touch with you as soon as we have received further supplies	*Wir haben Ihren Bedarf vorgemerkt und werden uns wieder mit Ihnen in Verbindung setzen, sobald wir weitere Lieferungen erhalten haben*
Refusal of order	***Ablehnung des Auftrags***
As a result of the small quantity ordered …	*Auf Grund der geringen Menge, die bestellt wurde, …*
Owing to a lack of raw materials …	*Wegen eines Mangels an Rohstoffen …*
Since we have run out of … (article / goods / material(s))	*Da wir keine(n) … (Artikel / Waren / Material(ien)) mehr haben*
We are sorry that our company will not be in a position to provide the services required on the terms outlined	*Es tut uns Leid, dass unsere Firma nicht in der Lage sein wird, die gewünschten Dienstleistungen zu den angegebenen Bedingungen zu erbringen*
As we would only be prepared to supply subject to favourable references …	*Da wir nur auf Grund von günstigen Referenzen zur Lieferung bereit wären, …*
As we would only supply these goods if payment is made in advance …	*Da wir diese Waren nur liefern würden, wenn eine Zahlung im Voraus geleistet wird, …*
Since our terms would (have to) be strictly cash …	*Da unsere Bedingungen strikt auf Barzahlung lauten (müssten),…*
… we're sorry we can't accept your order	*… bedauern wir, Ihren Auftrag nicht annehmen zu können*
… we regret to inform you that we must decline your order	*… bedauern wir Ihnen mitzuteilen, dass wir Ihre Bestellung ablehnen müssen*

	We're sorry but it won't be possible for us to manufacture the goods to the specifications stated	*Bedauerlicherweise wird es uns nicht möglich sein, die Güter zu den aufgeführten Spezifikationen herzustellen*
3	**(Repetition of) prices and discounts**	***Preise und Nachlässe (Wiederholung)***
	This is to confirm our commission / fees for the services requested as follows: (list)	*Hiermit möchten wir unsere Provision / Gebühren für die gewünschten Dienstleistungen wie folgt bestätigen: (Liste)*
	We are pleased to confirm that, as stated in our offer, we are prepared to allow a … % (e.g. 10 %) discount on the prices quoted	*Wir freuen uns zu bestätigen, dass wir, wie in unserem Angebot genannt, bereit sind, einen … %igen Nachlass (z. B. 10 %) auf die angebotenen Preise zu gewähren*
	(Modification of) prices	***(Änderung der) Preise***
	Owing to an increase in labour costs the prices quoted in your order are no longer valid	*Auf Grund einer Erhöhung der Lohnkosten sind die in Ihrem Auftrag angegebenen Preise nicht mehr gültig*
	We are unable to supply the goods at the price requested because the new (improved) model sells at a higher price	*Wir sind nicht in der Lage, die Waren zu dem gewünschten Preis zu liefern, weil das neue (verbesserte) Modell zu einem höheren Preis verkauft wird*
	We must draw your attention to the fact that we are compelled to make an additional charge of …	*Wir müssen Ihre Aufmerksamkeit auf die Tatsache lenken, dass wir gezwungen sind, eine zusätzliche Gebühr von … zu erheben*
	(Modification of) discounts	***(Änderung der) Nachlässe***
	You are no longer eligible for the discount claimed because the special offer has now expired	*Sie sind nicht mehr berechtigt, den geforderten Nachlass in Anspruch zu nehmen, weil das Sonderangebot jetzt ausgelaufen ist*
	We are unfortunately unable to allow you the reduction you ask for because our goods are already being sold at rock-bottom prices	*Wir sind leider nicht in der Lage, Ihnen den gewünschten Nachlass zu gewähren, weil unsere Waren bereits zu absoluten Tiefstpreisen verkauft werden*
	Since this is a repeat order you are now entitled to a discount of … % on the list price	*Da es sich hierbei um einen Nachfolgeauftrag handelt, sind Sie jetzt berechtigt, einen … %igen Nachlass auf den Listenpreis zu erhalten*
4	**(Repetition of) terms of delivery**	***(Wiederholung der) Lieferbedingungen***
	As stated in previous correspondence, our prices cover delivery CPT Newcastle	*Wie in unserer bisherigen Korrespondenz dargelegt, beinhalten unsere Preise die Lieferung CPT Newcastle*
	Delivery will be made, as agreed, CIP London Airport	*Die Lieferung erfolgt wie vereinbart CIP Flughafen London*
	The consignment will, in all probability, be ready for despatch on … (date)	*Die Sendung wird höchstwahrscheinlich am … (Datum) versandbereit sein*

	We undertake to have the goods ready for collection in good time for … (e.g. The Motor Show etc.)	*Wir verpflichten uns, die Waren rechtzeitig für die … (z.B. Autoausstellung usw.) zur Abholung bereitzuhalten*
	Modification of terms of delivery	***Änderung der Lieferbedingungen***
	Consignments of this nature can only be delivered FOB Hamburg at the price quoted	*Sendungen dieser Art können zum angebotenen Preis nur FOB Hamburg geliefert werden*
	We will assume that you accept these terms if we are not informed to the contrary by 1st June	*Wir nehmen an, dass Sie diese Bedingungen annehmen, wenn wir nicht bis zum 1. Juni Gegenteiliges von Ihnen hören*
	(Repetition of) terms of payment	***Zahlungsbedingungen (Wiederholung)***
	As already indicated in our offer our terms of payment are …	*Wie wir bereits in unserem Angebot angegeben haben, sind unsere Zahlungsbedingungen wie folgt: …*
	Please remit the invoice amount by bank transfer to our account no. … at (the) … Bank in … (location)	*Bitte zahlen Sie den Rechnungsbetrag per Banküberweisung auf unser Konto Nr. … bei der … Bank in … (Ort) ein*
	As agreed we are enclosing our 30/60/90-day sight draft, which we would ask you to accept and return to us	*Wie vereinbart, fügen wir unseren 30/60/90-Tage Sichtwechsel bei, den wir Sie bitten zu akzeptieren und an uns zurückzuschicken*
	… together with a copy of our General Conditions of Sale	*… zusammen mit einer Kopie (Ausgabe) unserer Allgemeinen Verkaufsbedingungen*
5	**(Repetition / modification of) date and mode of delivery**	***(Wiederholung / Änderung des) Datum(s) und (der) Lieferart***
	We confirm that delivery will be made by … (mode of delivery, e.g. by road / rail / air / ship etc.) within 6 weeks without fail	*Wir bestätigen, dass die Lieferung ganz bestimmt innerhalb von 6 Wochen durch … (Lieferart, z.B. per Lkw / Schiene / Luft / Schiff usw.) erfolgen wird*
	Please accept our apologies for the fact that we unfortunately cannot guarantee delivery within the period of time requested	*Bitte entschuldigen Sie die Tatsache, dass wir leider innerhalb des erbetenen Zeitraums keine Lieferung garantieren können*
	Delivery cannot be made before … (date)	*Die Lieferung kann nicht vor dem … (Datum) erfolgen*
6	**Technicalities – marks**	***Technische Einzelheiten – Markierungen***
	The crates have been numbered "EPD/40920A/Dover/1-25/EU" and marked "To be collected"	*Die Kisten sind mit „EPD/40920A/Dover/1-25/EU" nummeriert und mit der Aufschrift „Wird abgeholt" versehen worden*
	The containers etc. will be marked "Inflammable liquid", in accordance with your instructions	*Die Container usw. werden in Übereinstimmung mit Ihren Anweisungen mit der Aufschrift versehen: „Brennbare Flüssigkeit"*

	The usual marks have been used	*Die üblichen Markierungen wurden verwendet*
	For your convenience we have enclosed an order form for you to use when placing your next order	*Der Einfachheit halber haben wir ein Auftragsformular beigefügt, das Sie benutzen können, wenn Sie Ihre neue Bestellung aufgeben*
	We would request that you state the article numbers when placing your next order	*Wir möchten Sie bitten, die Artikelnummer anzugeben, wenn Sie Ihren nächsten Auftrag erteilen*
	Packing	***Verpackung***
	As per your instructions the goods have been despatched in …	*Gemäß Ihren Anweisungen wurden die Waren in … versandt*
	Your packing instructions will be strictly observed	*Ihre Verpackungsanweisungen werden strikt eingehalten*
	Shipping	***Verschiffung***
	As per your letter dated / of … the goods were shipped on board "MS Anastasia", which sets sail on … (date) and docks in … (name of port) on … (date)	*Gemäß Ihrem Brief vom … wurden die Waren an Bord der „MS Anastasia" verladen, die am … (Datum) auslaufen und am … (Datum) in … (Name des Hafens) eindocken wird*
	Unfortunately, it will only be possible for us to ship the goods by … (mode of shipment)	*Leider wird es uns nur möglich sein, die Waren durch … (Art des Versands) zu verschicken*
	Unless otherwise instructed we will ship the goods … (mode of shipment)	*Sofern wir nicht andere Anweisungen erhalten, werden wir die Güter durch … (Art des Versands) verschicken*
	It is standard practice to ship goods of this nature by … (mode of shipment)	*Es ist allgemeine Praxis, Waren dieser Art durch … (Art des Versands) zu versenden*
	We will notify your freight forwarders / shipping agent / shipping company etc. as soon as the goods are ready for collection	*Wir werden Ihre Spediteure / Ihren Schiffsagenten / Ihre Schifffahrtsgesellschaft usw. benachrichtigen, sobald die Waren abholbereit sind*
7	**Conditions to be fulfilled**	***Bedingungen, die erfüllt werden müssen***
	Please note that this order is subject to our General Conditions of Sale, a copy of which is printed on the back of our Order Form	*Bitte nehmen Sie zur Kenntnis, dass dieser Auftrag unseren Allgemeinen Verkaufsbedingungen unterliegt, von denen eine Abschrift auf der Rückseite unseres Auftragsformulars abgedruckt ist*
	… provided that you send us written confirmation that payment will be made by … (means of payment, e.g. documentary credit)	*… vorausgesetzt, dass Sie uns eine schriftliche Bestätigung senden, dass die Zahlung durch … (Zahlungsart, z. B. Dokumentenakkreditiv) erfolgen wird*

	Please arrange for the sum of … to be transferred to our account no. … at the … (bank) to enable us to start processing your order	*Bitte veranlassen Sie, dass die Summe von … auf unser Konto Nr. … bei der … (Bank) überwiesen wird, damit wir mit der Bearbeitung Ihres Auftrages beginnen können*
	Please advise us as regards … (e.g. shipping routes, shipping arrangements, customs regulations, import regulations etc.)	*Bitte geben Sie uns bezüglich … (z. B. Verschiffungsrouten, Verschiffungsabmachungen, Zollvorschriften, Importbestimmungen usw.) Bescheid*
	Our duplicate sales agreement is enclosed	*Unsere Vertragsdoppel ist beigefügt*
	Delivery	***Lieferung***
	We expect the goods to be delivered by + (date)	*Wir erwarten, dass die Güter bis … (Datum) geliefert werden*
8	**Request for confirmation**	***Bitte um Bestätigung***
	We trust we will be receiving your instructions with respect to …	*Wir vertrauen darauf, dass wir Ihre Anweisungen bezüglich … erhalten werden*
	Please confirm by fax if you have no objections to this arrangement	*Bitte schicken Sie uns Ihre Bestätigung per Fax, falls Sie gegen diese Abmachung keine Einwendungen erheben*
	Please advise us if our new offer meets / does not meet your approval	*Bitte unterrichten Sie uns, falls Sie mit unserem neuen Angebot einverstanden / nicht einverstanden sind*
	We will start processing your order as soon as you have consented to the(se) (new) terms	*Wir werden mit der Bearbeitung Ihres Auftrags beginnen, sobald Sie den (diesen) (neuen) Bedingungen zugestimmt haben*
9	**Polite ending**	***Höflicher Schluss***
	You will be receiving our advice of despatch in the next few days	*Sie erhalten unser Versandavis in den nächsten Tagen*
	We will be mailing you our advice of despatch in due course	*Wir werden Ihnen zu gegebener Zeit unsere Versandanzeige zuschicken*
	Thank you for your custom	*Vielen Dank für Ihren Auftrag*
10	**Enclosure(s)**	***Anlage(n)***
	General Conditions of Sale	*Allgemeine Verkaufsbedingungen*
	Pro-forma invoice	*Proforma-Rechnung*
	(Duplicate) Sales Agreement	*Vertragsdoppel*
	Contract of Sale	*Kaufvertrag*
	Draft(s)	*Entwurf*
	Bill(s) of exchange	*Wechsel (Tratte(n))*

Unit 6

Delivery

1 Reference to goods ordered	This is to inform you that … This is to advise you that … We are pleased to inform you that … We are pleased to confirm that … We are now able to confirm that …	the • articles • goods • machines • machinery • equipment • apparatus	ordered		as per your letter dated/of … (see enclosure) as per your letter/fax/e-mail dated/of … (see copy enclosed) as per the Order Form enclosed
			you have commissioned us to we have been commissioned to	manufacture supply	
	… has/have (now) been completed and … … is/are (now) ready and …				
2 Available for collection*	(The goods)	… will be made available to you for collection at	our premises our factory our plant our distribution centre our depot our warehouse	in … (location)	on … (date) in the next few … (e.g. days) in the course of this/next week
		… can (now) be collected at … can (now) be picked up at … are (now) available for collection at … have (now) been made available for collection at			at any time on the date stated/arranged/agreed, i.e. … (date) whenever you wish during office hours (9 am – 5 pm) at any time between 8 am and 6 pm at any time convenient to you subject to your notifying us 24 hours in advance
Ready for despatch*		… are now ready for despatch	Please let us have your forwarding instructions Please let us know how/when/how and when you wish to have them forwarded We await your forwarding instructions		

Advice of despatch*	(The goods)	... have (now) been ... will (now) be	sent forwarded shipped posted/ mailed despatched rushed	to you ...		
		... can (now) be	collected picked up	by your forwarding agents ... (name of forwarder)		
– mode of transport	... by	road rail air ship goods train (refrigerated) lorry (refrigerated) truck van low loader inland waterway vessel barge express air mail surface mail parcel post special messenger special courier motor-cycle despatch rider		... as	rail freight sea freight air freight package freight fast freight a groupage consignment/a consolidated shipment a whole container load a part container load a separate load bulk cargo	
	The goods will be sent as air freight on Lufthansa Flight No. ..., which leaves Düsseldorf Airport on ... (date) at ... (time) landing at ... (airport) on ... (date) at ... (time)					
	The goods	have been will be	loaded shipped	on board MV "Victoria", on board MS "Diana",	which is due to set sail for Hamburg which sets sail for Hamburg which is due to leave (the port of) Dover which is scheduled to leave Dover for Hamburg	on ... (date) by ... (date) at the end of the month within the next few days

– terms of delivery (Incoterm)	The goods have been shipped The goods will be shipped Delivery will be made	… (Incoterm + destination, e. g. CIF Dover/CIP Heathrow Airport) franco to your • premises • office • factory • plant • warehouse • depot • warehouse • site carriage forward carriage paid		as requested as instructed as arranged as agreed (in our Contract of Sale) as per your instructions as agreed • in our telephone conversation of … (date) • at our meeting in … (location) on … (date)	
	The goods ordered as per your letter/fax/e-mail dated/of … (date)	will be delivered to you	on … (date)	… (Incoterm + destination)	as requested as instructed as arranged as agreed (in our Contract of Sale) as per your instructions
	The goods ordered	were forwarded to you were shipped to you were sent to you	this morning yesterday last Friday		
– name of forwarder	The goods will be	delivered forwarded shipped transported packed and shipped	by … (name of forwarder)		
	Delivery will be	made effected			
	… (name of forwarder) will		deliver forward ship transport pack and ship	the goods the consignment the load etc.	

	We will have … (name of freight forwarder) Will arrange for … (name of forwarder) to We will instruct … (name of forwarder) to … (name of forwarder) will be instructed to	deliver forward ship transport pack and ship	the goods	
	We have arranged for	delivery to be made the goods to be shipped	by … (name of forwarder)	
– estimated time of arrival	The goods/consignment	will in all probability will most probably is/are expected to is/are due to	arrive be delivered reach … (location)	on … (date) by … (date) at the end of the month within the next … weeks (e.g. within the next three weeks)
	According to her sailing card MS Diana	is scheduled to	dock at arrive at reach	(the port of) Dover
	You will be able to	take delivery of collect pick up	the goods	on … (date) by … (date) within … (period of time) at the end of the month
	We will	notify contact get in touch with fax e-mail call (tele)phone	you as soon as the goods	have been loaded are on board are on their way have arrived in … (location) can be collected in … (location) can be picked up in … (location) have reached … (location)

– details of packing – shipping marks	The goods	have been packed are supplied are sent are despatched are forwarded are shipped	in (cardboard / fibreglass) boxes in (plywood) boxes in foam-lined boxes in collapsible cardboard boxes in (generously padded / wooden) boxes in (sturdy) (reinforced) (strongly boarded) crates in (tea) chests (lined with silver paper) in (solid wooden) (damp-proof) (nailed / battened) cases in polystyrene packing material in (100 litre) carboys in (canvas / paper / 3-ply reinforced paper) bags in (50 kg) sacks in (securely sealed) (air-tight) tins in (1,000 l) barrels in (sturdy / stout / sealed) (fibre) drums in bundles in bales (2 m × 5 m) in a container (in containers) on a pallet (on pallets)	with metal strapping with metal bands with double hooping (drums) reinforced by wire filled with wire wool lined with silver paper with thick padding to guard against knocks with cleats for extra strength lined with plastic lined with tinfoil with a foam rubber lining with chemical foam lining wrapped in foil sealed in vacuum-shrunk polythene	marked … with the usual marks
– packaging	The … (containers) are made of		environmentally friendly … (material) disposable … (material) bio-degradable … (material, e.g. plastic) (non-)recyclable … (material) (non-) returnable … (material) (sturdy / reinforced) cardboard (water-proof / water-resistant / heat-resistant) synthetic material (strong / sturdy) wood (2cm thick) metal (stainless) steel (wrought) iron (strong) wire		

		(thick) glass (strong/unbreakable/durable) plastic rubber waxcloth oilcloth corrugated paper waxed paper silver paper jute canvas
	The … (type of packing, e.g. pallets)	are charged at a flat rate of … (charge, e.g. £5) per unit are charged at … (charge, e.g. 5 euros) each are non-returnable can be returned to our plant/works/factory within … (period of time) for a refund, provided they are in good condition can be returned to our works carriage forward must be returned within 14 days if a refund is to be claimed will be picked up by our carrier when the next consignment is delivered, free of charge should be stored until collected by us
	Please return the empties/the pallets/the crates etc.	(carriage forward) to our depot with the next load
3 Request for packing instructions (and shipping marks)*	Please let us have We now require Would you now please let us have We await	your packing (and marking) instructions your instructions as regards packing (and shipping marks)
	Would you now please indicate Please advise us	how the goods are to be packed how you wish to have the goods packed (and marked) what packaging you require what material is to be used to pack the goods
	It is normal practice It is customary (in the trade)	to pack these goods in … to use … (material) to pack these goods
	Such goods	are normally packed in … (material) normally come packed in … are normally sent as bulk cargo

	Should we not hear from you to the contrary Unless otherwise instructed	we will pack the goods in … the goods will be packed in … we will assume that you wish to have the goods packed in this way we will assume that you have no objection to the goods being packed in this way the goods will be packed in this way	
– shipping marks	Please indicate Please advise us Please let us know Please instruct us as to	how you wish the boxes/crates/containers etc. to be marked what shipping marks you require	
	Should we not hear from you to the contrary Unless otherwise instructed	we will use the usual shipping marks the usual shipping marks will be used the boxes/crates/containers etc. will be marked in the usual way the boxes will be marked … (details of shipping marks, e.g. TWE/4035/JED/1-6/6 (for 6 containers))	
4 Reference to mode of payment*	As soon as	we have received your cheque for … we have received your banker's draft for … we have received your remittance for … (in payment of/in part-payment of our invoice) you have accepted and returned our (sight) draft (bill of exchange) for … the invoice amount has been transferred to our account no. … at (the) … Bank in … (location) your remittance in settlement of the enclosed Statement of Account • has been received • has been credited to our account the documentary credit in our favour has been opened we have been advised by our bank that the letter of credit (in our favour) has been opened	the goods will be despatched the goods will be forwarded the goods will be shipped the goods will be sent to you
– request for payment	We enclose our invoice/statement (no. … dated/of …) and would be grateful if you would settle it as agreed Our invoice no. … dated/from … (date) is enclosed for settlement Our statement for the period from … (date) to … (date) is enclosed for settlement Our statement as of 31 March .. is enclosed Our statement for … (period, e.g. January, the first/second/third/fourth quarter of … (year)) is enclosed for settlement Please • transfer the invoice amount to our account no. … at (the) … Bank within the time stipulated • remit We have drawn on you for the invoice amount of … at 30/60/90/180 d/s and enclose our draft for your acceptance		

Please accept and return the enclosed draft, after which the goods will be despatched

We have instructed our correspondent bank, (the) … Bank in … (location) to release the documents
- as soon as the draft has been accepted (D/A)
- on acceptance of the draft (D/A)
- on payment of the draft (D/P)

The documents will be released to you on payment/acceptance of the (enclosed) draft

5 Reference to documentation enclosed or sent separately*

In accordance with the conditions stipulated in the documentary credit As stipulated As agreed (in our Contract of Sale) As requested As instructed As arranged As agreed As per your instructions	we enclose the following documents: the following documents are enclosed: the following documents have been given to/handed over to (the) … Bank (name of seller's bank) in … (location)	e. g. – complete set of clean, on-board bills of lading (notify: …) (address of person to be notified) – original and three copies of the commercial invoice – insurance policy (certificate) – certificate of origin – customs declaration – export licence – certificate of analysis etc.

We enclose …
Please find enclosed …
Enclosed you will find …
We enclose 2, 3, 4, 5 etc. originals of the … (name of document, e. g. Commercial Invoice)
Our … (name of document, e. g. Commercial Invoice) is enclosed in duplicate/triplicate/quadruplicate/quintuplicate

Our pro-forma invoice is enclosed	to enable you to open the letter of credit to enable you to apply for an import licence We would request you to remit the sum due, after which the goods will be despatched to you immediately

The … (name of document(s))	has/have be forwarded to you will be forwarded to you	under separate cover by separate post by separate mail separately

6 Polite ending	We trust your order has been We hope your order has been	carried out executed processed	to your entire satisfaction	and look forward to the pleasure of serving you again and look forward to receiving further orders and hope to receive further orders and would be pleased to receive further orders
	We feel sure We trust We hope	that you will be pleased with the goods that the goods will be to your liking that the goods will suit your needs that you will be pleased with the high quality of our products that the goods will arrive punctually and in good condition that the consignment will arrive safely and on schedule		
	Please do not hesitate to	contact us get in touch with us let us know tell us		should you have any queries if you require further information
7 Enclosure(s)	Bill of Lading/Inland Waterways Bill of Lading/Consignment Note/Air Waybill/Commercial Invoice/Pro-forma Invoice/Consular Invoice/Customs Invoice/Insurance Policy/Insurance Certificate/Certificate of Origin/Customs Declaration/Packing List/Bill of Exchange (Draft)			

1	**Reference to goods ordered**	***Bezugnahme auf bestellte Waren***
	This is to advise you that the goods ordered as per your letter / fax / e-mail dated / of … (see copy enclosed) are (now) ready	*Hiermit teile(n) ich (wir) Ihnen mit, dass die gemäß Ihrem Brief / Fax / Ihrer E-Mail vom … (siehe beiliegende Kopie) bestellten Waren (jetzt) fertig sind*
	We are pleased to confirm that the machines, as per the Order Form enclosed, have now been completed	*Wir freuen uns, Ihnen zu bestätigen, dass die Maschinen gemäß beiliegendem Auftragsformular nunmehr fertiggestellt sind*
2	**Available for collection***	***Abholbereit / Fertig zur Abholung****
	The goods will be made available to you for collection at our premises in … (location) / on … (date) / in the course of this / next week	*Die Waren werden am … (Datum) / im Laufe dieser / der nächsten Woche in unseren Geschäftsräumen in … (Ort) zur Abholung bereitstehen / abholbereit sein*
	The goods can (now) be picked up at our distribution centre	*Die Waren können (jetzt) in unserem Vertriebszentrum abgeholt werden*
	Ready for despatch*	***Versandbereit / Fertig zum Versand****
	The goods are now ready for despatch. Please let us have your forwarding instructions	*Die Waren sind jetzt versandbereit / fertig zum Versand. Bitte geben Sie uns Ihre Versandanweisungen an*
	Advice of despatch*	***Versandavis / Versandmitteilung****
	The goods have (now) been shipped to you by … (mode of transport)	*Die Waren sind (jetzt) an Sie per … (Transportart) abgeschickt worden*
	The goods can (now) be picked up by your forwarding agents	*Die Waren können (jetzt) von Ihrem Spediteur abgeholt werden*
	Mode of transport	***Transportart***
	by road / rail / air / ship / goods train	*per Straße / Schiene / auf dem Luftweg / per Schiff / Güterzug*
	as rail freight / sea freight / air freight / package freight / fast freight / a groupage consignment / a consolidated shipment / bulk cargo	*als Bahnfracht / Seefracht / Luftfracht / Paketfracht / Eilfracht / Sammelgut / Sammeltransport / Massengut*
	The goods will be sent as air freight on Lufthansa Flight No. …, which leaves Düsseldorf Airport on … (date) at … (time) landing at … (airport) on … (date) at … (time)	*Die Waren werden als Luftfracht mit dem Lufthansa-Flug Nr. … geschickt, der am … (Datum) um … (Zeit) vom Flughafen Düsseldorf abgeht und am … (Datum) um … (Zeit) auf dem … (Flughafen) ankommt*
	Terms of delivery (Incoterms)	***Lieferbedingungen (Incoterms)***
	The goods have been shipped CIF Dover as requested	*Die Waren wurden wie gewünscht CIF Dover verschifft*
	Delivery will be made franco to your premises as per your instructions	*Die Lieferung erfolgt gemäß Ihren Anweisungen frei Haus / Ihren Geschäftsräumen*

	The goods ordered were shipped to you yesterday CIP London Airport as agreed	*Die bestellten Waren wurden gestern wie vereinbart CIP Flughafen London an Sie versandt*
	Name of forwarder	***Name des Spediteurs***
	The goods will be packed and shipped by … (name of forwarder)	*Die Güter werden von … (Name des Spediteurs) verpackt und versandt*
	We will arrange for … (name of forwarder) to deliver the goods	*Wir werden veranlassen, dass … (Name des Spediteurs) die Waren verschickt*
	Estimated time of arrival	***Geschätzte Ankunftszeit***
	The goods / consignment will in all probability arrive on … (date)	*Die Waren werden / Die Sendung wird höchstwahrscheinlich am … (Datum) ankommen*
	According to her sailing card MS Diana is due to dock at (the port of) Dover at the end of the month	*Laut Fahrplan soll die MS Diana Ende des Monats in (im Hafen von) Dover anlegen*
	You will be able to take delivery of the goods within the next three weeks	*Sie werden die Waren innerhalb der nächsten drei Wochen in Empfang nehmen können*
	We will get in touch with you as soon as the goods are on board	*Wir werden mit Ihnen Verbindung aufnehmen, sobald die Güter an Bord sind*
	Details of packing	***Einzelheiten der Verpackung***
	The goods have been packed in foam-lined boxes with metal strapping marked …	*Die Waren sind in Schaumstoff-gefütterten Kisten, die mit Metallbändern umwickelt und … markiert sind, verpackt worden*
	The goods are forwarded in foam-lined boxes with the usual marks	*Die Waren werden in Schaumstoff-gefütterten Kisten mit den üblichen Markierungen versandt*
	Packaging	***Verpackung***
	The containers are made of environmentally friendly material	*Die Behälter sind aus umweltfreundlichem Material hergestellt*
	Pallets are supplied at cost	*Die Paletten werden zum Selbstkostenpreis geliefert*
	Our pallets are non-returnable	*Bei unseren Paletten handelt es sich um Einwegpaletten*
	The pallets will be picked up by our carrier when the next consignment is delivered, free of charge	*Die Paletten werden von unserem Frachtführer kostenlos abgeholt, wenn die nächste Sendung geliefert wird*
	Please return the empties (carriage forward) to our depot	*Bitte schicken Sie das Leergut (unfrei) an unser Lager zurück*
3	**Request for packing instructions (and shipping marks)***	***Bitte um Versandanweisungen (und Versandmarkierungen)****
	We now require your instructions as regards packing (and shipping marks)	*Wir benötigen jetzt Ihre Anweisungen bezüglich der Verpackung (und der Versandmarkierungen)*

	Please advise us how you wish to have the goods packed (and marked)	*Bitte teilen Sie uns mit, wie wir die Waren verpacken (und markieren) sollen*
	It is normal practice to pack these goods in cardboard boxes	*Es ist üblich, diese Waren in Pappkartons zu verpacken*
	Should we not hear from you to the contrary, the goods will be packed in crates	*Falls wir nichts Gegenteiliges von Ihnen hören, werden die Güter in Lattenkisten verpackt*
	Shipping marks	***Versandmarkierungen***
	Please instruct us as to what shipping marks you require	*Bitte weisen Sie uns an, welche Versandmarkierungen Sie benötigen*
	Unless otherwise instructed the boxes will be marked … (e.g. "TWE/4035/JED/1-6/6" (for 6 containers))	*Falls Sie uns nicht anderweitig unterrichten, werden die Kisten mit… (z. B. „TWE/4035/JED/1-6/6" (bei 6 Containern)) markiert*
4	**Reference to mode of payment***	***Bezugnahme auf Zahlungsart****
	As soon as we have received your remittance for … (amount) (in payment of / in part-payment of our invoice) the goods will be shipped	*Sobald wir Ihre Überweisung für … (Betrag) (in Begleichung von / als Teilzahlung unserer Rechnung) erhalten haben, werden die Waren zum Versand gebracht*
	As soon as we have been advised by our bank that the letter of credit (in our favour) has been opened, the goods will be sent to you	*Sobald wir von unserer Bank unterrichtet werden, dass das Akkreditiv (zu unseren Gunsten) eröffnet worden ist, werden die Waren an Sie geschickt*
	Request for payment	***Bitte um Zahlung***
	Our statement for the period from … (date) to … (date) is enclosed for settlement	*Unser Kontoauszug für den Zeitraum vom … (Datum) bis … (Datum) ist zwecks Begleichung beigefügt*
	We have drawn on you for the invoice amount of … at 30/60/90/180 d/s and enclose our draft for your acceptance	*Wir haben für den Rechnungsbetrag von … mit einer Laufzeit von 30/60/90/180 Tagen einen Sichtwechsel auf Sie gezogen und fügen diesen bei, damit Sie ihn akzeptieren*
	We have instructed our correspondent bank, (the) … Bank in … (location) to release the documents as soon as the draft has been accepted / paid	*Wir haben unsere Korrespondenzbank, die … Bank in … (Ort) angewiesen, die Dokumente auszuhändigen, sobald der Wechsel akzeptiert / bezahlt worden ist*
5	**Reference to documentation enclosed or sent separately**	***Bezugnahme auf beigefügte oder getrennt übersandte Dokumente***

	In accordance with the conditions stipulated in the documentary credit we enclose the following documents: complete set of clean, on-board bills of lading (notify: …), original and three copies of the commercial invoice, insurance policy (certificate), certificate of origin, customs declaration and export licence	*In Übereinstimmung mit den im Dokumentenakkreditiv festgelegten Bedingungen fügen wir folgende Dokumente bei: kompletter Satz reiner an-Bord Konnossemente (zu benachrichtigen: …), die Original-Handelsrechnung mit drei Kopien, Versicherungspolice (Zertifikat), Ursprungszeugnis, Zollerklärung und Exportlizenz*
	As requested the following documents have been given to / handed over to (the) … Bank (name of seller's bank) in … (location) …	*Wunschgemäß sind folgende Dokumente der … Bank (Name der Bank des Verkäufers) in … (Ort) übergeben / ausgehändigt worden*
	Please find enclosed the documents required	*Beigefügt erhalten Sie die gewünschten Dokumente*
	Our … (name of document, e.g. Commercial Invoice) is enclosed in duplicate / triplicate / quadruplicate / quintuplicate	*Unser(e) … (Name des Dokuments, z.B. Handelsfaktura) ist in doppelter / dreifacher / vierfacher / fünffacher Ausfertigung beigefügt*
	Our pro-forma invoice is enclosed to enable you to open the letter of credit	*Unsere Proforma-Rechnung ist beigefügt, damit Sie das Akkreditiv eröffnen können*
6	**Polite ending**	***Höflicher Schluss***
	We trust your order has been carried out to your (entire) satisfaction and look forward to the pleasure of serving you again	*Wir sind zuversichtlich, dass Ihr Auftrag zu Ihrer (vollsten) Zufriedenheit ausgeführt worden ist, und freuen uns darauf, Sie wieder zu bedienen*
	We feel sure that the consignment will arrive safely and on schedule and would be pleased to receive further orders	*Wir sind überzeugt, dass die Sendung sicher und termingerecht ankommen wird, und würden uns freuen, weitere Aufträge von Ihnen zu erhalten*
	Please do not hesitate to contact us should you have any queries	*Bitte zögern Sie nicht, sich an uns zu wenden, falls Sie irgendwelche Fragen haben*
7	**Enclosure(s)**	***Anlage(n)***
	Bill of Lading / Inland Waterways Bill of Lading / Consignment Note / Air Waybill / Commercial Invoice / Pro-forma Invoice / Consular Invoice / Customs Invoice / Insurance Policy / Insurance Certificate / Certificate of Origin / Customs Declaration / Packing List / Bill of Exchange (Draft)	*Konnossement / Binnenschifffahrts-Konnossement / Frachtbrief / Luftfrachtbrief / Handelsrechnung / Proforma-Rechnung / Konsulatsrechnung / Zollrechnung / Versicherungspolice / Versicherungszertifikat / Ursprungszeugnis / Zollerklärung / Packliste / Wechsel (Tratte)*

Unit 7

Payment

A. Buyer

1 Acknowledgement of

– receipt of goods	We are pleased to confirm that we have (now) received … (goods) and your invoice We have (now) received the consignment of … (goods) together with your invoice We have (now) taken delivery of … (goods)	as per our order no. …	dated/of …		
	The consignment of … (goods)			has now arrived was delivered	• this morning • this afternoon • today

– performance of services	We are pleased to confirm that the	maintenance repair	work on	(… machine, plant, installation, equipment, apparatus etc.)	has now been completed/ carried out	as requested as stipulated to our satisfaction in accordance with our instructions
		servicing adjustment installation	of			

– examination of goods	The goods have (now) been	• checked • tested • examined • weighed • counted • inspected • sampled	and we are pleased to note that they are and found to be		as ordered as required as stipulated in our order as specified
			and we regret to inform you and we are sorry to note and we are sorry to tell you and we note with surprise and we note with dismay	that they are not that some of them are not	
	Having (thoroughly) • checked • tested • examined • inspected	the goods	we are pleased to confirm that they are we are unfortunately obliged to inform you that (some of) the goods are not we must unfortunately point out that (some of) the goods are not		
	A thorough • examination of the goods • inspection		has	revealed shown confirmed	that they are that they (unfortunately) are not
	Checks carried out on the goods		have		

– reference to invoice/bill/statement	Thank you for We have received With reference to	the above-mentioned statement for … (period, e.g. the quarter ending 30 June ..) your statement for January .. your January statement your statement of account for the period … (e.g. 1–15 January ..)	showing a balance in your favour of … (amount)			
	Your invoice/bill/statement	has (now) been checked	against our (own) records against our books against our Goods Inwards records by our accountant by our Chief Accountant by our Accounts Department	and found to be (in)correct (in the following point(s):)		
		corresponds to tallies with does not correspond to does not tally with	our (own) records our books			
	Your invoice Your bill Your invoice no. … enclosed Your Commercial Invoice no … Your statement Your … (e.g. January, February etc.) statement Your statement for the quarter ending … (date) Your quarterly statement Your statement for the first/second/third/fourth quarter of … (e.g. this year, 2004 etc.)	for … (amount)	will be has been	paid settled	by … (date) within … (period of time) within the time specified as per contract as agreed as requested as instructed as stipulated	
	The sum of … (amount) The invoice amount (of …) The above-mentioned sum (of …)			remitted transferred	to you to your account (no. … at (the) … Bank)	as per contract as agreed as requested as instructed as stipulated

2 Reference to mode of payment – cheque/ international giro/IMO/ banker's draft	We enclose our	cheque international giro international money order (IMO) banker's draft		for … (amount)		by way of payment in (part-)payment of your invoice no. …/your statement … as the first of three (equal) instalments in payment of … in settlement of your invoice no. …/your statement …			
– transfer	We have instructed our bank to We have instructed (the) … Bank in … to Our bank has been instructed to Our bankers will	remit transfer credit		the invoice amount the sum in question the sum of … (e.g. $2,000) the amount of … (e.g. $2,000) the above-mentioned sum (of …)		to you to your account (no. … at (the) … Bank)	by SWIFT by mail transfer by telegraphic transfer		
	Your account	no. … at (the) … Bank in … (location)		will be has been	credited	with the invoice amount with the sum in question with the sum of … (e.g. $2,000) with … (amount, e.g. $2,000)			
	… (amount, e.g. $2,000) The sum of … (amount) The invoice amount The sum in question The above-mentioned sum (of …)					to your account no. … at (the) … Bank in … (location)			
	This is to inform you that We are pleased to inform you that We are pleased to advise you that Please note that	we have • settled • paid	your invoice your bill your statement	no … dated /of …	for … (amount)	by	remitting transferring crediting	… (amount, e.g. $2,000) the sum of … (amount)	to your account
							crediting your account with the sum of … (amount)		
		we have now	balanced cleared settled	our account with you			trans-ferring	the sum of … (amount) … (amount)	to you to your account at … (bank)

– draft (bill of exchange)	Please draw on us	at 30/60/90 d/s (days after sight)	in settlement of in payment of	your invoice your statement our account the above-mentioned invoice/ statement/account	and send us your draft for acceptance	
	We enclose your draft	for … (amount),	which we have	duly accepted	and will honour	at maturity on the due date
	We are returning your draft		which has been		and will be honoured	
– automatic debit transfer	We note that payment is to be made by automatic debit transfer			on receipt of the goods on receipt of invoice		
3 Reference to discrepancies*	Having checked your	invoice statement	against	our (own) records our books	we must point out that … it would seem that … we note that … we must draw your attention to the fact that …	
	Having compared your		with			

… your … (e. g. January) statement has been wrongly totalled
… you have made an arithmetical error in calculating
- the invoice amount
- the balance due as per your … (e. g. January, latest etc.) statement

… you have miscalculated … (e. g. the discount, the invoice amount, the amount due according to your statement for the quarter ending March 31st)
… the goods you have charged us for do not
- tally with
- correspond to

those supplied

… you have overcharged/undercharged us by … (amount)
… we have been overcharged/undercharged by … (amount)
… you have charged us for … (goods, Item 5 etc.) twice, three times etc.
… you have not included our credit note for … (amount) dated/of …
… you have allowed /granted a(n) … (e. g. cash/quantity/initial order etc.) discount of (only) … % instead of … % as promised
… Items 3 and 9 of your statement have been incorrectly charged
… Items 3 and 9 of your invoice dated/of … have been incorrectly priced
… there has been an error in totalling the invoice amount, resulting in your overcharging us by … (amount, e. g. $50)
… you have debited us with … (amount) instead of crediting us with this sum
… your monthly/quarterly statement shows a balance in your favour of … (amount) instead of … (amount) according to our records

... you have omitted to include
- the discount of ... % to which we are entitled (as we were supplied with substitutes and not with the goods originally ordered)
- two (etc.) credit items, i. e. credit note no. CR20 dated/of ... for ... (amount) and your customer loyalty bonus of ... % for 5 years of custom

... you have omitted to include the quantity discount of 10 % granted on orders
- for more than ... (number) units
- exceeding ... (number) units

... your packing list shows that 144 bottles of Château Neuf du Pape 1997 were supplied, whereas on your invoice you charge us for 150 bottles

... you have based your charges on the exchange rate for the ... (currency, e. g. euro) valid on ... (date, e. g. the delivery date), whereas ... (date, e. g. the order date) was agreed

... you have based your charges on the current price list instead of the one valid when our order was placed

... you have charged us ... (e. g. interest, VAT etc.)
- at ... % instead of ... %
- at the wrong rate
- on the wrong items
- on Item 3 instead of Item 6

... you have charged us for packing which has now been returned to you

... you have charged us for ... (e. g. packing, insurance, unloading etc.) at the normal rate (of ..., e. g. $10 per crate), whereas a preferential rate of ... (details of rate) was agreed

... you have sent us a draft for ... (amount) instead of for ... (amount)

... you have sent us a sight draft for 60 days instead of 90 days

... your draft is unsigned

... the words and figures on your draft differ

– amendments*

We are returning	your invoice your statement your bill	and would request you to and would ask you to and would be pleased if you would	amend it correct it	and return it to us send it back to us	for settlement for payment

We have therefore (only)	remitted transferred sent you a cheque for	... (amount)	and would request you to	amend your records accordingly acknowledge this in writing correct the statement enclosed and return it to us double-check your statements/invoices in future ensure that such inaccuracies • do not recur • do not happen again

We are (therefore) offsetting We have (therefore) offset We will (therefore) offset We will (therefore) be offsetting	the extra amount charged the amount of … (amount) … (amount)	against	the sum due as per your invoice/ statement (no. …) the sum due as per this invoice/ statement your next statement your next invoice your next bill
We are (therefore) deducting We have (therefore) deducted We will (therefore) deduct We will (therefore) be deducting		from	

Please We would therefore request you to We would therefore be grateful if you would	take this into account bear this in mind	when sending us your next when making up your next	invoice statement
	send us a credit note for the difference send us a statement showing the correct balance send us an amended statement send us a corrected statement amend your statement/invoice accordingly correct your statement to show the correct balance correct your invoice/statement to show the correct amount due confirm that the invoice amount is, in fact, … (amount) confirm that the statement should, in fact, show a balance of … (amount) in your favour		

As soon as When After	we have received	your corrected your amended the correct an accurate	invoice statement bill	we will remit the sum owing we will settle it it will be settled it will be paid we will clear our account with you we will settle our account with you payment will be made we will send you our remittance we will have your account credited accordingly

4 Polite ending	Please acknowledge receipt of Please confirm that you have received	our remittance our cheque the draft with our acceptance payment		
	Please let us know Please contact us Please do not hesitate to contact us	if you don't receive if you do not receive should you not receive	our remittance our cheque the draft the amount transferred payment	on time by … (date) within … (period of time) by the time stated as promised
		if there are any queries should you have any queries		
	We look forward to receiving We trust we will soon be receiving We will consider this matter to be settled as soon as we have received		your amended/corrected invoice/statement etc.	
5 Enclosure(s)	Cheque/International Giro/IMO/Banker's Draft/Draft (Bill of Exchange)/Invoice/Statement/Bill			

B. Seller

1 Reference to invoice/statement*	We enclose our invoice/statement (no. … dated/of …) for goods supplied against your order no. … dated/of … for settlement We enclose our invoice/statement (no. … dated/of …) and would be grateful if you would settle it as agreed Our invoice no. … dated/of … for … (amount) is enclosed for settlement Our statement for the period from … (date) to … (date) is enclosed for settlement Our statement as of 31 March .. is enclosed Our statement for … (period, e.g. January, the first/second/third/fourth quarter of … (year) is enclosed for settlement	
	On payment of … (our invoice/statement, amount) On receipt of your remittance for … (amount)	the goods will be • despatched • forwarded • shipped the goods will be handed over to our forwarders for delivery the goods will be forwarded to you we will have the goods delivered to you
	If payment is made • by … (date) • within … (period)	you may deduct the usual discount of … % a … % discount is granted

	Please check the enclosed statement for all goods and services provided up to and including … (date).		As the sum due is less than … (e.g. $100) please carry this total forward to next month's account	
	We are drawing on you	for … (amount) for this amount	at 30/60/90	days' sight d/s
	Please arrange for … (amount) to be Please have this amount		remitted transferred	to us to our account at (the) … Bank in … (location)
	Please arrange for payment of this amount We would appreciate settlement of the total amount due We would ask you to remit/transfer the amount due		in the near future in the next few days by … (date) within … (period) as arranged at your earliest convenience	
2 Acknowledgement of – receipt of payment*	We have received We are pleased to confirm that we have (now) received	your remittance for … (amount) your cheque for … (amount) your banker's draft for … (amount) your international giro for … (amount) your IMO (international money order) for … the draft for … (amount) the sum of … (amount)	in payment of in settlement of	our invoice no. … for all invoices up to and including … (date) our … (e.g. January) statement our statement for the … (first/second/third/fourth) quarter of … (year)
	We are now able to confirm This is to confirm As requested, we are sending you confirmation	that your remittance for … (amount) in payment/settlement of … (e.g. invoice no. 321 dated/of) …) has been received that all monies owed in respect of … (e.g. invoices for the quarter ending 30 June .. / our January statement) have now been received		
		that your account with us is	fully paid up balanced cleared	
– part-payment*	We have received your remittance/cheque/IMO/banker's draft/transfer for … (amount)		in part-payment of by way of part-payment of as the first/second etc. instalment of the sum owing as per	our invoice for … (amount) our statement for the period up to and including … (date, e.g. 30 June ..)
	The balance of … (amount) The next/final instalment of …	is due on … (date)		

3 Reference to receipt for payment*	Our receipt is enclosed			
	Our receipt for … (amount) Our receipt for the sum of … (amount)	in payment of in settlement of	our invoice no. … our … (e.g. January) statement our statement for the … (first/second/third/fourth) quarter of … (year) our statement dated/of …	is enclosed is attached
	We enclose We have enclosed We are enclosing Enclosed you will find	our receipt our receipt for … (amount) our receipt for the sum of … (amount)	in payment of in settlement of	our invoice no. … our … (e.g. January) statement our statement for the … (first/second/third/fourth) quarter of … (year) our statement dated/of …
4 Reference to discrepancies/errors/amendments*	With reference to	your remittance for … (amount) dated/of … the sum of … (amount) transferred to us on … (date)	we must point out that … it would seem that … we note that … we must draw your attention to the fact that …	
	… you have not • paid/remitted • transferred • arranged for payment of — the full amount (of …) as per our invoice/statement no. … dated/of … for … (amount) … you have omitted to sign your cheque for … (amount) … your cheque for … (amount) is unsigned … your cheque is undated … your cheque is post-dated … your cheque has been wrongly made out … your cheque has only been made out for … (amount) instead of … (amount) as per our invoice/statement no. … dated/of … for … (amount) … you have paid … (wrong amount) instead of … (right amount) … the words and figures on your cheque differ … you have not stated what invoice/statement you are paying … you have not stated what goods you are paying for … there has been (what seems to be) a clerical error on your part, since … (details, e.g. the invoice you refer to is not the one sent to you on … (date) … you have taken a discount of … % to which you are not entitled, as our special offer was only valid until … (date) … you have taken a quantity discount of … %, whereas your order is for less than … (number) units, kg, dozen, gross etc. … you have transferred the invoice amount/the amount due according to our statement • without accepting to pay the bank charges incurred • but have had the bank charges debited to us			

… We are (therefore)	returning your … (e.g. cheque, etc.) sending you a copy of … (e.g. the credit note, the debit note, the letter from our bank etc.)	and would request you to and would ask you to	send us one for the correct amount arrange for payment of the correct amount have the correct amount transferred to our account remit the correct sum remit the amount due

We enclose	a debit note	for … (amount) for this amount for the sum in question for the amount in question	and will amend our next	statement invoice bill	accordingly

We would therefore	request you to ask you to be grateful if you would	send us a let us have your	cheque for remittance for	… (amount) this amount the sum in question the sum due the amount due	at your earliest convenience by return as soon as possible in due course
		arrange for payment of			by SWIFT by bank transfer etc.

Having checked our Having re-checked our Having cross-checked our	statement invoice	against	our records the forwarding agent's records the original order your order dated/of … your amended order	we note that we agree that	there has (indeed) been an error our statement/invoice/it is (indeed) incorrect our statement/invoice/it contains some errors our statement/invoice/it does (indeed) contain some errors our statement/invoice/it must be corrected the invoice amount/sum due has (indeed) been miscalculated/incorrectly calculated you have (indeed) been overcharged/undercharged by … (amount) we have (indeed) omitted to include … (e.g. your credit note for …, a discount of … % etc.)

		We enclose	an amended statement/invoice our corrected statement/invoice an amended draft for … (amount) our credit note for … (amount) our forwarder's receipt a copy of our forwarding agent's letter
5	Polite ending	Thank you for your attention to this matter Thank you for choosing to place your order with … (name of seller's company) We would be grateful if you would attend to this matter at the earliest opportunity We trust there will be no recurrence of this (unfortunate) error in the future Please accept our apologies for this unfortunate oversight on our part We apologise for the inaccuracies in our statement/invoice and assure you there will be no recurrence of this in the future We would request you to … (e.g. provide a full description of the articles for which payment is made, quote our invoice, etc.) number when making payment in future Please quote the … (e.g. order, reference, customer, article, batch) number when making payments in future We would be grateful if you would remember to include the … (e.g. order, reference, article, batch) number in all future correspondence with us	
6	Enclosure(s)	Receipt/Invoice/Statement/Draft/(Copy of) Forwarder's Receipt etc.	

A. Buyer

1	**Acknowledgement of receipt of goods**	***Bestätigung des Erhalts der Waren***
	We have (now) taken delivery of the goods as per our order no. 876 dated 10 January …	*Wir haben (jetzt) die Lieferung der Waren gemäß unserem Auftrag Nr. 876 vom 10. Januar .. erhalten*
	– performance of services	***– Erfüllung von Leistungen***
	We are pleased to confirm that the maintenance work on the electrical equipment has now been completed in accordance with our instructions	*Wir freuen uns zu bestätigen, dass die Wartungsarbeiten an der elektrischen Ausrüstung jetzt in Übereinstimmung mit unseren Anweisungen beendet worden sind*
	– examination of goods	***Prüfung der Waren***
	The goods have (now) been checked and we are pleased to note that they are as ordered	*Die Waren sind (nun) geprüft worden, und wir freuen uns festzustellen, dass Sie dem Auftrag entsprechen*
	The goods have (now) been inspected and we regret to inform you that they are not as specified	*Wir haben die Waren (jetzt) überprüft und bedauern Ihnen mitzuteilen, dass sie nicht unseren Angaben entsprechen*
	Having (thoroughly) checked the goods, we are pleased to confirm that they are as stipulated in our order	*Nachdem wir die Waren (gründlich) untersucht haben, freuen wir uns zu bestätigen, dass sie den Angaben in unserem Auftrag entsprechen*
	A thorough examination of the goods has revealed that they are not as required	*Eine gründliche Prüfung der Waren hat ergeben, dass sie nicht den Anforderungen entsprechen*
	– reference to invoice / bill / statement	***– Bezugnahme auf Rechnung / Kontoauszug***
	Thank you for the above-mentioned statement for the quarter ending 30 June …, showing a balance in your favour of $1,000	*Vielen Dank für den obengenannten Kontoauszug für das am 30. Juni .. endende Quartal, der einen Saldo zu Ihren Gunsten von 1.000 $ aufweist*
	Your invoice has (now) been checked against our (own) records and found to be incorrect in the following points:	*Ihre Rechnung ist (nun) mit unseren (eigenen) Aufzeichnungen verglichen worden, und wir stellten fest, dass sie in folgenden Punkten unrichtig ist:*
	Your invoice bill has (now) been checked by our Chief Accountant and found to be incorrect	*Ihre Rechnung ist (jetzt) von unserem Hauptbuchhalter geprüft und für unrichtig befunden worden*
	Your statement does not tally with our books	*Ihr Kontoauszug stimmt nicht mit unseren Büchern überein*
	Your Commercial Invoice no. 989 for $5,000 will be paid as per contract	*Ihre Handelsrechnung Nr. 989 über 5.000 $ wird vertragsgemäß bezahlt*

	The above-mentioned sum of $1,000 has been remitted to your account no. 897654 at the NatWest Bank as instructed	*Die obengenannte Summe von 1.000 $ ist anweisungsgemäß auf Ihr Konto Nr. 897654 bei der NatWest Bank überwiesen worden*
2	**Reference to mode of payment**	***Bezugnahme auf Rechnungsart***
	We enclose our banker's draft for $5,000 by way of payment	*Wir fügen als Zahlung unseren Bankscheck über 5.000 $ bei*
	We enclose our international money order (IMO) for $5,000 as the first of three (equal) instalments in payment of your invoice	*Wir fügen als erste der drei (gleichen) Raten unsere internationale Postanweisung (IMO) über 5.000 $ in Begleichung Ihrer Rechnung bei*
	We have instructed our bank to credit the amount of $2,000 to your account no. 109876 at the Chemical Bank in New York by S.W.I.F.T.	*Wir haben unsere Bank angewiesen, den Betrag von 2.000 $ Ihrem Konto Nr. 109876 bei der Chemical Bank in New York durch S.W.I.F.T. gutzuschreiben*
	This is to inform you that we have settled your statement no. 768 of March 3 .. by transferring the sum of $6,500 to your account	*Hiermit teilen wir Ihnen mit, dass wir Ihren Kontoauszug Nr. 768 vom 3. März .. durch Überweisung der Summe von 6.500 $ auf Ihr Konto beglichen haben*
	We are pleased to advise you that we have paid your invoice by transferring $2,000 to your account	*Wir freuen uns Ihnen mitzuteilen, dass wir Ihre Rechnung durch Überweisung von 2.000 $ auf Ihr Konto bezahlt haben*
	Please draw on us at 60 d/s in settlement of the above-mentioned account and send us your draft for acceptance	*Bitte ziehen Sie auf uns einen 60 Tage-Sichtwechsel in Begleichung der obengenannten Rechnung und schicken Sie uns Ihre Tratte zum Akzept*
	We enclose your draft for $4,000, which has been duly accepted and will be honoured at maturity	*Wir fügen Ihren Wechsel für 4.000 $ bei, der ordnungsgemäß akzeptiert wurde und bei Fälligkeit eingelöst wird*
	We note that payment is to be made by automatic debit transfer on receipt of invoice	*Wir nehmen zur Kenntnis, dass die Zahlung bei Erhalt der Rechnung durch Bankeinzugsverfahren erfolgen soll*
3	**Reference to discrepancies***	***Bezugnahme auf Unstimmigkeiten****
	Having checked your statement against our (own) records we must point out that …	*Nachdem wir Ihren Kontoauszug mit unseren (eigenen) Aufzeichnungen verglichen haben, müssen wir darauf hinweisen, dass …*
	you have miscalculated the discount	*Sie den Nachlass falsch berechnet haben*
	you have overcharged / undercharged us by $100	*Sie uns 100 $ zu viel / zu wenig berechnet haben*
	you have not included our credit note for $100 dated August 10 ..	*Sie unsere Gutschrift über 100 $ vom 10. August .. nicht berücksichtigt haben*

items 3 and 9 of your statement have been incorrectly charged	*die Positionen 3 und 9 Ihres Kontoauszugs nicht richtig belastet worden sind*
you have debited us with $250 instead of crediting us with this sum	*Sie uns 250 $ belastet haben statt uns diese Summe gutzuschreiben*
You have omitted to include the quantity discount of 10 % granted on orders for more than 2,000 units	*Sie vergessen haben, den Mengenrabatt von 10 %, der uns für Aufträge von mehr als 2.000 Stück gewährt wird, einzubeziehen*
you have based your charges on the current price list instead of the one valid when our order was placed	*Sie Ihre Gebühren auf Grund der laufenden Preisliste berechnet haben, statt diejenige zugrunde zu legen, die gültig war, als unser Auftrag erteilt wurde*
the words and figures on your draft differ	*die Wörter und Zahlen auf Ihrem Wechsel voneinander abweichen*
– amendments*	*– Änderungen**
We are returning your invoice and would request you to amend it and send it back to us for settlement	*Wir schicken Ihnen Ihre Rechnung zurück und bitten Sie, diese abzuändern und uns zwecks Zahlung wieder zuzusenden*
We have therefore sent you a cheque for $6,500 only and would request you to correct the statement enclosed and return it to us	*Wir haben Ihnen deshalb einen Scheck über lediglich 6.500 $ zugesandt und bitten Sie, den beigefügten Kontoauszug zu berichtigen und an uns zurückzugeben*
We are (therefore) offsetting the extra amount charged before against the sum due as per your current statement	*Wir verrechnen (deshalb) den vorher berechneten Zusatzbetrag mit der gemäß Ihrem laufenden Kontoauszug fälligen Summe*
We are (therefore) deducting $150 from your next statement	*Wir werden (daher) 150 $ von Ihrem nächsten Kontoauszug abziehen*
We would therefore request you to send us a credit note for the difference	*Wir bitten Sie daher, uns für die Differenz eine Gutschrift zuzusenden*
We would therefore be grateful if you would take this into account when making up your next invoice	*Wir wären Ihnen deshalb dankbar, wenn Sie dies berücksichtigen würden, wenn Sie Ihre nächste Rechnung ausstellen*
Please send us an amended statement	*Bitte schicken Sie uns einen berichtigten Kontoauszug*
As soon as we have received your amended statement we will remit the sum owing	*Sobald wir Ihren berichtigten Kontoauszug erhalten haben, werden wir Ihnen die geschuldete Summe überweisen*
After we have received an accurate invoice we will have your account credited accordingly	*Sobald wir eine korrekte Rechnung erhalten haben, werden wir den entsprechenden Betrag Ihrem Konto gutschreiben*

4	Polite ending	*Höflicher Schluss*
	Please confirm that you have received the draft with our acceptance	*Bitte bestätigen Sie, dass Sie den Wechsel mit unserem Akzept versehen erhalten haben*
	Please do not hesitate to contact us should you have any queries	*Bitte zögern Sie nicht, mit uns Kontakt aufzunehmen, wenn Sie irgendwelche Fragen haben*
	We look forward to receiving your corrected invoice	*Wir sehen der Übersendung Ihrer berichtigten Rechnung entgegen*
	We will consider this matter to be settled as soon as we have received your amended invoice	*Wir werden dafür sorgen, dass diese Angelegenheit erledigt wird, sobald wir Ihre berichtigte Rechnung erhalten haben*
5	Enclosure(s)	*Anlage(n)*
	Cheque	*Scheck*
	International Giro	*Internationaler Postscheck*
	IMO	*Internationale Postanweisung*
	Banker's Draft	*Bankscheck*
	Draft (Bill of Exchange)	*Tratte (Wechsel)*
	Invoice	*Rechnung*
	Statement	*Kontoauszug*

B. Seller

1	Reference to invoice / statement*	*Bezugnahme auf Rechnung / Kontoauszug**
	We enclose our statement no. 785 dated May 5 .. for goods supplied against your order no. AT786 of June 6 .. for settlement	*Wir fügen zwecks Zahlung unseren Kontoauszug Nr. 785 vom 5. Mai .. für Waren bei, die gemäß Ihrem Auftrag Nr. AT786 vom 6. Juni .. geliefert wurden*
	We enclose our invoice and would be grateful if you would settle it as agreed	*Wir fügen unsere Rechnung bei und wären Ihnen dankbar, wenn Sie diese wie vereinbart begleichen würden*
	Our statement for the period from 1 April to 30 June is enclosed for settlement	*Unser Kontoauszug für den Zeitraum vom 1. April bis 30. Juni ist zwecks Zahlung beigefügt*
	On payment of $3,000 the goods will be handed over to our forwarders for delivery	*Bei Zahlung von 3.000 $ werden die Waren unserem Spediteur zur Lieferung übergeben*
	On receipt of your remittance for $500 the goods will be shipped	*Bei Erhalt Ihrer Überweisung von 500 $ werden die Waren versandt (verschifft)*
	If payment is made by 31 January you may deduct the usual discount of 3 %	*Wenn die Zahlung bis zum 31. Januar erfolgt, können Sie den üblichen Nachlass von 3 % abziehen*

	We are drawing on you for $4,500 at 90 days' sight	*Wir ziehen auf Sie einen 90-Tage-Sicht-wechsel für 4.500 $*
	We would appreciate settlement of the total amount due in the next few days	*Wir würden eine Begleichung des fälligen Gesamtbetrages in den nächsten Tagen begrüßen*
2	**Acknowledgement of receipt of payment**	***Bestätigung des Erhalts der Zahlung***
	We are pleased to confirm that we have (now) received your international giro for $3,500 in payment of our invoice	*Wir freuen uns zu bestätigen, dass wir (nunmehr) Ihren internationalen Postscheck für 3.500 $ in Begleichung unserer Rechnung erhalten haben*
	This is to confirm that all monies owed in respect of invoices for the quarter ending 30 June .. have now been received	*Hiermit bestätigen wir, dass alle geschuldeten Beträge im Zusammenhang mit Rechnungen für das am 30. Juni .. endende Quartal jetzt eingegangen sind*
	– part-payment	***– Teilzahlung***
	We have received your transfer for $5,000 in part-payment of our invoice for $7,500	*Wir haben Ihre Überweisung von 5.000 $ als Teilzahlung unserer Rechnung über 7.500 $ erhalten*
	We have received your remittance for $1,000 as the first instalment of our statement for the period up to and including 30 June ..	*Wir haben Ihre Überweisung von 1.000 $ als erste Rate unseres Kontoauszugs für den Zeitraum bis einschließlich 30. Juni .. erhalten*
	The balance of $2,500 is due on 31 August ..	*Der Saldo von 2.500 $ ist am 31. August .. fällig*
3	**Reference to receipt for payment**	***Bezugnahme auf Zahlungserhalt***
	Our receipt for the sum of $2,000 in payment of our statement of January 31 .. is enclosed	*Unsere Empfangsbescheinigung für die Summe von 2.000 $ in Begleichung unseres Kontoauszugs vom 31. Januar .. ist beigefügt*
	We are enclosing our receipt for the $5,000 transferred in settlement of our invoice no. 8987	*Wir fügen unsere Empfangsbescheinigung für die 5.000 $ bei, die in Begleichung unserer Rechnung Nr. 8987 überwiesen worden sind*
4	**Reference to discrepancies / errors / amendments***	***Bezugnahme auf Unstimmigkeiten / Fehler / Änderungen****
	With reference to your remittance for $4,500 dated .. we must point out that you have not paid the full amount of $6,000 as per our invoice no. 4532 of 28 February ..	*Wir beziehen uns auf Ihre Überweisung von 4.500 $ vom … und müssen darauf hinweisen, dass Sie nicht den vollen Betrag von 6.000 $ gemäß unserer Rechnung Nr. 4532 vom 28. Februar .. bezahlt haben*
	Your cheque is post-dated	*Ihr Scheck ist rückdatiert*
	Your cheque has only been made out for $4,000 instead of $4,100 as per our statement no. 989 dated 31 December ..	*Ihr Scheck ist nur auf 4.000 $ statt auf 4.100 $ gemäß unserem Kontoauszug Nr. 989 vom 31. Dezember .. ausgestellt worden*

	You have not stated what invoice you are paying	*Sie haben nicht aufgeführt, welche Rechnung Sie bezahlen*
	There has been what seems to be a clerical error on your part, since the invoice you refer to is not the one sent to you on March 31	*Scheinbar ist in Ihrem Büro ein Fehler gemacht worden, da die Rechnung, auf die Sie sich beziehen, nicht diejenige ist, die wir Ihnen am 31. März zusandten*
	You have taken a quantity discount of 5 %, whereas your order is for less than 500 units	*Sie haben einen Mengenrabatt von 5 % in Anspruch genommen, obwohl Ihr Auftrag sich auf weniger als 500 Stück bezieht*
	We are (therefore) returning your cheque and would request you to send us one for the correct amount	*Wir senden Ihnen (daher) Ihren Scheck zurück und bitten Sie, uns einen für den korrekten Betrag zuzuschicken*
	We enclose a credit / debit note for $159 and will amend our next statement accordingly	*Wir fügen eine Gutschrifts- / Lastschriftsanzeige über $159 bei und werden unseren nächsten Kontoauszug entsprechend berichtigen*
	We would therefore request you to let us have your remittance for the sum in question in due course	*Wir bitten Sie daher, uns Ihre Überweisung für die infrage stehende Summe zu gegebener Zeit zukommen zu lassen*
	We would therefore request you to arrange for payment of this amount by SWIFT	*Wir bitten Sie daher, die Zahlung dieses Betrages per SWIFT zu veranlassen*
	Having checked our statement against the original order we agree that it is, indeed, incorrect	*Nachdem wir unseren Kontoauszug mit dem Originalauftrag verglichen haben, geben wir zu, dass er tatsächlich nicht richtig ist*
	Having re-checked our invoice against the forwarding agent's records we note that our invoice must be corrected	*Nachdem wir unsere Rechnung erneut mit den Aufzeichnungen des Spediteurs verglichen haben, stellen wir fest, dass unsere Rechnung berichtigt werden muss*
	Having cross-checked our statement against your amended order we agree that you have indeed been overcharged / undercharged by $250	*Nachdem wir unseren Kontoauszug und Ihren berichtigten Auftrag genauestens überprüft haben, sind wir auch der Meinung, dass Sie tatsächlich mit 250 $ zu viel / zu wenig belastet worden sind*
	We enclose an amended statement	*Wir fügen einen berichtigten Kontoauszug bei*
	We enclose an amended draft for $5,000	*Wir fügen einen berichtigten Wechsel über 5.000 $ bei*
5	**Polite ending**	***Höflicher Schluss***
	Thank you for your attention to this matter	*Vielen Dank, dass Sie dieser Sache Ihre Aufmerksamkeit geschenkt haben*

	We trust there will be no recurrence of this (unfortunate) error in the future	*Wir sind zuversichtlich, dass dieser (unglückliche) Fehler sich in Zukunft nicht wiederholen wird*
	We apologise for the inaccuracies in our statement and assure you there will be no recurrence of this in the future	*Wir entschuldigen uns für die Unstimmigkeiten in unserem Kontoauszug und versichern Ihnen, dass sich dieses in Zukunft nicht wiederholen wird*
6	**Enclosure(s)**	*Anlage(n)*
	Receipt	*Empfangsbescheinigung*
	Invoice	*Rechnung*
	Statement	*Kontoauszug*
	Draft	*Wechsel*
	(Copy of) Forwarder's Receipt	*(Kopie der) Spediteurübernahmebescheinigung*

Unit 8

Delay in Delivery

A. Buyer

1 Reference to delayed order	On ... (date) Six/seven/eight weeks ago on ... (date)	we I our company	ordered placed an order with your company for placed a firm order with your company for requested you to supply us with		... (goods)
			commissioned you to commissioned your company to	make ... (e.g. a tailor-made stock-recording system) erect ... (e.g. a building, a monument etc.) build ... (e.g. a warehouse, a road) construct ... (a building) design ... manufacture ... carry out work on ... (details of work, e.g. the central heating system ...) carry out maintenance work on ... (e.g. our generator) repair ... service ... maintain ... inspect ... test ... check ... overhaul ... write a report on ... assess the efficiency of ...	

With reference to our order no. ... for ... We refer to our order no. ... for ... We are writing in connection with our order for ...	... (goods)	dated/of ...

With reference to the above-mentioned order ...

According to	the contract of sale, the sales agreement,	a copy of which is enclosed, (see enclosed copy)	the delivery period agreed was	... (period of time, e.g. 3 weeks)
			the delivery date agreed was	... (date, e.g. 1 June ..)

It was stipulated in	the contract the contract of sale the sales agreement	that delivery was to be made that the work was to be performed that this work was to be • carried out • done	by … (date)/within … (period)
The delivery date/ period stipulated in		was … (date/period)	
The date as per		by which the work was to be performed was … (date)	
This has now been exceeded by	… (period of time, e.g. 3 weeks)		
The goods Our order Delivery of our order The report The work	is/are now	3 weeks overdue behind schedule	
Our order for … (goods) dated/of … The goods we ordered on … (date) The goods ordered as per our order no. … dated/of …	still hasn't/haven't has/have still not	arrived been delivered	
The work This work Work on … (details of work, e.g. on the generator)	still hasn't been has still not been	carried out performed done started completed	
Despite your assurance that Although we were assured that	the goods would arrive the goods would be delivered we would be able to take delivery of the goods the work would be carried out		on the date agreed on time punctually on schedule by … (date) within … (period of time) in good time for … (e.g. the Essen Trade Fair on 1 June ..)

	... we must point out that ... we must draw your attention to the fact that ... we regret to say that		they	still haven't have still not	arrived been delivered reached us
			it the work the ... work (e. g. repair work)	still hasn't been has still not been	done carried out performed
	The consignment of ... (goods)	ordered on ... (date)	as per our order no. ...	still hasn't has still not	arrived at our premises been delivered
		referred to above			
	We must point out that We must draw your attention to the fact that	the goods were ordered the order was placed	subject to its/their arriving on condition that it/they arrived on condition that the work was • done • carried out • performed • started • completed		by ... (date) within ... (period)
		the contract of sale provides for delivery the sales agreement provides for performance of this service/work			
	We specifically requested that	the work be carried out delivery be made that this work be performed			
2 Cancellation of order*	Since As In view of the fact that	you have not kept to the terms of you have broken the terms of you have failed to honour the terms of	the contract of sale the sales agreement our agreement our arrangement	we have no alternative but to we have no choice but to we are unfortunately obliged to we are unfortunately compelled to	cancel our order cancel this and all further orders cancel this and all other outstanding orders cancel this and all other unfilled orders discontinue our business relationship with your company
		you are in breach of contract you have not seen fit to give us an explanation for the delay no explanation for the delay has been forthcoming you have given us neither an explanation nor a (new) delivery date no attempt whatsoever has been made on your part to explain the delay			

	Any goods All goods	now delivered now supplied	will (therefore) be	returned sent back	to you to your premises	carriage forward at your expense
				refused	and returned to you and sent back to you	
				placed at your disposal stored at your expense	pending your instructions	
				stored until … (date), after which time they will be disposed of		
	Your company's	• personnel • staff • technicians		refused access to the	• machine • machinery • equipment • apparatus	
	… we (therefore) have … we will (therefore) have		no alternative but to no choice but to	refuse your company's personnel access to the machinery, etc. return the goods, carriage forward send the goods back at your expense refuse to take delivery of the goods place the goods at your disposal store the goods at your expense dispose of the goods in the manner most convenient to us		
	… we are (therefore) … we will (therefore) be		obliged to compelled to			
3 Importance of prompt delivery*	As Since In view of the fact that We wish to remind you that We would point out that You will (no doubt) appreciate that Please remember that		any further delay will cause us considerable inconvenience any (further) delay may well result in our losing orders any (further) delay may well result in our losing business our customers might well look elsewhere for their goods our customers are already looking elsewhere for their goods a machine which is out of action means a loss of custom/business for our company our customers cannot reasonably be asked to wait any longer our customers cannot reasonably be expected to wait any longer we ourselves must keep to our own delivery dates we have a commitment towards our own customers we stand to lose business as a result of this delay we cannot reasonably ask our own customers to wait any longer we cannot reasonably expect our customers to wait any longer we ourselves are under pressure from our customers to deliver without any further delay our customers are no longer prepared to wait			

- our customers have been complaining about the delay in delivery
- our customers are threatening us with legal action
- our customers are threatening to sue us
- we are losing credibility with our customers
- some of our customers are now threatening to cancel their orders
- some of our customers are on the point of cancelling their orders
- some of our customers have already cancelled their orders
- a major customer has already cancelled
- our import licence expires in … (period, e. g. 3 weeks)
- the goods must arrive in time for the … (e. g. summer season, Christmas break, holiday period)

4 Request for explanation of delay*

- Please tell us why
- Please explain why
- Please let us know why
- We would welcome an explanation as to why
- We would very much like to know why

+

- the goods are delayed
- the goods still haven't been delivered
- the goods have still not been delivered
- we have not yet taken delivery of the goods
- the goods have (still) not arrived (yet)
- the work still hasn't been carried out
- the work has still not been performed

- An explanation as to why

+

- would be most appreciated
- would be most helpful
- could be passed on to our customers

- No explanation as to why

+

- has been offered to date
- has been given to us to date
- has been forthcoming

- We fail to understand
- We cannot imagine
- We are at a loss to understand

+

- why you have not contacted us to explain why
- why you have offered us no explanation as to why
- why no explanation has been given to us as to why
- why no attempt on your part has been made to explain why

	Please explain to us why the goods are so late Please give us your reasons for the delay Please let us know what has happened to the goods Please tell us what has become of the goods We would very much like to know why the goods have not (yet) arrived We would very much like to know why this work has not (yet) been carried out We would very much welcome your explanation as to why the goods (still) haven't arrived Please let us have any information you may have regarding the current whereabouts of • the goods • your personnel • your technician(s)
	When were the goods despatched? When was the consignment collected? Is the carrier at fault? Is the freight forwarder to blame?

In view of	your reliable service in the past our long-standing business relationship the quality of your service up to now your company's otherwise good reputation the fact that there have been no problems of this nature to date	we can only assume that we can only imagine that	there must be an important reason for the delay there has been an error of some sort your employee(s) has (have) been held up the goods have been held up somewhere en route to our premises the goods must have been lost in transit the consignment has been misdirected our order has been stolen our order has become mixed up with someone else's

5 Request for delivery by a certain date*	... nevertheless ... whatever the case may be ... whatever may have happened ... regardless of the circumstances	we must have the goods the work must be • done • carried out • performed we must insist on delivery we must have your (firm) assurance that delivery will be made we must be certain that the goods will reach our premises delivery must now be made the goods must now be delivered we must insist that delivery be made	by ... (date) within ... (period)	at the latest at the very latest without fail

	The latest delivery date that we can accept is … (date) The latest date for performance of this work is … (date) Please ensure that delivery is made by … (date)/within … (period) We can only make use of the goods if they arrive by …/within … Our customers are only prepared to wait for the goods for another … (period, e.g. 3 days) We are only prepared to wait for this work to be done until … (date) The very latest date by which delivery of the goods must be made is … (date), after which time we will have no further use for them		
6 Consequence(s) of (further) delay*	… failing this we will have no alternative but to cancel our order (see "2. Cancellation of order" for further expressions)*		
	If you are unable to deliver within the time stated Failure to supply the goods within this time will mean that We must point out that	we will have to it will be necessary for us to	extend the validity of the documentary credit re-negotiate the terms of payment sell the goods at a lower price reduce the price of the goods by … %
	Should this final deadline not be kept If you are unable to meet this deadline If this deadline is not met If delivery is not made • by … (date, e.g. this date) • within … (period, e.g. this period) If the work is not done by … (date) Should the goods not reach our premises by the time stated In the event of delivery not being made • by this time/date • within this time In the event of the work not being performed • by this time • within this time Failure to meet this deadline will mean that	we will have no alternative but to we will have no choice but to we will unfortunately be obliged to we will unfortunately be compelled to we will not hesitate to	cancel our order cancel this and all further orders cancel this and all other outstanding orders cancel this and all other unfilled orders discontinue our business relationship with your company place this and all future orders elsewhere obtain the goods from another supplier buy the goods elsewhere report your company to your local chamber of commerce commission another company to carry out the work lodge a complaint with the … (nationality, e.g. British) Consulate/Embassy contact your country's trade mission in … (buyer's country, e.g. Germany) make a formal complaint to … (e.g. your consulate in our country, your embassy, your local chamber of commerce, your trade mission in our country) put the matter in the hands of our solicitors take appropriate steps to recoup our losses take legal action

hold you liable for any losses incurred
sue you for loss of business
sue you for loss of custom
sue you for breach of contract
sue you for damages
seek compensation
seek legal redress

Failure to meet this deadline
- will lead to our cancelling the order
- will result in our + ing (see list above for further expressions, e.g. ... our discontinuing our business relationship with your company)

There is now no point in delivering the goods unless you are able to offer a sizeable reduction in price

We will now only grant your personnel access to our
- machine
- machinery
- equipment
- apparatus

if a ... (e.g. 10 %) reduction in price is granted

In view of our loss of custom to date we are no longer willing to take the goods at the original price
We are only willing to accept delivery of the goods now if you reduce your price by ... (e.g. $50 per unit/10 %)
The goods will now only be accepted if there is a substantial price reduction
As this delay puts you in breach of contract we will only accept the goods if the price is reduced by ... (e.g. $50 per unit/10 %)

Any additional expense incurred by us as a result of this delay will be
All additional costs to our company resulting from this delay will be

deducted from your invoice/statement
charged to you
passed on to you for settlement

7 Polite ending

We trust that we will be hearing from you in the very near future
We expect to hear from you by ... (date)/within ... (period)
We would welcome your comments on this matter
Please let us know by return how you stand on this
Please let us know by return when the goods will arrive and why they have been delayed
Please let us know by return why the work has not been carried out and when it will be performed
We are convinced that the delay is as a result of some minor mishap and expect to be hearing from you shortly
As soon as we have received your explanation and the goods we are sure that things will return to normal between our two companies
Prompt delivery of the goods is all that is needed to settle this matter
We regret having to cancel, but you will appreciate that we have no other choice
We very much regret that we have had to cancel our order but must point out that the delay was through no fault of our own

B. Seller

1 Tell the buyer that delivery will/may be delayed*	Regarding As regards With regard to In respect of In connection with	your order for … (goods) order no. … dated/of … your order no. … for … (goods) dated/of … the consignment of … (goods) the … (e.g. maintenance, repair) work on … (machine, machinery, equipment, apparatus, plant etc., e.g. the water purification plant) the installation of … (machine, machinery, equipment, apparatus, e.g. the water purification plant)			
	… we unfortunately have to … we are unfortunately obliged to	tell you inform you let you know point out draw your attention to the fact	that,	owing to circumstances (entirely) beyond our control, as we ourselves are waiting for (raw) materials to be delivered, as our own suppliers have not yet delivered the goods ordered, as a result of a strike on the part of … (the French dockers), as a consequence of the hurricane in … (location), owing to a fire in our … (part of company, e.g. warehouse), as a result of the death of … (employee, e.g. our Head of Despatch, Ms Tomkins),	delivery of the goods … the consignment … performance of this service … this work …
	… could … might … might well … will … will probably … will most probably … will unfortunately	be delayed be later than expected take longer than planned take longer than envisaged			
	… might not be … might well not be … can't be … cannot be … won't be … will not be	carried out done performed started completed		on time in time for … (e.g. the exhibition) on schedule by the time agreed within the time agreed	

2 Acknowledge receipt of buyer's letter	Thank you for your letter dated / of … We refer to your letter dated / of … We have received your letter dated / of … With reference to your letter dated / of …	regarding as regards with regard to in respect of in connection with	your order for … (goods) order no. … dated / of … your order no. … for … (goods) dated / of … the consignment of … (goods) the … (e. g. maintenance, repair) work on … (machine, machinery, equipment, apparatus, plant etc., e. g. the water purification plant) the installation of … (machine, machinery, equipment, apparatus, e. g. the water purification plant)
	Thanks for telling us that Thank you very much for informing us that Thank you for letting us know that	the goods haven't arrived (yet) the goods (ordered) have not arrived yet you still haven't taken delivery of the goods you have not yet taken delivery of the goods	
– first (brief) apology for delay	We are sorry to note that We are extremely sorry to note that We note with regret that We very much regret that We are most surprised and sorry to note that We are dismayed to learn that		
	Sorry for the delay We are sorry that the goods are late We are sincerely sorry for this delay We • realise / • appreciate / • understand how inconvenient this must be for you We understand the difficulties this delay must be causing you We fully appreciate your predicament We have every understanding for the difficult circumstances your company is now in We realise that this has placed you in a difficult position May we first of all express our sincere regret that this has happened Please accept our apologies for this We sincerely apologize for this		

3	Release the buyer from the contract*	Therefore For this reason Under the circumstances In view of this	we are prepared to we are willing to we will	release you from your contract with us cancel your order with us permit you to withdraw from the contract	if necessary should you so wish should you so require	We would ask you to confirm this in writing Please let us know what you decide in writing Please let us have you decision on this in writing You will appreciate that we will need to have your final decision on this in writing
4	Explain the delay	The delay has been brought about by The delay is as a result of This delay has come about because of The delay has been caused by This delay is due to As a result of Owing to		the breakdown of our computer system a fire on our premises the fact that our premises were recently broken into a clerical error by a member of our staff a misunderstanding on the part of … (name of person) an illegible fax the fact that your first letter must have got lost in the post an error on the part of the Post Office, which omitted to forward our mail to our company's new address, which is as follows: (address) industrial action in the … industry (e.g. in the metalworking industry) industrial action on the part of (the) … (e.g. on the part of air traffic controllers) a • rail strike • dock • shipping • road hauliers' • airline pilots' • Post Office workers' a strike by airport personnel a strike at … (port, airport, railway station, container terminal etc., e.g. Düsseldorf Airport) a strike in … (location, e.g. Paris) an air traffic controllers' strike a wild-cat strike by … (e.g. French lorry drivers) a go-slow in the … industry (e.g. in the textile industry) an overtime ban in the … industry (e.g. in the road haulage industry) a work-to-rule by … (e.g. by Deutsche Telekom)		

the (sudden) illness of … (e.g. a partner, one of our senior executives, a close relative, a technician, an employee etc.)
the death of … (e.g. a partner, one of our senior executives, a close relative)
a fire in our … (e.g. warehouse, showroom, office building, plant, office, Goods Outwards Department etc.)
a plane crash at … (name of airport, e.g. Munich) Airport
a collision in the … (name of sea, ocean etc. e.g. The English Channel)
the sinking of … (name of ship, e.g. SS Hermione) in … (location, e.g. the North Sea off the coast of Aberdeen)
a collision on the … (name of river/inland waterway, e.g. the Rhine, the Rhein-Herne Kanal)
the civil unrest in … (location, e.g. eastern Europe)
a civil war in … (location)
a state of emergency in … (location)
the closure of … (e.g. the Brenner Pass, the Panama Canal, the A40 motorway from Germany to the Netherlands)
the closure of the factory manufacturing these goods
the breakdown of all (tele)communications with … (location, e.g. Calais)
an earthquake in … (location)
a drought in … (location)
a hurricane in … (location)
a typhoon in … (location)
a forest fire (forest fires) in … (location)
(heavy) (widespread) flooding in … (location)
the … (name of river, e.g. the Danube) breaking its banks in … (location)
a plague of locusts in … (location)
the bankruptcy of one of our major trading partners
the insolvency of one of our suppliers
a lack of skilled labour
a shortage of qualified personnel
unexpectedly great demand for these goods
a sudden lack of demand for these goods
a rush of incoming orders
the devaluation of the … (currency)
the revaluation of the … (currency)
a rise in interest rates

			the introduction of exchange controls the introduction of export licences for these goods a change in the law a change in customs regulations a tightening of customs regulations export restrictions an export ban on these goods	
– refer to enclosure(s)	Please refer to the enclosed … (enclosure(s), e.g. press cutting etc.) for further information, (see … enclosed)			
5 Give date for delivery or part-delivery	Having We have now We have in the meantime	contacted got in touch with spoken to made contact with been given an explanation by obtained an explanation from received a report from	our forwarders (see forwarder's receipt enclosed) our carrier the shipping company the Deutsche Bahn AG the airport authorities in … (location) the port authorities in … (location) our suppliers our representative in … (location, e.g. your country) our agent in … (location, e.g. your country) the manufacturer the factory the factory manager our production manager the production department our plant manager our sales representative the warehouse a reliable business associate in … (location)	who/which tell(s) us that …
	… (and) (we) have now … (and) (we) have in the meantime	been reliably informed by found out from been told by been given an assurance by		that …
	… we are now able to say that …			

... delivery may be expected ... delivery may most certainly be expected ... you may expect delivery ... you may count on delivery ... the goods will be delivered ... the (maintenance/repair/service) work will be carried out ... servicing of the machinery will have been completed ... the machine will (in all probability) be operational ... the equipment will be back in operation ... the computer system will be up and running ... the machine will be working normally ... our service personnel will have completed their work on the machine ... the report will be ready	by ... (date) within ... (period of time)	at the latest
... your letter/fax/e-mail must have crossed with our advice of despatch (see enclosure)	we therefore assume that we are therefore certain that it is therefore safe to say that	the goods are in transit the goods are well on their way the goods are now in your country the goods have now crossed the border the vessel with your goods will have docked in ... (port) by now you will now have taken delivery of the goods the goods will have reached you by now you will now be in possession of the goods the work will have been carried out by now

	... a third/half/50 %/ two thirds/75 % ... the major part ... the first instalment	of the goods ordered of the consignment of your order	will be sent to you will be rushed to you will be delivered to you will arrive will reach you will be posted to you	by express by special delivery by special messenger by air mail by air freight separately as a special consignment	by ... (date) within ... (period of time)	at the latest
		of the work to be done of the ... (e.g. maintenance/repair/ service) work		will have been • carried out • done • completed		
	... your order will be given priority ... your order will be processed in the normal way as soon as things return to normal					
	... your order will be dealt with as fast as possible and that			• you will be sent an advice of despatch • should be receiving the goods • should have received the goods		in the next few days by ... (date)
	... under the circumstances, we are unfortunately unable to give priority to your order but you may expect delivery			by ... (date) within ... (period of time)		and the balance by .../within ...
	The rest The balance The remaining goods		will be sent to you will be delivered to you will arrive will reach you	by ... (date) within ... (period of time)		at the latest without fail
	The remaining work to be done The next/second/third etc./final instalment of your order		will have been carried out will have been done will have been completed			
6 Grant a concession (or concessions)*	Under the circumstances In order to make up for the inconvenience caused In view of our long-standing business relationship Since we have been doing business for several/many years now			we are reducing our price for this consignment by ... % we are prepared to lower the price for ... (goods) by ... % we are willing to supply the goods ... (better Incoterm, e.g. CIP buyer's city) we will service the equipment free of charge for ... (period of time, e.g. 6 months) we are willing to extend the guarantee period by a further 6 months. There will be no extra charge for the new up-dated model		

7 Second apology for the delay	As already said As mentioned at the beginning of this letter/ message to you Please let us once again say that	we are sorry about we are very sorry about we apologize for we wish to apologize for we offer you our sincerest apologies for we sincerely regret we most sincerely regret we deeply regret we very much regret	the delay the mix-up the lack of punctuality	which was due to no fault of our own which was due to circumstances beyond our control which was entirely our own fault due to an unfortunate misunderstanding • on our part • on your part
	We (once again) May we (once again) Please let us (once again)	offer you our sincerest apologies for		
8 Polite ending – reassure the buyer	We promise that We assure you that We guarantee that You may rest assured that You have our word that You may be sure that We undertake to ensure that We will do our very best to ensure that We will do our utmost to make certain that Everything in our power will be done to ensure that We will take appropriate steps to ensure that	it won't happen again such a thing will not happen again there will be no such delays in future there will be no recurrence of such a delay all goods ordered will reach you punctually in future all … (e. g. maintenance / repair / service) work will be carried out punctually in future your reports will arrive on schedule in future our forwarders / carriers / shipper will deliver your consignments on time your orders will be given priority your orders will be handled by a different carrier / forwarder / shipper etc.		
	We'll make certain that We will ensure that We will do our very best to ensure that We will do our utmost to ensure that Everything in our power will be done to ensure that We will take appropriate steps to ensure that	it doesn't happen again there are no such delays in future there is no recurrence of such a delay all goods ordered reach you punctually in future such a thing does not happen again all … (e. g. maintenance / repair / service) work is carried out punctually in future your reports arrive on schedule in future our forwarders / carriers / shipper deliver(s) your consignments on time your orders are given priority your orders are handled by a different carrier / forwarder / shipper etc.		

	Please do not hesitate to contact us	should you have any further queries should the goods not arrive as promised should there be any further delays if the consignment does not arrive on schedule if you do not take delivery of the goods by … / within …	
	Please tell us Please contact us Please let us know We would be grateful if you would contact us We would appreciate it if you would let us know We would very much like to be informed	as soon as once when	the goods arrive the consignment arrives our technician arrives (our technicians arrive) work has started on … (details , e. g. the machine) servicing of the equipment has been completed
9 Enclosure(s)	Advice of despatch Forwarder's receipt Press cutting (Extract from) Insurance agent's report (Extract from) Customs regulations etc.		

Delay in Delivery

A. Buyer

1	**Reference to delayed order**	***Bezugnahme auf verspäteten Auftrag***
	The goods we ordered on 1 June .. still haven't arrived	*Die von uns am 1. Juni .. bestellten Waren sind noch nicht angekommen*
	Eight weeks ago on February 20 .. we placed an order with your company for 100 mobile phones	*Vor acht Wochen, am 20. Februar .., erteilten wir Ihrer Firma einen Auftrag über 100 Mobiltelefone*
	On 1 June .. our company commissioned you to construct a security gate on our premises	*Am 1. Juni .. beauftragte unsere Firma Sie mit dem Bau eines Sicherheitstors für unser Werksgelände*
	With reference to the above-mentioned order, a copy of which is enclosed, the delivery period agreed was 3 weeks	*Unter Bezugnahme auf den oben erwähnten Auftrag, von dem eine Kopie beigefügt ist, war die vereinbarte Lieferzeit 3 Wochen*
	This has now been exceeded by 14 days	*Diese ist jetzt um 14 Tage überschritten*
	The goods are now 3 weeks overdue	*Die Waren sind nun 3 Wochen überfällig*
	Work on the electricity generator has still not been started	*Die Arbeit am Stromgenerator ist noch nicht begonnen worden*
	Despite your assurance that we would be able to take delivery of the goods on schedule …	*Trotz Ihrer Zusicherung, dass wir in der Lage sein würden, die Lieferung der Waren termingemäß entgegenzunehmen …*
	Although we were assured that the work would be carried out in good time for the Essen Trade Fair on 1 June ..	*Obwohl uns versichert wurde, dass die Arbeiten rechtzeitig für die Essener Handelsmesse am 1. Juni .. ausgeführt würden*
	We regret to say that the work still hasn't been done	*Wir bedauern, Ihnen mitzuteilen, dass die Arbeiten immer noch nicht durchgeführt worden sind*
	We must point out that the goods still haven't been delivered	*Wir müssen darauf hinweisen, dass die Waren immer noch nicht geliefert wurden*
	We must draw your attention to the fact that the goods were ordered subject to their arriving by 30 June ..	*Wir müssen Ihre Aufmerksamkeit auf die Tatsache lenken, dass die Waren unter der Bedingung bestellt wurden, dass sie bis zum 30. Juni .. ankämen*
	We specifically requested that the work be carried out within 4 weeks	*Wir baten ausdrücklich darum, die Arbeiten innerhalb von 4 Wochen auszuführen*
2	**Cancellation of order***	***Stornierung des Auftrags****
	Since you have not kept to the terms of the contract of sale we have no alternative but to cancel our order	*Da Sie sich nicht an die Vertragsbedingungen gehalten haben, haben wir keine andere Wahl, als unseren Auftrag zu stornieren*

	In view of the fact that you have failed to honour the terms of our agreement, we are unfortunately obliged to cancel this and all other outstanding orders	*Angesichts der Tatsache, dass Sie die Bedingungen unserer Abmachung nicht eingehalten haben, sind wir leider genötigt, diesen Auftrag und alle anderen ausstehenden Aufträge zu stornieren*
	As you are in breach of contract, we have no choice but to cancel this and all further orders	*Da Sie Vertragsbruch begangen haben, haben wir keine andere Wahl, als diesen und alle weiteren Aufträge zu stornieren*
	As you have given us neither an explanation nor a (new) delivery date, we are unfortunately compelled to discontinue our business relationship with your company	*Da Sie uns weder eine Erklärung noch ein (neues) Lieferdatum gegeben haben, sind wir leider gezwungen, unsere Geschäftsbeziehung mit Ihrer Firma abzubrechen*
	Any goods now delivered will (therefore) be returned to you, carriage forward	*Alle nun gelieferten Waren werden (daher) unfrei an Sie zurückgeschickt*
	All goods now delivered will (therefore) be placed at your disposal pending your instructions	*Alle jetzt gelieferten Waren werden Ihnen (daher) zur Verfügung gestellt, wofür wir Ihre Anweisungen erwarten*
	Your company's personnel will be refused access to the machinery	*Dem Personal Ihrer Gesellschaft wird der Zutritt zu den Maschinen verwehrt*
3	**Importance of prompt delivery***	***Wichtigkeit prompter Lieferung****
	As any further delay will cause us considerable inconvenience …	*Da jede weitere Verzögerung uns erhebliche Unannehmlichkeiten verursachen wird, …*
	In view of the fact that our customers might well look elsewhere for their goods …	*Angesichts der Tatsache, dass unsere Kunden sich möglicherweise anderweitig mit den Waren eindecken …*
	We would point out that we ourselves are under pressure from our customers to deliver without any further delay	*Wir möchten darauf hinweisen, dass wir selbst von unseren Kunden unter Druck gesetzt werden, ohne weitere Verzögerung zu liefern*
	You will (no doubt) appreciate that we stand to lose business as a result of this delay	*Sie werden (zweifellos) verstehen, dass wir Gefahr laufen, als Ergebnis dieser Verzögerung Geschäftsanteile zu verlieren*
4	**Request for explanation of delay***	***Bitte um Erklärung der Verzögerung****
	Please tell us why the goods are delayed	*Bitte teilen Sie uns mit, warum Sie mit den Waren in Verzug sind*
	We would welcome an explanation as to why we have not yet taken delivery of the goods	*Wir würden eine Erklärung darüber begrüßen, warum wir die Lieferung der Waren noch nicht entgegennehmen konnten*

	We would very much like to know why the work still hasn't been carried out	*Wir würden gern wissen, warum die Arbeiten immer noch nicht ausgeführt wurden*
	An explanation as to why the goods (still) haven't arrived (yet) would be most appreciated	*Eine Erklärung darüber, warum die Waren (immer noch) nicht angekommen sind, würden wir sehr begrüßen*
	No explanation as to why the work still hasn't been carried out has been offered to date	*Uns ist bis heute noch keine Erklärung gegeben worden, weshalb die Arbeit immer noch nicht ausgeführt wurde*
	We are at a loss to understand why no explanation has been given to us as to why we have not yet taken delivery of the goods	*Wir können überhaupt nicht verstehen, warum wir keine Erklärung darüber erhalten haben, weshalb die Lieferung der Waren noch nicht erfolgt ist*
	Please give us your reasons for the delay	*Bitte geben Sie uns Ihre Gründe für die Verzögerung an*
	We would very much welcome your explanation as to why the goods (still) haven't arrived	*Wir würden es sehr begrüßen, Ihre Erklärung darüber zu erhalten, warum die Güter (immer noch) nicht angekommen sind*
	When were the goods despatched?	*Wann wurden die Güter versandt?*
	Is the freight forwarder to blame?	*Trifft den Spediteur die Schuld?*
	In view of your reliable service in the past, we can only assume that there must be an important reason for the delay	*Angesichts Ihres zuverlässigen Service in der Vergangenheit können wir nur annehmen, dass es einen wichtigen Grund für die Verzögerung geben muss*
	In view of the fact that there have been no problems of this nature to date, we can only imagine that the goods have been held up somewhere en route to our premises	*Angesichts der Tatsache, dass bis heute Probleme dieser Art nicht aufgetreten sind, können wir uns nur vorstellen, dass die Waren irgendwo auf dem Weg zu unseren Geschäftsräumen aufgehalten worden sind*
5	**Request for delivery by a certain date***	***Bitte um Lieferung bis zu einem bestimmten Datum****
	Whatever the case may be, we must insist on delivery within 7 days at the latest	*Wie die Sachlage auch sein mag, müssen wir auf Lieferung innerhalb von spätestens 7 Tagen bestehen*
	Our customers are only prepared to wait for the goods for another 3 days	*Unsere Kunden sind nur bereit, weitere 3 Tage auf die Güter zu warten*
6	**Consequence(s) of (further) delay***	***Folge(n) einer (weiteren) Verzögerung****
	If you are unable to deliver within the time stated, we will have to extend the validity of the documentary credit	*Wenn Sie nicht in der Lage sind, innerhalb der festgesetzten Zeit zu liefern, müssen wir die Gültigkeit des Dokumentenakkreditivs verlängern*

	Failure to supply the goods within this time will mean that it will be necessary for us to sell them at a lower price	*Sollten die Waren nicht innerhalb dieses Zeitraums geliefert werden, bedeutet dies, dass wir sie zu einem niedrigeren Preis verkaufen müssen*
	If you are unable to meet this deadline we will unfortunately be obliged to cancel this and all further orders	*Wenn Sie diesen letzten Termin nicht einhalten können, werden wir leider genötigt sein, diesen und alle weiteren Aufträge zu stornieren*
	Should the goods not reach our premises by the time stated, we will have no alternative but to obtain them from another supplier	*Sollten die Waren unsere Geschäftsräume nicht bis zum festgesetzten Termin erreichen, haben wir keine andere Wahl, als sie von einem anderen Lieferanten zu beziehen*
	In the event of the work not being performed by this time, we will unfortunately be compelled to put the matter in the hands of our solicitors	*Falls die Arbeiten bis zu diesem Zeitpunkt noch nicht ausgeführt sind, sind wir leider gezwungen, die Angelegenheit unseren Anwälten zu übergeben*
	Failure to meet this deadline will lead to our cancelling the order	*Falls dieser letzte Termin nicht eingehalten wird, werden wir den Auftrag stornieren*
	Failure to meet this deadline will result in our discontinuing our business relationship with your company	*Falls dieser letzte Termin nicht eingehalten wird, werden wir unsere Geschäftsbeziehung mit Ihrer Firma beenden*
	There is now no point in delivering the goods unless you are able to offer a sizeable reduction in price	*Es besteht jetzt keine Veranlassung mehr, die Waren zu liefern, es sei denn, Sie können uns einen nennenswerten Preisnachlass gewähren*
	We are only willing to accept delivery of the goods now, if you reduce your price by $50 per unit	*Wir sind nur bereit, die Lieferung der Waren jetzt noch anzunehmen, wenn Sie Ihren Preis um 50 $ pro Stück reduzieren*
	Any additional expense incurred by us as a result of this delay will be deducted from your statement	*Alle zusätzlichen Kosten, die uns auf Grund dieser Verzögerung entstehen, werden von Ihrem Kontoauszug / Ihrer Abrechnung abgezogen*
7	**Polite ending**	***Höflicher Schluss***
	We trust that we will be hearing from you in the very near future	*Wir sind zuversichtlich, dass wir sehr bald von Ihnen hören werden*
	Please let us know by return when the goods will arrive and why they have been delayed	*Bitte teilen Sie uns umgehend mit, wann die Güter ankommen werden und warum ihre Lieferung sich verzögert hat*
	We regret having to cancel, but you will appreciate that we have no other choice	*Wir bedauern, stornieren zu müssen, aber Sie werden verstehen, dass wir keine andere Wahl haben*

B. Seller

1	**Tell the buyer that delivery will / may be delayed***	***Sagen Sie dem Käufer, dass die Lieferung sich verzögern wird / sich möglicherweise verzögert****
	Regarding your order for mobile phones, we unfortunately have to tell you that, owing to circumstances (entirely) beyond our control, delivery of the goods might well be delayed	*Hinsichtlich Ihres Auftrags auf Mobiltelefone müssen wir Ihnen leider mitteilen, dass auf Grund von Umständen, die (völlig) außerhalb unserer Kontrolle liegen, durchaus die Möglichkeit besteht, dass sich die Lieferung der Waren verzögert*
	With regard to order no. 897 dated 20 July .. we are unfortunately obliged to draw your attention to the fact that, as our own suppliers have not yet delivered the goods ordered, delivery will probably take longer than planned	*Hinsichtlich des Auftrags Nr. 897 vom 20. Juli .. sind wir leider genötigt, Ihre Aufmerksamkeit auf die Tatsache zu lenken, dass die Lieferung voraussichtlich länger als geplant dauern wird, da unsere eigenen Lieferanten die bestellten Güter noch nicht zugestellt haben*
	In respect of the installation of a complete alarm system, we unfortunately have to inform you that, owing to a fire in our warehouse, we are unable to complete the work on schedule	*Was die Anbringung eines kompletten Alarmsystems anbelangt, müssen wir Ihnen leider mitteilen, dass wir wegen eines Feuers in unserem Lager nicht in der Lage sind, die Arbeit termingerecht zu beenden*
2	**Acknowledge receipt of buyer's letter**	***Bestätigen Sie den Erhalt des Schreibens des Käufers***
	Thank you for your letter of June 9 .. regarding your order for modems	*Vielen Dank für Ihren Brief vom 9. Juni .. bezüglich Ihrer Bestellung für Modems*
	Thank you (very much) for informing us that the goods haven't arrived (yet)	*Wir danken Ihnen (sehr) für die Mitteilung, dass die Waren (noch) nicht angekommen sind*
	– first (brief) apology for delay	***– erste (kurze) Entschuldigung für die Verzögerung***
	We are sorry to note that the goods (ordered) have not arrived yet	*Es tut uns Leid festzustellen, dass die (bestellten) Güter noch nicht angekommen sind*
	We are sorry that the goods are late	*Wir bedauern, dass die Waren zu spät ankommen*
	We understand the difficulties this delay must be causing you	*Wir verstehen die Schwierigkeiten, welche diese Verzögerung Ihnen zwangsläufig verursacht*
	Please accept our apologies for this	*Bitte nehmen Sie unsere diesbezügliche Entschuldigung entgegen*

3	**Release the buyer from the contract***	***Entbinden Sie den Käufer vom Vertrag****
	Under the circumstances we are prepared to release you from your contract with us, if necessary. We would ask you to confirm this in writing	*Unter diesen Umständen sind wir bereit, Sie nötigenfalls von Ihrem Vertrag mit uns zu entbinden. Wir bitten Sie aber, dies schriftlich zu bestätigen.*
4	**Explain the delay**	***Erklären Sie die Verzögerung***
	The delay is as a result of the breakdown of our computer system	*Die Verzögerung ist auf eine Störung in unserem Computersystem zurückzuführen*
	The delay has been brought about by the fact that your first letter must have got lost in the post	*Die Verzögerung ist durch die Tatsache entstanden, dass Ihr erster Brief in der Post verlorengegangen sein muss*
	The delay has been caused by industrial action in the metalworking industry	*Die Verzögerung wurde durch Arbeitskampfmaßnahmen in der metallverarbeitenden Industrie verursacht*
	… (by) the closure of the factory manufacturing these goods	*… (durch) die Schließung der Fabrik, die diese Waren herstellt*
	… (by) the bankruptcy of one of our major trading partners	*… (durch) den Konkurs eines unserer Haupthandelspartner*
	… (by) a shortage of qualified personnel	*… (durch) einen Mangel an qualifiziertem Personal*
	… (by) a rush of incoming orders	*… (durch) eine Flut neuer Bestellungen*
	– refer to enclosure(s)	***– beziehen Sie sich auf die Anlage(n)***
	Please refer to the enclosed press cutting for further information	*Bitte entnehmen Sie weitere Informationen dem beigefügten Presseausschnitt*
5	**Give date for delivery or part-delivery**	***Geben Sie das Datum für die Lieferung oder Teillieferung an***
	Having contacted our forwarders (see forwarder's receipt enclosed), who have told us that the goods are in transit, we are now able to say that delivery may be expected by the end of the week at the latest	*Nach Rücksprache mit unserem Spediteur (siehe beigefügte Spediteurübernahmebescheinigung), der uns mitteilte, dass die Waren unterwegs sind, können wir Ihnen jetzt mitteilen, dass mit der Lieferung spätestens bis Ende der Woche gerechnet werden kann*
	We have, in the meantime, spoken to the shipping company, which told us that you may count on delivery within 7 days	*Wir haben in der Zwischenzeit mit der Versandfirma gesprochen, die uns mitteilte, dass Sie mit der Lieferung innerhalb von 7 Tagen rechnen können*
	We have now obtained an explanation from our sales representative, who tells us that the computer system will be up and running within 48 hours at the latest	*Wir haben nunmehr eine Erklärung von unserem Verkaufsvertreter erhalten, der uns mitteilt, dass die Computeranlage spätestens in 48 Stunden wieder funktionsbereit sein wird*

	Your letter / fax / e-mail must have crossed with our advice of despatch (see enclosure)	*Ihr Brief / Fax / Ihre E-Mail muss sich mit unserer Versandanzeige gekreuzt haben (siehe Anlage)*
	We therefore assume that the goods are well on their way	*Wir nehmen deshalb an, dass die Waren jetzt unterwegs sind*
	The first instalment of your order will be rushed to you as a special consignment	*Die erste Teillieferung Ihres Auftrags wird Ihnen als Sondersendung sofort zugehen*
	Your order will be given priority	*Wir werden Ihren Auftrag bevorzugt ausführen*
	Your order will be dealt with as fast as possible	*Ihr Auftrag wird so schnell wie möglich bearbeitet*
	You will be sent an advice of despatch in the next few days	*Sie werden in den nächsten Tagen eine Versandanzeige zugeschickt bekommen*
	Under the circumstances, we are unfortunately unable to give priority to your order but you may expect a part-delivery by 15 August .. and the balance 2 weeks later	*Unter diesen Umständen sind wir leider nicht in der Lage, Ihrem Auftrag Priorität einzuräumen, aber Sie können bis zum 15. August .. mit einer Teillieferung rechnen und den Rest 2 Wochen später erhalten*
	The balance will arrive by November 30 .. without fail	*Der Rest wird ganz sicher bis zum 30. November .. ankommen*
6	**Grant (a) concession(s)***	***Gewähren Sie (eine) Konzession(en)****
	Under the circumstances we will service the equipment free of charge for 6 months	*Unter diesen Umständen werden wir die Anlage 6 Monate lang kostenlos warten*
	In order to make up for the inconvenience caused we are reducing our price for this consignment by 10 %	*Um Sie für die verursachten Unannehmlichkeiten zu entschädigen, reduzieren wir unseren Preis für diese Sendung um 10 %*
7	**Second apology for the delay**	***Zweite Entschuldigung für die Verzögerung***
	As already said, we are sorry about the delay which was due to no fault of our own	*Wie bereits gesagt, bedauern wir die Verzögerung sehr, für die wir selbst nichts können*
	Please let us once again say that we apologize for the mix-up, which was entirely our own fault	*Bitte lassen Sie uns noch einmal sagen, dass wir uns für die Verwechslung entschuldigen, für die wir voll verantwortlich waren*
	May we (once again) offer you our sincerest apologies for the lack of punctuality due to an unfortunate misunderstanding on our part	*Wir möchten uns nochmals für den Mangel an Pünktlichkeit entschuldigen, der auf ein bedauerliches Missverständnis unsererseits zurückzuführen ist*

8	**Polite ending – reassure the buyer**	***Höflicher Schluss – Beruhigen Sie den Käufer***
	You may rest assured that there will be no such delays in future	*Sie können versichert sein, dass solche Verzögerungen sich in Zukunft nicht wiederholen werden*
	We undertake to ensure that your orders will be given priority	*Wir sichern Ihnen zu, dass Ihre Aufträge bevorzugt bearbeitet werden*
	We will take appropriate steps to ensure that all goods ordered will reach you punctually in future	*Wir werden geeignete Schritte unternehmen um sicherzustellen, dass alle bestellten Waren Sie in Zukunft pünktlich erreichen werden*
	Everything in our power will be done to ensure that there is no recurrence of such a delay	*Wir werden alles in unserer Macht Stehende tun um sicherzustellen, dass eine solche Verzögerung sich nicht wiederholen wird*
	Please do not hesitate to contact us should you have any further queries	*Bitte zögern Sie nicht, uns anzusprechen, sollten Sie weitere Fragen haben*
	Please let us know if there are any further delays	*Bitte teilen Sie uns mit, ob es noch weitere Verzögerungen gibt*
	We would be grateful if you would contact us as soon as the goods arrive	*Wir wären Ihnen dankbar, wenn Sie mit uns Kontakt aufnehmen würden, sobald die Waren eintreffen*
	We would very much like to be informed when work has started on the machine	*Wir würden sehr gern erfahren, wenn mit der Arbeit an der Maschine angefangen worden ist*
9	**Enclosure(s)**	***Anlage(n)***
	Advice of despatch Forwarder's receipt Press cutting (Extract from) Insurance agent's report (Extract from) Customs regulations etc.	*Versandavis* *Spediteurübernahmebescheinigung* *Presseausschnitt* *(Auszug aus dem) Bericht des Versicherungsvertreters* *(Auszug aus den) Zollbestimmungen* *usw.*

Unit 9
Complaints

A. Buyer – Making a Complaint

1 Confirm receipt of goods	We have just received the We have now taken delivery of	… (goods) the consignment of …	ordered on … (date) as per our order no. … dated/of … (date) for which we placed an order on … (date)		
	The … (goods) The consignment of … (goods)	as per our order no … as requested/ordered in our letter dated/of …	has/have now • arrived • reached us is/are now on our premises was/were delivered to us • today • yesterday • two days ago etc.		
	The above-mentioned	consignment goods	was delivered on … (date) were delivered on … (date)	and forwarded to and passed on to and delivered to and collected by and picked up by	our customer(s) our client(s) Messrs (name of customers) The Metal Box Company Ltd etc.
		equipment machinery		and put into service by and installed by and used by	
Confirm performance of service	The maintenance work The repair work The repairs	carried out on	… (machine, equipment, building etc., e.g. the DTYD mini-bar)	is/are now • complete • finished	
	The installation of The servicing of The redecorating of The (re)painting of The renovation of (AE) The remodeling of (e.g. a shop) etc.			has/have now been • completed • finished • concluded	
	Work on				
	The … (e.g. machine(s), equipment, building etc.)	has/have now been	installed repaired serviced overhauled (re)painted renovated etc.		

2 Say what is wrong – goods*	When we opened the When our Goods Inwards Department opened the When our customer(s) opened the When opening the On opening the Upon opening the After opening the		box(es) case(s) container(s) package(s) etc. *(see Unit 6 "Delivery")*	he she we they	found that saw that discovered that	the DTYD mini-bar was article no. … was articles nos. … were one item was the goods were	damaged below standard not up to scratch etc.
				it was apparent that it was evident that it was noticed that it was quite obvious that			
	On Upon While Whilst	examining inspecting checking testing	the goods the articles the material(s) the delivery the machine the equipment etc.	we saw that we found that we discovered that it was noticed that it became apparent that it became clear that		some of the goods were many of the goods were most of the goods were some/many/most of them were all of the goods were the machine was the equipment was it was they were	
			the bottle(s) the cask(s) the drum(s) the carboy(s) the tin(s) the container(s)			it they one of them several of them some of them most of them all of them	was/were damp was/were leaking was/were leaky was/were unsealed was/were open was/were half-empty was/were empty was/were wet had leaked

This is most likely because This is probably due to the fact that	the goods were	dropped crushed • in the ship's hold • in the container • on board the plane left outside • in the rain • in the sunlight poorly packed roughly handled (in transit) badly made incorrectly sealed badly sealed loaded and unloaded too many times sent (against our instructions) as a groupage consignment/ consolidated shipment

When	testing trying out running using operating working with	the machine, the equipment etc.	for a short time for some time for … (period, e.g. two hours, for several minutes)	we saw that we found that we discovered that we realised that it was noticed that it became apparent that it became clear that	it was	inefficient noisy too slow etc.

After	using running working with operating printing with copying with cutting with etc.	it did not	meet our requirements come up to our expectations perform as expected

– services*	On Upon When	examining inspecting checking	the … work (e. g. repair work, maintenance work, paintwork etc.) the … (specific details, e. g. the finish, the workmanship, the surface, the texture etc.)	we saw that we found that we discovered that we realised that it was noticed that it became apparent that it became clear that	it was	not up to standard below standard of inferior quality poorly executed poorly performed completed to poor standard
					it did not	meet our requirements meet our standards come up to our expectations comply with EU standards correspond to our specifications
	We must also point out that We also regret to say that We also feel obliged to tell you that It is also our unpleasant duty to inform you that			your technician(s) your employee(s) your repairman/men your staff your personnel	was/ were	aggressive clumsy etc.
– proof*	We enclose We have included We will be posting/mailing you You will be receiving		a photograph/photographs of a sample/samples of a report on an independent assessor's report on the carrier's receipt the bill of lading the survey report copies of … (e. g. all documents) authenticated by … (e. g. a consulate) in connection with		the damage etc.	as proof by way of proof as evidence by way of evidence for your information to substantiate our claim to show you what we mean to illustrate our point

3	Ask for an explanation	Please Will you therefore We would therefore ask you to	explain why this let us know why this let us have an explanation as to why this	has happened happened has come about came about could happen could come about	as soon as possible by return immediately by … (+ date, e. g. the end of the week) within … (+ period of time, e. g. the next 48 hours)
		We would welcome your comments on this We look forward to receiving your comments on this matter Please let us have your version of events Please let us have your explanation of what happened We expect to be receiving a full and detailed explanation as to why and how this came about We trust we will be receiving your explanation of what has happened Please let us have a full explanation of what took place We require a full explanation as to how such damage could take place We require a full explanation as to how the goods could become … (e. g. damaged, scratched, wet etc.)			
		A full explanation of events Your explanation as to how such a thing could happen	will have to be given to us is now required is now necessary is now vital		before any further business is done before we can continue doing business with you before any further orders are placed if our companies are to continue doing business with each other if the matter is to be settled for the matter to be settled
4	Consequences for the buyer's company	We trust you understand that Needless to say You will, of course, appreciate that You will, no doubt, appreciate that It goes without saying that	this has caused us a lot of trouble this has been very annoying for us this has caused us considerable inconvenience we have been greatly inconvenienced by this we have suffered a considerable financial loss as a result of this these goods cannot be sold at the price stated we cannot sell these goods at the price agreed we will only be able to sell these products if the price is reduced substantially we can only hope to sell these goods if the price is lowered considerably we stand to lose our good name if we put these goods on sale we stand to lose business if we cannot supply our customers with the right goods there is no market for goods of this quality		

		our customers will not accept goods of inferior quality our customers will reject these goods and turn to another supplier our competitors will gain an edge over us if we put such goods on sale we will lose our competitive edge on the … (e. g. local) market if we offer such goods we will lose our market share if we offer these goods for sale we cannot offer these products to our customers we will be inundated with complaints if we pass these products on to our customers we are unable to get on with our daily business without this equipment our … (name of equipment, system etc., e. g. our mailmerge system) is unable to function without … (product) we will not be able to manufacture … (product) until the … (equipment/machine etc.) is installed/repaired/adjusted etc.	
	We have no alternative but to We have no choice but to We are unfortunately obliged to We will have no alternative but to We will have no choice but to We will unfortunately be obliged to	request a complete refund cancel our order and obtain the goods from another supplier withhold payment until (a) suitable replacement(s)/substitute(s) is/are provided take legal action put the matter in the hands of our solicitors take appropriate steps to recoup our losses	
	We reserve the right to	hold you liable for any losses incurred sue you for loss of business sue you for loss of custom sue you for breach of contract sue you for damages seek compensation seek legal redress	if the matter is not settled without delay if the matter is not settled to our entire satisfaction should you be unable to suggest a suitable solution
5 Return the goods to the seller*	We are returning the (damaged) goods to you The (faulty) goods will be returned to you The (defective) goods are being returned to you You will be receiving the (unsaleable) goods	carriage forward at your expense and risk	

		Since As In view of the fact that	we have no use for these goods we are unable to use/sell these goods the goods are unsaleable these goods are taking up warehouse space we are unable to store the damaged goods	please arrange to have them collected please arrange to have them picked up we would ask you to instruct your carrier to collect them	as soon as possible by return immediately by … (+ date, e.g. the end of the week) within … (+ period of time, e.g. the next 7 days)
		… otherwise	we will be obliged to we will have no alternative but to we will have no choice but to	return them to you send them back have them forwarded to you	carriage forward at your expense and risk
	– goods to be collected by seller*	The goods have been placed at your disposal	at our branch in … (location) in our warehouse in … (location) on our premises in … (location)	and we would ask you to have them collected Please arrange for them to be picked up	as soon as possible by return immediately by … (+ date, e.g. the end of the week) within … (+ period of time, e.g. the next 7 days)
		Should your representative wish to Should you wish to	examine them inspect them have them examined have them inspected examine the work inspect the work see for yourself/himself/herself	our premises are open from … (time, e.g. 9 am) to … (time, e.g. 5 pm) please call us/our office/me on … (telephone number) to arrange for an appointment	
6	Request the seller to take appropriate action*	Please (therefore) We would (therefore) ask you to We must (therefore) ask you to We must (therefore) insist that you	investigate the matter find out what has happened look into this make enquiries solve this problem settle the matter find a solution (to this problem) let us know what can be done to rectify the situation		as soon as possible immediately by … (+ date, e.g. the end of the week) within … (+ period of time, e.g. the next 48 hours)

	ensure that the right goods arrive	in good condition in perfect condition safely		
	make sure that the work is • done • completed • finished	to good standard as per contract satisfactorily		
Under the circumstances In view of the (extent of) the damage In view of the urgency of the situation As we ourselves are under pressure from our customers In order for us not to miss our own delivery deadlines To enable us to meet the delivery date(s) promised to our customers	please we would ask you to we must ask you to we must insist that you	send us let us have rush us arrange for us to receive	a replacement replacements a substitute substitutes the missing product(s) the missing goods the missing part(s) the equipment etc.	as soon as possible by return immediately by … (+ date, e.g. the end of the week) within … (+ period of time, e.g. the next 48 hours) on the next available flight to … (airport) on the next ship to … (location)
Since we are committed to deliver • by … (date) • within … (period of time)	please ensure that	we receive we are sent we are supplied with		
As we need to have the equipment up and running in good time for … (e.g. the opening of our new branch, the exhibition etc.)	please we would ask you to we must ask you to we must insist that you	repair adjust check and adjust re-adjust re-install complete the work on send a technician to • attend to • see to • deal with	the equipment the machine(s) the machinery the product(s) etc.	as soon as possible immediately by … (+ date, e.g. the end of the week) within … (+ period of time, e.g. the next 48 hours)

Under the circumstances In view of the (extent of) the damage			we must cancel the entire order and request you to refund the invoice amount
Please (therefore) arrange to have Please (therefore) have We therefore wish you to have We must insist that you have		your agent/ representative	visit our premises/our office/the factory etc. call on us examine the goods assess the extent of the damage view the site look at the work carried out see for himself/herself
We will only consider We are only prepared to consider We are only willing to consider		keeping the goods accepting the work carried out accepting work of this standard	if you grant (us) a … % (e.g. 20 %) reduction in price if you reduce the price by … % if the price is reduced by … % if you are prepared to sell us the article(s) for $200 (per unit) if you include … (e.g. an extra 6 months' warranty etc.) if a reduction in price of … % is granted
We will only	be prepared to be able to be willing to be in a position to	keep the goods accept work of this quality pay the price agreed in the contract of sale	if you agree to change your terms of delivery to … (better Incoterm, e.g. CIP buyer's city) if you grant us … (e.g. 3 months') credit if you agree to maintain the equipment free of charge for … (e.g. 1 year) if you increase the warranty period on the goods by … (e.g. 6 months) if you include free on-site maintenance for … (e.g. 12 months) with your offer if you include free after-sales service for … (e.g. 12 months) with your offer if you grant us free access to your telephone hotline (for 12 months)
We must ask you to We must therefore insist that you		refund the (entire) invoice amount refund the sum of … (amount) already paid refund the invoice amount and collect the consignment at your expense and risk	

7 Polite ending

Please We hope that you will be able to We trust that you will We expect you to	sort this out look into this (matter) deal with the matter investigate the matter attend to this (matter)	immediately in the (very) near future as soon as possible without delay by … (date) within … (period of time)
We hope to receive We look forward to receiving	your answer your comments your version of events your explanation of what happened a full explanation the results of your investigation your suggestions as regards solving this matter	

This matter will need to be sorted out This problem will need to be solved This matter will need to be settled A solution to this problem will need to be found	in the (very) near future without delay	and to our complete satisfaction and to the entire satisfaction of all concerned	before we place any more orders with you before any more orders are placed with your company if our (hitherto satisfactory) business relations are to continue if we are to continue dealing with each other if our companies are to continue doing business with each other

We must point out that We would add that	any further business with your company any further dealings with your company the continuation of our business relationship	will depend upon how this matter is settled
	your handling of this matter	will determine whether we will be able to continue dealing with you in future

You will no doubt understand that no other course of action was open to us
We feel sure you will understand that, under the circumstances, we have had no choice but to act in this way
We trust you will appreciate the difficult position you have placed us in and hope that every effort will be made to find a solution as soon as possible

8	Enclosure(s)*	Our customer's letter of complaint Photograph(s) Sample(s) Independent Assessor's Report Freight Forwarder's Report Carrier's Receipt Bill of Lading Survey Report Sales Agreement etc.

B. Seller – Dealing with a Complaint

1	Acknowledge receipt of the buyer's letter immediately	We have (just) received Many thanks for Thank you for In reply to In response to In answer to	your letter/fax/e-mail/ message dated/of …	regarding with regard to in connection with	order no … the above-mentioned order/ consignment/goods the shipment of … (goods) the consignment of … (goods) the … (product, e.g. DTYD mini-bar) work done on … (details, e.g. your computer system) maintenance work carried out on … (details) service work performed on … (details) etc.	
		We received				yesterday 2 days ago etc.
		Your letter/fax/ e-mail/message dated/of …	regarding with regard to in connection with	order no … the shipment of … (goods) the consignment of … (goods) the … (product, e.g. DTYD mini-bar) work done on … (details, e.g. your computer system) maintenance work carried out on … (details) service work performed on … (details) etc.	has (now) been passed on to us has been forwarded to us	by … (e.g. a representative/ agent)

2	Say you are sorry that the buyer is dissatisfied	We're sorry We are sorry We regret We are dismayed We are surprised … and (we) (are) sorry … and (we) regret … and (we) are dismayed … and (we) are most surprised	that to hear that to learn that to discover that to find that	the goods arrived bent/broken/chipped etc. the equipment is not working (properly) the machine is not performing as expected some articles are missing you received the wrong goods
		… since this is the first complaint we have received about … (details of product/work etc.) … as no other customer has experienced • any problems with … (details of product/service) to date • any problems of this nature … in view of the fact that this is an extremely reliable model/version etc. … since we have been using this form of packaging for the past … (e.g. 10) years without any problems whatsoever … as we have been dealing with this haulage company for many years now and have had no cause for complaint … given that Mr/Miss/Ms Jones has been employed with us for several years now and his/her work has given no cause for complaint		
		We note with regret that … and note with regret that	you are unhappy with you are dissatisfied with you are not satisfied with you are not pleased with	our service the work carried out by our technician(s) the performance of the machine
3	Say that the matter will be dealt with	We'll find out what's been happening We will look into this matter This matter will be attended to Your complaint will be investigated	straight away immediately without delay within the next 24/48 hours	
	– the matter is being dealt with	We are now looking into the matter and The matter is now being dealt with and This matter is now receiving attention and Your complaint is now being investigated and We are making enquiries into this matter and	the freight forwarders the hauliers the carrier the driver responsible for delivering this consignment the police	have/has been contacted
		The insurance company will be sending us/you a claim form for the loss/damage etc.		

– the matter has been dealt with	Since receiving your letter/fax/e-mail/ message	we have (now) looked into the matter we have (now) enquired into the matter we have (now) investigated the matter we have made enquiries regarding … (details, e.g. the damage) we have enquired about … (details, e.g. the missing items) with … (person, e.g. the freight forwarders)		… and found out that … … and ascertained that … … and discovered that …
	As soon as we got your After receiving your As soon as we had received your	letter/fax/e-mail/ message	we looked into the matter we enquired into the matter we investigated the matter we made enquiries regarding … (details)	
4 Ask for more time to investigate the complaint*	As it will take some time for us Since it will take a few days	to find out to ascertain	what went wrong … what has been happening … what has happened … who is at fault … how this could happen …	
		to get to the root of this …		
	As Since In view of the fact that	it will take a few days before we can say what's been happening … we have not yet been able to contact … (person/company etc.) … investigations of this nature take some time … we have not yet received the • freight forwarder's • carrier's • haulage company's • insurance company's • police report … the … report has not arrived yet … we are still waiting for the … (details) …		
	… please … we would ask you to … we would be (most) grateful if you would … we would (very much) appreciate it if you would	give us more time allow us more time give us a few more days let us have a little more time let us have some more time	to look into this to look into the matter to investigate your claim to make enquiries to deal with your complaint	
5 Request proof*	Any proof (of … e.g. the damage) Any evidence (of … e.g. negligence)	you may have you may have to substantiate your claim you are able to provide us with	will help (our investigations) will be of help will be of (great) assistance to us will greatly assist us	

	We require We will need It will be necessary to supply us with Our representative/agent will need to see	proof of your claim evidence to prove your claim evidence to substantiate your claim any evidence you may have to prove your claim	before any action can be taken on our part before we can proceed any further before we can take any further steps
	Please let us have Please send us Please allow our representative/agent to see	all the proof you have all the evidence you have any evidence you may have to prove your claim anything of relevance to your claim	to help us with our enquiries to help us with our investigations to enable us to take appropriate action
6 Explain*	We have now found out that We have now discovered that We are now able to tell you that Our investigations have now shown that Our enquiries have revealed that The shipping company's report has revealed that Our representative/agent has discovered that	the damage was as a result of the damage was caused by	an error on our part an oversight on our part a problem with packing an accident in transit an accident when the goods were being unloaded in … (location) a storm an earthquake a power cut in the freight forwarder's warehouse a fire in … (e.g. our/the freight forwarder's warehouse, showroom, office building, plant, office, Goods Outwards Department etc.) a plane crash at … (name of airport, e.g. Munich) Airport a collision in the … (name of sea, ocean etc. e.g. The English Channel) a collision on the … (name of river/inland waterway, e.g. the Rhine) an earthquake in … (location) a hurricane in … (location) a typhoon in … (location) (heavy) (widespread) flooding in … (location) negligence on the part of one of our employees, who has now been dismissed

	From what you say about the From the information you have given us on the Judging by your description of the On the basis of your description of the	breakage chipping cracks damage deficiencies dents discolouration imperfections irregularities roughness rust marks rusty spots scratches shortcomings stains tarnishing warping (sea) water damage etc.	it sounds as if it would seem that we feel sure that	this problem is the result of this problem has come about because of	rough handling of the equipment an operating error on your part a mistake when using … (details) overuse of the equipment overloading overheating incorrect storage storing the … (e. g. materials) at the wrong temperature excessive humidity on your premises operating the equipment at too low a voltage not using the machine in the way intended etc.
		problem fault malfunction			
7 Apologise*	We're sorry about We apologise for Please accept our apologies for We sincerely apologise for	what went wrong the trouble you have had the inconvenience caused any inconvenience this may have caused this oversight this misunderstanding the mishap the damage this (these) error(s) (on our part) this (these) mistake(s) (on our part) the poor service the poor workmanship our employee's (employees') behaviour. He/She/They has/have been (severely) reprimanded			

	We very much regret We deeply regret	what has happened that this should have happened		
	Thanks Many thanks Thank you Please accept our sincere thanks We wish to thank you	for letting us know for telling us about this for bringing this matter to our attention for drawing our attention to this problem for alerting us to this problem		
	It won't It certainly won't It certainly will not You may rest assured that it will not We will do our best to ensure that it will never	happen again recur		
	The invoice amount	has been will be	transferred to your account in full refunded to you	
	We enclose	our remittance our cheque a credit note	for … (amount) for the full invoice amount	
8 Explain that you are not at fault*	This can only have happened Damage of this nature can only have happened Such damage can only have been caused	after the goods left our premises by the goods being left in the rain/snow/in strong sunlight by heavy smoke by misuse by incorrect use by rough handling in transit in an accident in a fire	We are thus in no way responsible for this damage We therefore cannot be held responsible for this This damage is therefore through no fault of our own We are consequently unable to accept liability in this case	

	Our • enquiries • investigations have shown that The insurance company's report indicates quite clearly that The arbitrator's report states that The police report clearly proves that According to the report drawn up by … (name of person/company) According to the survey submitted by … (name of person/company)	we are our company is our staff are our employee(s) is/are	not to blame so not at fault therefore in no way at fault so in no way to blame for the damage so entirely blameless so not responsible for the fault/malfunction consequently	we cannot accept your claim we are unable to accept your claim we are unable to make an adjustment any repairs carried out will be charged to you in full
		the damage was caused in transit so the goods were roughly handled therefore this damage has nothing to do with us so		
	Since, in his/her/their (independent) report, … (name) conclude(s) that the damage	must have occurred can only have occurred	in your warehouse on your premises in one of your vehicles while the goods were in your possession	
– you are partly at fault*	As, according to the … 's (e.g. the independent assessor's) report,	the product was faulty … the product was not in perfect order when it reached you … the item in question was damaged as a result of poor packing … we are partly to blame for the damage … we cannot exclude the possibility that we are partly to blame … the equipment was malfunctioning when it left our premises … the equipment was not correctly installed … etc.		
	… we are prepared to accept part of the cost of replacing/repairing the machine … we are prepared to accept the cost of replacing • the damaged part(s) • the faulty component(s) … we are willing to pay … (amount, e.g. $5,000) towards the cost of repairs … we are prepared to accept … % (e.g. 50 %) of the replacement costs … we will arrange for the work to be • completed at our expense • repeated … we will have the work done again at cost price			

– you are at fault	Since As In view of the fact that	it's our fault we made a mistake we are at fault we are to blame you are in no way to blame for this defect the damage happened on our premises the damage happened while we were still responsible for the goods the damage happened while the goods were in our custody our employee(s) carried out the work to poor standard	we are prepared to cover the cost of replacing/repairing the machine we are prepared to accept the cost of replacing the damaged part(s)/the faulty component(s) we are willing to pay the repair costs we are prepared to pay for a replacement (for replacements) we will arrange for the work to be completed/repeated at our expense we will have the work done again at no extra charge
9 Suggest a solution – replacements/substitutes*	We suggest we send you We are sending you We have sent you We will be sending you We are rushing you	a replacement consignment replacements for the damaged/faulty/sub-standard etc. goods goods of a similar nature substitutes suitable substitutes an up-dated version our new improved model	by express by return by special delivery by special messenger on the next available flight to … (location) on the next train/ship to … (location)

It They	will arrive	by … (date)	without fail	There will be no extra charge for this You will only be charged … (e.g. forwarding costs, for insurance etc.)
	should be with you should reach you should arrive		at the (very) latest	

– ex gratia concessions*	Although the product is/the goods are no longer under guarantee The guarantee on the goods has already expired, nevertheless Despite the fact that the guarantee period for the goods has now expired	we are willing to we are prepared to	repair replace exchange	it them	free of charge at no extra cost at cost price for the price of materials only
	Please ship/forward/send the goods to our … (location, e.g. service centre in Nuremberg, warehouse in Berlin etc.) for them to be repaired Please return the faulty goods to us, carriage forward The goods will be repaired and returned to you, carriage paid				

– expert(s)*	We are sending	an expert a(n expert) technician a team of technicians (the Head of) our maintenance team our trouble-shooter an engineer a team of engineers	to repair to check to test to overhaul to re-install	the machine the equipment the unit etc.

Should If	he she they	finds that discovers that find that discover that	we are at fault it is our fault we are to blame the fault is due to us	the repairs will be carried out free of charge
			we aren't at fault it is not our fault we are not to blame the fault is not due to us the fault is as a result of misuse the machine has been used wrongly	we will be obliged to charge you for this work you will be charged for the repairs at the normal rate we will invoice you accordingly

– goodwill*	The work will be	done again re-done carried out again finished completed	at our expense at no extra charge at the cost of materials only for a nominal fee	as a gesture of our goodwill
	The machine The equipment	will be	checked inspected tested serviced re-adjusted re-installed overhauled	

– operating tips*	The instruction manual The operating instructions The "Technical Tips" leaflet	enclosed included with this letter which we have sent to you • under separate cover • by separate post	contains useful information on this problem will most certainly be of help to you deals with this problem in detail	We suggest you refer to the section entitled … (title)

	We suggest you call our service hotline on … (telephone number) to obtain expert advice on problems of this nature We enclose a leaflet on our • toll-free customer service hotline, which is open 24 hours a day. • service telephone number which can be used during normal working hours • fax service, which can be used to obtain • technical data sheets • expert advice • answers to FAQs (frequently asked questions)				
– financial concessions*	Under the circumstances In view of our excellent business relations to date	we are willing to we are prepared to	grant you a … % (e.g. 20 %) discount on the sales price waive the transport costs supply the goods … (better Incoterm e.g. CPT buyer's warehouse) let you have the newer more expensive model at the price of the old one grant you … (period, e.g. 3 months') credit to enable you to sell the goods		
– release from contract*	Since you state that you have no use whatsoever for the goods As you are unwilling to wait for an independent assessment of the matter		we are terminating our contract with you. The goods will be collected by our forwarders we are releasing you from the Contract of Sale and would request you to return the goods to us		
10 Suggest arbitration*	Since we are unable to agree on this As we are unable to reach an agreement	we suggest that	the damage the work the machine the equipment	be examined by be assessed by	an (independent) expert an arbitrator a team of independent experts … (name), a recognised authority in this field
	As the contract provides for the settlement of disputes by arbitration As we have already agreed to settle any disputes by arbitration In view of the fact that the Sales Agreement stipulates that disputes be settled by arbitration		we have taken we will take we will be taking	the necessary steps appropriate action	and suggest that …
			we have called in we have contacted we have approached	… (name of expert/firm)	
	… we accept his/her/their findings … we abide by his/her/their decision				
11 Polite ending	We look forward to hearing from you soon Please let us have your comments on this matter at your earliest convenience You will be receiving further information from us in the course of the next few days We will be contacting you in the very near future with a complete explanation of what has happened				

We feel sure that the … (document/photographs etc.) enclosed will serve to confirm our explanation of events and would welcome your comments on this matter
We hope our suggestion meets your approval and look forward to receiving your comments
We trust that the course of action we recommend will serve to settle the matter amicably and to the satisfaction of all parties concerned
(In the meantime) please do not hesitate to contact us should you have any further queries
You may rest assured that your next order will not give you grounds for complaint
We look forward to doing further business with you in the future
We hope to have the pleasure of serving you in the future

12 Enclosure(s)

Photograph(s)/Sample(s)
Freight forwarder's report
Independent assessor's report
Carrier's receipt
Copy of the bill of lading
Insurance company's report
Survey report
Authenticated copy/copies of … (document(s))

A. Buyer – Making a Complaint

1	**Confirm receipt of goods**	***Bestätigen Sie den Erhalt der Waren***
	We have just received the goods ordered on December 1 ..	*Wir haben soeben die Waren, die am 1. Dezember .. bestellt wurden, erhalten*
	We have now taken delivery of the consignment as per our order no. 987 dated 6 May ..	*Wir haben jetzt die Warensendung gemäß Auftrag Nr. 987 vom 6. Mai .. entgegengenommen*
	The goods as per our order no. 321 have now arrived	*Die gemäß Auftrag Nr. 321 bestellten Waren sind jetzt angekommen*
	The consignment of bananas as ordered in our letter of 3 March .. was delivered to us today	*Die Sendung Bananen, die wir mit unserem Schreiben vom 3. März .. bestellt hatten, wurde uns heute geliefert*
	The above-mentioned goods were delivered on 1 June .. and forwarded to our customer	*Die obengenannten Waren wurden am 1. Juni .. geliefert und unserem Kunden zugestellt*
	The above-mentioned equipment was delivered on 15 January .. and put into service by Messrs Hartmann & Braun	*Die obengenannte Anlage wurde am 15. Januar .. geliefert und von der Firma Hartmann & Braun in Dienst gestellt*
	Confirm performance of service	***Bestätigen Sie die erbrachte Leistung***
	The maintenance work carried out on the DTYD mini-bar has now been completed	*Die an der DTYD Mini-Bar ausgeführte Wartungsarbeit ist nun fertiggestellt worden*
	The machines have now been serviced	*Die Maschinen sind jetzt gewartet worden*
2	**Say what is wrong***	***Sagen Sie, was falsch ist****
	When we opened the box we found that the DTYD mini-bar was damaged	*Als wir die Kiste öffneten, stellten wir fest, dass die DTYD-Minibar beschädigt war*
	On opening the cases we saw that one item was of inferior quality	*Beim Öffnen der Kisten sahen wir, dass ein Posten von minderer Qualität war*
	When our customers opened the containers they discovered that the goods were sub-standard	*Als unsere Kunden die Container öffneten, stellten sie fest, dass die Waren nicht dem Standard entsprachen*
	On examining the articles we found that some of them were imperfect	*Als wir die Artikel prüften, stellten wir fest, dass einige von ihnen fehlerhaft waren*
	While testing the equipment it became apparent that it was unreliable	*Während wir die Ausrüstung prüften, stellte sie sich als unzuverlässig heraus*
	This is most likely because the goods were roughly handled in transit	*Dies ist höchstwahrscheinlich darauf zurückzuführen, dass die Waren auf dem Transport unsachgemäß behandelt wurden*

	This is probably because the goods were sent (against our instructions) as a consolidated shipment	*Dies ist wahrscheinlich darauf zurückzuführen, dass die Waren (entgegen unseren Anweisungen) als Sammeltransport geschickt wurden*
	This is probably due to the fact that the goods were poorly packed	*Wahrscheinlich beruht dies auf der Tatsache, dass die Waren schlecht verpackt wurden*
	When testing the machine for a short time we saw that it was inefficient	*Als wir die Maschine kurz testeten, stellten wir fest, dass sie unzulänglich arbeitete*
	– services*	*– Dienstleistungen**
	When checking the workmanship it was noticed that it was not up to standard	*Als wir die Verarbeitung prüften, wurde festgestellt, dass sie nicht dem Standard entsprach*
	It is also our unpleasant duty to inform you that your technician was clumsy	*Auch ist es unsere unangenehme Pflicht Ihnen mitzuteilen, dass Ihr Techniker sich ungeschickt angestellt hat*
	– proof*	*– Beweis**
	We enclose a photograph of the damage as proof	*Wir fügen als Beweis eine Fotografie des Schadens bei*
	We will be mailing you an independent assessor's report on the damage as evidence	*Wir werden Ihnen als Beweis den Bericht eines unabhängigen Gutachters über den Schaden zukommen lassen*
3	**Ask for an explanation**	***Bitten Sie um eine Erklärung***
	Please explain why this has happened as soon as possible	*Bitte erklären Sie so bald wie möglich, warum dies passiert ist*
	We would welcome your comments on this	*Wir würden Ihre diesbezügliche Stellungnahme begrüßen*
	Please let us have your version of events	*Bitte legen Sie uns die Vorkommnisse aus Ihrer Sicht dar*
	Please let us have a full explanation of what took place	*Bitte lassen Sie uns eine ausführliche Erklärung dessen zukommen, was vorgefallen ist*
	Your explanation as to how such a thing could happen will have to be given to us before any further orders are placed	*Bevor weitere Aufträge erteilt werden, erwarten wir von Ihnen eine Erklärung darüber, wie so etwas passieren konnte*
4	**Consequences for the buyer's company**	***Konsequenzen für die Gesellschaft des Käufers***
	We trust you understand that this has caused us a lot of trouble	*Wir gehen davon aus, dass Sie Verständnis dafür haben, dass uns dies eine Menge Ärger verursacht hat*
	Needless to say we will only be able to sell these products if the price is reduced substantially	*Es erübrigt sich zu sagen, dass wir diese Produkte nur verkaufen können, wenn der Preis erheblich reduziert wird*

	You will, of course, appreciate that we have been greatly inconvenienced by this	*Sie werden natürlich verstehen, dass wir hierdurch erhebliche Unannehmlichkeiten hatten*
	You will, no doubt, appreciate that we will lose our competitive edge on the local market if we offer such goods	*Sie werden zweifellos verstehen, dass wir auf dem örtlichen Markt unseren Wettbewerbsvorteil einbüßen werden, wenn wir solche Waren anbieten*
	We have no alternative but to request a complete refund	*Wir haben keine andere Wahl, als um vollständige Rückerstattung zu bitten*
	We are unfortunately obliged to withhold payment until suitable substitutes are provided	*Wir sind leider gezwungen, die Zahlung zurückzuhalten, bis geeigneter Ersatz geliefert wird*
	We will have no alternative but to take legal action	*Wir werden keine andere Wahl haben, als gerichtliche Schritte einzuleiten*
	We will unfortunately be obliged to take appropriate steps to recoup our losses	*Wir sehen uns leider gezwungen, geeignete Schritte zu unternehmen, um unsere Verluste wieder hereinzuholen*
	We reserve the right to hold you liable for any losses incurred, if the matter is not settled without delay	*Wir behalten uns das Recht vor, Sie für jegliche entstandenen Verluste haftbar zu machen, falls die Angelegenheit nicht unverzüglich geregelt wird*
5	**Return the goods to the seller***	***Schicken Sie die Waren an den Verkäufer zurück****
	We are returning the damaged goods to you carriage forward	*Wir schicken die beschädigten Güter unfrei an Sie zurück*
	Since we have no use for these goods, please arrange to have them collected as soon as possible	*Da wir für diese Güter keine Verwendung haben, sorgen Sie bitte dafür, dass Sie sobald wie möglich abgeholt werden*
	In view of the fact that these goods are taking up warehouse space, please arrange to have them picked up immediately	*Im Hinblick auf die Tatsache, dass diese Waren Lagerfläche beanspruchen, veranlassen Sie bitte, dass sie unverzüglich abgeholt werden*
	... otherwise we will be obliged to have them forwarded to you at your expense and risk	*... andernfalls sind wir gezwungen, sie Ihnen auf Ihre Kosten und Gefahr zugehen zu lassen*
	– goods to be collected by seller*	***– Waren, die vom Verkäufer abgeholt werden sollen****
	The goods have been placed at your disposal at our branch in Munich and we would ask you to have them collected as soon as possible	*Die Waren sind Ihnen in unserer Filiale in München zur Verfügung gestellt worden, und wir bitten Sie, diese sobald wie möglich abholen zu lassen*
	Should you wish to examine them, our premises are open from 8 am to 4 pm	*Sollten Sie eine Besichtigung der Waren vornehmen wollen, können Sie dies in unseren Geschäftsräumen von 8 Uhr morgens bis 4 Uhr nachmittags tun*

6	**Request the seller to take appropriate action***	***Bitten Sie den Verkäufer, geeignete Maßnahmen zu ergreifen****
	We must therefore ask you to look into this as soon as possible	*Wir müssen Sie deshalb bitten, dies sobald wie möglich zu untersuchen*
	We must insist that you investigate the matter immediately	*Wir müssen darauf bestehen, dass Sie die Angelegenheit unverzüglich untersuchen*
	We would therefore ask you to ensure that the right goods arrive in perfect condition within the next 48 hours	*Wir möchten Sie deshalb bitten sicherzustellen, dass die richtigen Waren innerhalb der nächsten 48 Stunden in perfektem Zustand ankommen*
	To enable us to meet the delivery dates promised to our customers we must insist that you rush us substitutes on the next available flight to Munich Airport	*Um sicherzustellen, dass wir die unseren Kunden versprochenen Lieferdaten einhalten können, müssen wir darauf bestehen, dass Sie uns die Ersatzstücke mit dem nächstmöglichen Flug zum Flughafen München befördern*
	In view of the extent of the damage, we must cancel the entire order and request you to refund the invoice amount	*Angesichts des Schadensumfangs müssen wir den gesamten Auftrag stornieren und Sie bitten, uns den Rechnungsbetrag zurückzuerstatten*
	We therefore wish you to have your agent visit our premises	*Bitte veranlassen Sie deshalb, dass Ihr Vertreter unsere Geschäftsräume aufsucht*
	We will only consider keeping the goods if you grant us a 20 % reduction in price	*Wir werden eine Abnahme der Waren nur in Betracht ziehen, wenn Sie uns einen Preisnachlass von 20 % gewähren*
	We are only prepared to consider accepting work of this standard if the price is reduced by 15 %	*Wir sind nur bereit, die Annahme einer Arbeit dieser Qualität in Erwägung zu ziehen, wenn der Preis um 15 % reduziert wird*
	We will only be willing to pay the price agreed in the contract of sale if you agree to change your terms of delivery to CIP … (buyer's city)	*Wir sind nur bereit, den im Kaufvertrag vereinbarten Preis zu zahlen, wenn Sie bereit sind, unsere Lieferbedingung in CIP … (Stadt des Käufers) umzuändern*
	We must therefore insist that you refund the entire invoice amount	*Wir müssen daher darauf bestehen, dass Sie den gesamten Rechnungsbetrag zurückerstatten*
7	**Polite ending**	***Höflicher Schluss***
	Please sort this out immediately	*Bitte klären Sie dies sofort*
	We trust that you will deal with the matter without delay	*Wir sind zuversichtlich, dass Sie die Sache unverzüglich bearbeiten*

	We hope to receive a full explanation by the beginning of next week	*Wir hoffen, bis Anfang nächster Woche eine umfassende Erklärung zu erhalten*
	This matter will need to be settled in the very near future and to our complete satisfaction before we place any more orders with you	*Diese Angelegenheit muss in nächster Zukunft zu unserer vollsten Zufriedenheit geklärt werden, bevor wir Ihnen weitere Aufträge erteilen*
	We would add that any further dealings with your company will depend upon how this matter is settled	*Wir möchten hinzufügen, dass weitere Geschäfte mit Ihrer Firma davon abhängen werden, wie diese Angelegenheit geregelt wird*
	We feel sure you will understand that, under the circumstances, we have had no choice but to act in this way	*Sie werden sicher verstehen, dass wir unter diesen Umständen keine andere Wahl hatten, als so zu handeln*
8	**Enclosure(s)***	***Anlage(n)****
	Our customer's letter of complaint Sample(s) Independent Assessor's Report Freight Forwarder's Report Carrier's Receipt Bill of Lading Survey Report	*Beschwerdebrief unseres Kunden* *Muster* *Bericht des unabhängigen Gutachters* *Bericht des Frachtspediteurs* *Bescheinigung des Frachtführers* *Konnossement* *Gutachterbericht*

B. Seller – Dealing with a Complaint

1	**Acknowledge receipt of the buyer's letter immediately**	***Bestätigen Sie sofort den Erhalt des Briefes des Käufers***
	We have just received your fax of January 9 .. regarding the above-mentioned order	*Wir haben soeben Ihr Fax vom 9. Januar .. bezüglich des obengenannten Auftrags erhalten*
	We received your e-mail dated 9 January .. in connection with the DTYD mini-bar yesterday	*Wir haben gestern Ihre E-Mail vom 9. Januar .. im Zusammenhang mit der DTYD Minibar erhalten*
	Your letter with regard to maintenance work carried out on the PA95 fuel pump has been forwarded to us by our representative	*Ihr Brief bezüglich der Wartungsarbeit an der PA95 Kraftstoffpumpe ist uns von unserem Vertreter zugeleitet worden*
2	**Say you are sorry that the buyer is dissatisfied**	***Drücken Sie Ihr Bedauern aus, dass der Käufer nicht zufrieden ist***
	We're sorry that the goods arrived broken	*Es tut uns Leid, dass die Waren beschädigt angekommen sind*
	We note with regret that you are not satisfied with our service	*Wir stellen mit Bedauern fest, dass Sie mit unserem Service nicht zufrieden sind*

	We regret to learn that the machine is not performing as expected	*Wir bedauern zu erfahren, dass die Maschine nicht erwartungsgemäß funktioniert*
	We are surprised and sorry to find that you received the wrong goods	*Wir sind überrascht und bedauern festzustellen, dass Sie die falschen Güter erhalten haben*
	... since this is the first complaint we have received about this product	*... da dies die erste Beschwerde ist, die wir im Zusammenhang mit diesem Produkt erhalten haben*
	... as we have been dealing with this haulage company for many years now and have had no cause for complaint	*... da wir seit vielen Jahren mit dieser Lkw-Spedition zusammenarbeiten und keinen Grund zur Klage hatten*
3	**Say that the matter will be dealt with**	***Sagen Sie, dass die Angelegenheit bearbeitet wird***
	We'll find out what's been happening straight away	*Wir werden sofort herausfinden, was passiert ist*
	We will look into this matter immediately	*Wir werden die Sache unverzüglich untersuchen*
	Your complaint will be investigated within the next 48 hours	*Ihre Beschwerde wird innerhalb der nächsten 48 Stunden untersucht*
	– the matter is being dealt with	***– die Angelegenheit wird bearbeitet***
	We are now looking into the matter and the freight forwarder has been contacted	*Wir untersuchen die Angelegenheit jetzt und haben bereits Kontakt mit dem Frachtspediteur aufgenommen*
	Your complaint is now being investigated and the driver responsible for delivering this consignment has been contacted	*Ihre Beschwerde wird derzeit untersucht, und wir haben bereits mit dem Fahrer, der für die Lieferung dieser Sendung zuständig war, Kontakt aufgenommen*
	– the matter has been dealt with	***– die Angelegenheit ist bearbeitet worden***
	Since receiving your message we have now investigated the matter and found out that ...	*Nach Erhalt Ihrer Nachricht haben wir die Angelegenheit untersucht und herausgefunden, dass ...*
	After receiving your letter we made enquiries regarding the fault and discovered that ...	*Nachdem wir Ihren Brief erhalten hatten, stellten wir bezüglich dieses Fehlers Nachforschungen an und fanden heraus, dass ...*
4	**Ask for more time to investigate the complaint***	***Bitten Sie um mehr Zeit, um die Beschwerde zu untersuchen****
	As it will take some time for us to find out what went wrong ...	*Da es einige Zeit dauern wird, bis wir herausgefunden haben, was falsch gelaufen ist, ...*
	Since it will take a few days to get to the root of this ...	*Da es einige Tage dauern wird, um dieser Angelegenheit auf den Grund zu kommen ...*
	As investigations of this nature take some time ...	*Da Nachforschungen dieser Art einige Zeit in Anspruch nehmen ...*

	In view of the fact that we have not yet received the haulage company's report ...	*Angesichts der Tatsache, dass wir den Bericht der Speditеurfirma noch nicht erhalten haben ...*
	... we would be most grateful if you would give us a few more days to investigate your claim	*... wären wir Ihnen sehr dankbar, wenn Sie uns noch ein paar Tage Zeit ließen, um Ihre Forderung zu untersuchen*
5	**Request proof***	***Bitten Sie um Beweise****
	Any proof of the damage you may have will help our investigations	*Jeder Beweis des Schadens, den Sie möglicherweise haben, wird uns bei unseren Nachforschungen helfen*
	We require proof of your claim before any action can be taken on our part	*Wir benötigen einen Beweis für Ihren Anspruch, bevor unsererseits irgendetwas unternommen werden kann*
	Our agent will need to see evidence to substantiate your claim before we can take any further steps	*Unser Vertreter benötigt einen Beweis, der Ihre Forderung erhärtet, bevor wir weitere Schritte unternehmen können*
	Please send us all the evidence you have to help us with our investigations	*Bitte senden Sie uns alle Beweise, die Sie haben, um uns bei unseren Nachforschungen zu helfen*
6	**Explain***	***Erklären Sie****
	We have now discovered that the damage was as a result of ...	*Wir haben jetzt herausgefunden, dass der Schaden das Ergebnis war von ...*
	Our enquiries have revealed that the damage was caused by an accident when the goods were being unloaded in ...	*Unsere Nachforschungen haben ergeben, dass der Schaden durch einen Unfall verursacht worden ist, als die Waren in ... ausgeladen wurden*
	From what you say about the imperfections, it sounds as if this problem is the result of incorrect storage	*Was Sie über die Unzulänglichkeiten sagen, scheint anzudeuten, dass dieses Problem das Ergebnis unkorrekter Lagerung ist*
	Judging by your description of the damage, it would seem that this problem has come about because of excessive humidity on your premises	*Nach Ihrer Beschreibung des Schadens zu urteilen scheint es, dass dieses Problem auf zu starke Feuchtigkeit in Ihren Geschäftsräumen zurückzuführen ist*
7	**Apologise***	***Entschuldigen Sie sich****
	We're sorry about what went wrong	*Wir bedauern den Fehler*
	We apologize for any inconvenience this may have caused	*Wir entschuldigen uns für jegliche Unannehmlichkeiten, die Ihnen möglicherweise entstanden sind*
	We very much regret that this should have happened	*Wir bedauern sehr, dass dies passieren konnte*
	It won't happen again	*Es wird nicht wieder vorkommen*
	You may rest assured that it will not recur	*Sie können sicher sein, dass dies nicht wieder vorkommen wird*

8	**Explain that you are not at fault***	***Erklären Sie, dass es nicht Ihre Schuld ist****
	This can only have happened after the goods left our premises. We are thus in no way responsible for this damage	*Dies kann nur passiert sein, nachdem die Waren unser Gebäude verliessen. Wir sind daher in keiner Weise für diesen Schaden verantwortlich*
	Such damage can only have been caused by the goods being left in the rain. We therefore cannot be held responsible for this	*Ein derartiger Schaden kann nur dadurch entstanden sein, dass die Waren im Regen gelassen wurden. Wir können daher hierfür nicht verantwortlich gemacht werden*
	Such damage can only have been caused by rough handling. We are consequently unable to accept liability in this case	*Ein solcher Schaden kann nur durch unsachgemäße Behandlung verursacht worden sein. Wir sind infolgedessen nicht in der Lage, in diesem Fall eine Haftung zu übernehmen*
	Our enquiries have shown that we are not to blame, so we cannot accept your claim	*Unsere Nachforschungen haben ergeben, dass wir nicht verantwortlich gemacht werden können, so dass wir nicht in der Lage sind, Ihre Forderung zu akzeptieren*
	The arbitrator's report states that our staff are in no way at fault so we are unable to make an adjustment	*Aus dem Bericht des Schlichters (auch Schadensgutachters) geht hervor, dass unser Personal in keiner Weise fehlerhaft gehandelt hat, so dass wir nicht in der Lage sind, eine Regelung herbeizuführen*
	Since, in her independent report, Frau Dr. Hermann concludes that the damage can only have occurred in one of your vehicles, any repairs carried out will be charged to you in full	*Da Frau Dr. Hermann in Ihrem unabhängigen Gutachten zu dem Schluss kommt, dass der Schaden nur in einem Ihrer Fahrzeuge aufgetreten sein kann, werden Ihnen alle ausgeführten Reparaturen voll in Rechnung gestellt werden*
	– you are partly at fault*	***– Sie sind teilweise Schuld****
	As, according to the independent assessor's report, the item in question was damaged as a result of poor packing, we are prepared to accept part of the cost of repairing the machine	*Da gemäß dem Bericht des unabhängigen Schadensgutachters der in Frage stehende Posten auf Grund schlechter Verpackung beschädigt wurde, sind wir bereit, einen Teil der Reparaturkosten für die Maschine zu übernehmen*
	Since we cannot exclude the possibility that we are partly to blame, we are willing to pay $500 towards the cost of repairs	*Da wir die Möglichkeit nicht ausschließen können, dass wir einen Teil der Schuld tragen, sind wir bereit, 500 $ der Reparaturkosten zu zahlen*

	As, according to the assessor's report, the equipment was not correctly installed, we will arrange for the work to be completed at our expense	*Da nach Aussagen des Berichts des Schadensgutachters die Anlage nicht richtig installiert war, werden wir veranlassen, dass die Arbeit auf unsere Kosten fertiggestellt wird*
	– you are at fault*	***– Sie sind Schuld****
	Since it's our fault we are prepared to cover the cost of repairing the machine	*Da es sich um unseren Fehler handelt, sind wir bereit, die Kosten für die Reparatur der Maschine zu übernehmen*
	In view of the fact that you are in no way to blame for this defect, we are willing to pay the repair costs	*Angesichts der Tatsache, dass Sie in keiner Weise für diesen Schaden verantwortlich gemacht werden können, sind wir bereit, die Reparaturkosten zu bezahlen*
9	**Suggest a solution**	***Schlagen Sie eine Lösung vor***
	– replacements / substitutes*	***– Ersatz****
	We suggest we send you a replacement consignment by express	*Wir schlagen vor, dass wir Ihnen per Express eine Ersatzsendung schicken*
	We have sent you goods of a similar nature by special delivery	*Wir haben Ihnen eine Sonderlieferung von Waren ähnlicher Art zugesandt*
	We are rushing you suitable substitutes on the next available flight to New York	*Wir schicken Ihnen sofort geeignete Ersatzstücke mit dem nächstmöglichen Flug nach New York*
	They will arrive by February 28 .. without fail. There will be no extra charge for this	*Sie werden auf jeden Fall bis 28. Februar .. ankommen. Hierfür werden keine Zusatzgebühren berechnet*
	– ex gratia concessions*	***– Konzessionen auf Kulanzbasis****
	Although the product is no longer under guarantee, we are prepared to repair it at no extra cost	*Obwohl das Produkt nicht mehr der Garantie unterliegt, sind wir bereit, es zu reparieren, ohne zusätzliche Kosten zu berechnen*
	Please ship the goods to our service centre in Nuremberg for them to be repaired free of charge	*Bitte schicken Sie die Güter an unser Service-Centre in Nürnberg, damit sie dort kostenlos repariert werden*
	– expert(s)*	***– Experte(n)****
	We are sending an expert to repair the machine	*Wir schicken Ihnen einen Fachmann, der die Maschine repariert*
	We are sending a team of technicians to test the unit	*Wir schicken Ihnen ein Team von Technikern, um die Anlage zu testen*
	Should he find that we are at fault, the repairs will be carried out free of charge	*Sollte er der Meinung sein, dass wir Schuld sind, werden die Reparaturen kostenlos ausgeführt*

	If they discover that the fault is not due to us, you will be charged for the repairs at the normal rate	*Wenn sie herausfinden, dass wir nicht für den Fehler verantwortlich sind, werden wir Ihnen die Reparatur zum normalen Satz in Rechnung stellen*
	– goodwill*	***– Goodwill / Kulanz****
	The work will be done again at our expense as a gesture of our goodwill	*Die Arbeit wird als Geste des guten Willens auf unsere Kosten erneut durchgeführt*
	The equipment will be re-adjusted for a nominal fee as a gesture of our goodwill	*Die Anlage wird als Geste unseres guten Willens zu einer Pauschalgebühr wieder in Ordnung gebracht*
	– operating tips*	***– Betriebshinweise****
	The instruction manual enclosed contains useful information on this problem. We suggest you refer to the section entitled "Trouble-shooting"	*Die beigefügte Bedienungsanleitung enthält nützliche Informationen zu diesem Problem. Wir schlagen vor, dass Sie das Kapitel „Trouble-shooting" (Problemlösungen) konsultieren*
	We enclose a leaflet on our toll-free customer service hotline, which is open 24 hours a day.	*Wir fügen einen Prospekt über unsere gebührenfreie Kundendienst-Hotline bei, die 24 Stunden am Tag zur Verfügung steht*
	– financial concessions*	***– Finanzielle Konzessionen****
	Under the circumstances we are prepared to waive the transport costs / reduce the price by 15 %	*Unter den gegebenen Umständen sind wir bereit, auf die Transportkosten zu verzichten / den Preis um 15 % zu reduzieren*
	The invoice amount has been transferred to your account in full	*Der Rechnungsbetrag ist Ihrem Konto in voller Höhe gutgeschrieben worden*
	We enclose a credit note for $500	*Wir fügen eine Gutschriftsanzeige über 500 $ bei*
	– release from contract*	***– Entbindung vom Vertrag****
	Since you state that you have no use whatsoever for the goods, we are terminating our contract with you. The goods will be collected by our forwarders	*Da Sie angeben, dass Sie keinerlei Verwendung für die Güter haben, beenden wir hiermit unseren Vertrag mit Ihnen. Die Waren werden von unserem Spediteur abgeholt.*
10	**Suggest arbitration***	***Schlagen Sie eine Entscheidung durch einen Schlichter vor****
	As we are unable to reach an agreement, we suggest that the damage be assessed by a team of independent experts	*Da wir zu keiner Einigung kommen können, schlagen wir vor, dass der Schaden von einem unabhängigen Expertenteam begutachtet wird*
	As the contract provides for the settlement of disputes by arbitration, we have taken the necessary steps and will accept the arbitrator's findings	*Da der Vertrag eine Beilegung von Streitigkeiten durch Schlichtung vorsieht, haben wir die nötigen Schritte unternommen und werden den Befund des Schiedsmannes akzeptieren*

11	**Polite ending**	***Höflicher Schluss***
	Please let us have your comments on this matter at your earliest convenience	*Bitte lassen Sie uns Ihre Stellungnahme zu dieserAngelegenheit sobald wie möglich zukommen*
	We will be contacting you in the very near future with a complete explanation of what has happened	*Wir werden in Kürze mit Ihnen Kontakt aufnehmen und alles erklären, was vorgefallen ist*
	We trust that the course of action we recommend will serve to settle the matter amicably and to the satisfaction of all parties concerned	*Wir sind zuversichtlich, dass die von uns empfohlene Verfahrensweise dazu beitragen wird, die Angelegenheit freundschaftlich und zur Zufriedenheit aller betroffenen Parteien zu regeln*
12	**Enclosure(s)**	***Anlage(n)***
	Independent assessor's report	*Bericht des unabhängigen Schlichters*
	Carrier's receipt	*Bescheinigung des Frachtführers*
	Copy of the bill of lading	*Kopie des Konnossements*
	Insurance company's report	*Bericht der Versicherungsgesellschaft*
	Survey report	*Gutachterbericht*

Unit 10

Delay in Payment

Seller

1 Reference to overdue invoice/ account	We refer to With reference to We are writing in connection with You have no doubt overlooked the fact that It has most probably escaped your notice that It has doubtless escaped your attention that	our the above-mentioned the above	invoice(s) statement statement of account bill		no. dated/ of … nos. … and … dated/of …		for … (amount, e.g. £1,500.95) for the sum of … (amount) showing an outstanding balance of … (amount) in our favour
	We are sorry to say that our We are sorry to note that our We regret to inform you that our This is to inform you that our	invoice(s) statement(s) statement(s) of account					
	… has not been paid yet … is still overdue … has not yet been settled … is now … (period of time, e.g. 2 weeks) overdue … has now been overdue for … (period of time, e.g. 10 days)	Please note that We would point out that We wish to point out that We would remind you that We trust you will recall that			payment was due it was agreed that payment would be made our sales agreement provides for payment according to our general conditions of sale payment was to be made		on … (date) by … (+ date) at the latest within … (+ period of time) at the latest
2 Refer to previous reminder(s) (copy/ copies enclosed)*	We are writing (once again) We regret that we are (once again) obliged to write to you We refer to our (two/three) previous letter(s) dated … (date(s), e.g. 15 and 31 January ..), a copy/ copies of which is/are enclosed,	in connection with our with regard to our on the subject of our		(above-mentioned)	invoice(s) statement(s) of account bill(s)	no./nos. … dated/of …	for … (amount, e.g. £1,500.95) for the sum of … (amount) showing an outstanding balance of … (amount) in our favour

… which	has not been paid yet is still overdue is still outstanding is as yet unpaid has not yet been settled has now been overdue for … (period of time, e.g. 10 days) is now … (period of time, e.g. 2 weeks) overdue	despite the reminder(s) sent to you on … (date(s)) despite the (two/three) reminder(s) you have received	(see copy/copies enclosed) (see enclosure(s))

We must point out that We are sorry to say that We regret to say that Please note that	this is the second/ third etc.	letter/fax to you time we have had to write to you occasion on which it has proved necessary to write to you	in this connection with regard to this matter

in connection with with regard to	the outstanding amount the outstanding balance the sum due the sum owing your account our invoice(s) our statement(s) (of account)

We have now been waiting for	our invoice(s) statement(s) (of account) bill(s)	to be paid to be settled	for … (+ period of time, e.g. two months) since … (+ point in time, e.g. 15 January)

Our invoice no. … for … (amount) Our (January) statement	has (now) been outstanding has (now) been due for payment is now … (period of time, e.g. 8 weeks) overdue

– no response to previous correspondence	Although Despite the fact that	you have already received	a two three several a number of repeated	reminder(s)	we have (still) heard nothing from you … we have received no reply … you (still) have not contacted us … our letters/faxes/e-mails have gone unanswered … you have not responded to our request(s) for payment … you have made no attempt (whatsoever) to contact us …
		a two three several a number of repeated	reminder(s)	has/have been sent to you	
	As Since In view of the fact that Given that	we have received you have sent us your company has sent us	neither an explanation nor a remittance neither the amount owing nor an explanation of the delay neither the sum due nor any indication of why payment has not been forthcoming no explanation (whatsoever) as to why payment has not been made		we …/it … (see "6. Consequences of non-payment")
		you	have neither sent a remittance	nor made any attempt to explain the delay	
		you are now your company is now	10 days two weeks etc.	in arrears … in arrears with payment …	
		we have heard nothing (at all) from you		for … (+ period of time, e.g. two months) since … (+ point in time, e.g. 15 January)	

– promises have not been kept	Although you assured us Despite your (repeated) assurances	that payment would be made promptly that payment would be made in full that your cheque was in the post that your remittance would arrive • by … (+ date) • within … (+ period of time) that you had instructed your bank to transfer the sum in question to our account that the amount owing would be paid in 4 equal instalments at weekly/monthly intervals that the (new) draft drawn upon you would be accepted and honoured at maturity that an extension of 4 weeks would give you enough time to raise the outstanding amount	we have received no payment to date we have only received … (amount) so far we have not received the (fourth and) final instalment of … (amount) we have only received one/two/three instalments up to now we are still waiting for your remittance to arrive we are still waiting for the next/final instalment we (still) have not received it
3 Express surprise that this should happen*	As Since In view of the fact that Given that	payment has not been delayed before your remittances have usually/always arrived on time you have always paid regularly up to now there have been no problems of this nature previously you have not been in arrears to date this is the first time that payment has been late all previous payments have been made on time you have always been prompt in settling your accounts your account has always been cleared punctually you have always been a reliable customer we have always considered you to be a reliable customer	we have not contacted you until now we have waited some time before contacting you we can only assume that this is due to an oversight on your part we assume you have overlooked our invoice/statement (of account) we must assume that there has been a misunderstanding of some sort we must assume that non-payment of our invoice is due to an error
	We can't imagine We cannot imagine We are at a loss to understand	what has gone wrong why payment has not been made why we have not received your remittance why we have heard nothing from you (so far) what has stopped you from contacting us	

4	Request an explanation	Why has our invoice/statement (of account) not been paid? Would you please tell us why we have received no payment to date?				
		Please tell us Please let us know Please explain We would (very much) welcome an explanation as to We look forward to receiving your explanation as to		why you haven't paid why payment is delayed why you still haven't paid our invoice/statement (of account) why our invoice/statement (of account) is still unpaid what has prevented you from paying	–	
		Your explanation as to			would be very much appreciated	
		Your reasons for non-payment				
		If you are unable to pay		please explain what has happened at least give us your reasons for non-payment		
		We may well be able to help you It may be possible to come to an agreement It might be possible to agree on new terms		if you're going through a bad patch if you (your company) have (has) run into (financial) difficulties if we are given an explanation for the delay in payment if you are experiencing problems of a financial nature		
5	Request payment and set a deadline*	We must therefore request that We must therefore insist that Please make sure that Please therefore ensure that	you pay payment be made you make a minimum payment of … (amount/percentage, e. g. $2,000/33 %) of the sum outstanding we receive your remittance for … (amount) the amount in question is transferred to our account you clear your account		by … (+ date) within … (+ period of time)	at the latest at the very latest without fail
					immediately by return without delay without any further delay	
		Please transfer Please remit	… (amount) the sum of … (amount) this amount	to our account no. … at (the) … Bank, sorting code …	by … (+ date) within … (+ period of time) immediately without delay without any further delay	

Deadlines	We will give you We will let you have We are prepared to allow you		two more days to pay another 10 days to pay a further two weeks to pay until the end of the month to pay	after which … (see "6. Consequences of non-payment") after which time … (see "6. Consequences of non-payment") whereupon … (see "6. Consequences of non-payment")
	We are prepared to We are willing to	give you grant you allow you extend the deadline for (final) payment by	two more weeks another two weeks a further 10 days	
	If we don't receive payment If we have not received payment If payment has not been made If the sum of … (amount) has not been credited to our account Should payment not have been made Should the amount in question not have been remitted to us		by … (+ date) within … (+ period of time)	we … (see "6. Consequences of non-payment")
	We are giving you another … days to pay We are setting you a (final) deadline for payment of … (number) days			after which … (see "6. Consequences of non-payment") after which time … (see "6. Consequences of non-payment")
	We must insist that payment be made		within the next … (period of time, e.g. 48 hours) by … (+ point in time, e.g. 12 noon on Friday 10th November ..)	
6 Consequences of non-payment*	If you do not pay If you do not settle If you are unable to settle If we do not receive the amount due on If payment is not forthcoming for Should you not settle Should you fail to pay Should it transpire that you are, in fact, unable to settle		our invoice(s) our statement (of account) your account our bill(s)	–
	Failure to pay Failure to settle			may well mean that

... we'll ... we will ... we'll have to ... we will have to ... we will be obliged to ... we will be compelled to ... it may well be necessary to ... we will have no choice but to ... it may well prove necessary to ... we will have no alternative but to	re-consider our terms of business with you revise all arrangements with your company change the terms on which we are able to do business with you revise our terms of trade with your company deal with your company on a different basis in future stop doing business with you terminate all business relations with your company stop all further deliveries cancel your credit terms cancel the generous credit terms you have been granted stop doing business with you on open account terms change our terms to "cash with order" only deal with your company on a "cash with order" basis insist on "cash with order" terms insist on payment in advance deal with your company on "cash against documents" terms insist that any further orders are on "cash against documents" terms require you to return the goods for which you have not paid draw a sight draft on your company and present it to your bankers for collection report your company to • the ... (buyer's city, e.g. London) Chamber of Commerce • your country's trade mission in ... (location) • your country's consulate/embassy in ... (location)	
	take the necessary steps to recover • the sum owing • the sum in question • the sum outstanding • the amount due • all outstanding monies	... together with interest at a rate of ... % p.a. and an administration charge of ... (amount, e.g. $50.00) ... to which interest will be added at the current rate (of ... %) together with an administrative fee of ... (amount)
	take legal action put the matter in the hands of our solicitors institute legal proceedings turn the matter over to an agent for collection use a collection agency to recover the debt	

		... we very much hope that it will not be necessary to take steps ... we would not like to take any action ... we are anxious to avoid taking any steps ... we feel sure that action can be avoided	which might cause your company • serious harm • irreversible which might endanger your company's reputation as a result of which your company's standing might suffer which might jeopardise future business which could lead to serious disadvantages for your company in the future		
7	Regret that a reminder is necessary*	We regret having to write to you again ... We are sorry that it has proved necessary to write to you once more ... We very much regret having to broach this matter with you yet again ... We had hoped it would not be necessary to contact you again in this matter ...			
		... (we) feel sure that ... and are certain that ... and are convinced that	the delay is as a result of	an oversight a misunderstanding an error	on your part
		Much as we regret having to contact you again, we must insist on payment	• by the date stated • within the time stated		
8	Polite ending	We trust you will be remitting the sum in question in the next few days We look forward to receiving your remittance in the (very) near future We expect to be receiving payment by the time stated We are confident that we will shortly be receiving the amount owed We feel sure that there is a simple explanation for the current situation We very much hope that this matter will be settled swiftly and to the satisfaction of all concerned We feel sure that the matter will be settled amicably in the very near future			
		Since this is the first time that payment has been delayed As there has never been a delay in payment on your part before In view of our satisfactory (business) relations in the past As we have now been doing business with each other for a considerable time	we feel sure we are convinced we do not doubt	that this problem will soon be solved that this matter will be settled in the very near future that an amicable solution will be found	
		If payment has already been made Should your remittance have crossed with this reminder Should your account/our invoice(s)/our statement (of account) have been settled in the meantime	please disregard this letter/fax/e-mail please ignore the contents of this letter/fax/e-mail please consider the matter to have been settled		
9	Enclosure(s)	Invoice(s) No. .../Nos. ... and ... Statement(s) (of Account) of/dated ... Our letter(s) of/dated... and ...			

Buyer

1 Reference to overdue invoice/account/reminder(s)	We refer to With reference to We are writing in connection with	your the above-mentioned the above	invoice(s) statement statement of account bill(s)	no. … dated/of … nos. … and … dated/of …	for … (amount, e.g. £1,500.95) for the sum of … showing an outstanding balance of … (amount) in your favour	
	… and your letter(s)/fax(es)/e-mail(s) of/dated … (and …)		in this connection requesting payment in which you point out that payment is now due/overdue indicating that payment was due on … (date)			
	Thanks for Thank you for Many thanks for We have received	your letter/fax/e-mail dated/of …	referring to • invoice(s) no. (nos.) … (and …) dated/of … for … (amount) • your … (e.g. February) statement (of account) dated/of … asking us to pay … (details) requesting payment of … (details) requesting that we settle … (details) in which you point out that payment of … (details) is now due/overdue indicating that payment of … (details) • was due on … (date) • has been due since … (date)			
2 First apology and explanation why payment is late*	We wish to apologise We would like to apologise We sincerely apologise Please accept our apologies	for the delay	in paying in settling	your invoice(s)/statement (of account) … (amount) your invoice(s) no./nos. … dated/of … for … (amount) your statement for the period 1 January to 31 March .. amounting to … your statement of account no. … dated/of … for … (amount) your bill(s) no./nos. … dated/of … for … (amount)		
			in balancing in clearing	our account (with you/your company)		
		for the fact that	your invoice(s) no./nos. … dated/of … for … (amount) your statement of account no. … dated/of … for … (amount) your bill(s) no./nos. … dated/of … for … (amount) your statement for the period 1 January – 31 March .. amounting to … (amount)		has/have not (yet) been	paid settled paid
			our account		has not (yet) been	balanced settled cleared

– explanation(s) (buyer is at fault)*	We have not paid your invoice(s)/statement (of account) because We have not yet paid your invoice(s)/statement (of account) because We have not been able to settle our account because Payment has been delayed because You have not received payment because Payment has not yet been made because We have not been able to clear our account because Your invoice(s)/your statement (of account) has (have) remained unsettled because We are behind schedule with our payments because We are in arrears with payment because	owing to as a result of as a consequence of	a breakdown in our computer system a fire on our premises the fact that our premises were recently broken into industrial action by the ... (name of union, e.g. office workers'/postal workers') union the fact that your invoice/statement (of account) was mislaid a clerical error by one of our staff a mistake when transferring the invoice amount/amount due (when referring to a statement) to your account an accounting error on our part a misunderstanding on our part an oversight by one of our staff an error by our bank the rise in interest rates the current credit squeeze the new taxation laws in this country a rapid rise in unemployment in this area the collapse of the ... (e.g. steel) industry here the problems in the ... (e.g. retail) trade here a sudden increase in the price of raw materials an unexpected rise in the price of petrol/diesel leading to higher transport costs a massive rise in the price of ... (commodity/raw material, e.g. coal) a massive drop in the price of ... (commodity/raw material, e.g. sugar) the fluctuating price of ... (commodity/raw material, e.g. coffee) on the world market the poor ... (crop, e.g. grape) harvest the destruction of the entire ... (name of crop, e.g. wheat) harvest as a result of ... (natural catastrophe, e.g. flooding) a sudden drop in demand for ... (product/service, e.g. synthetics/tailor-made software)

an unexpected lack of demand for … (product/service)
a drop in demand for … (commodity/product/service)
the instability of the … (currency, e.g. the Australian dollar)
the devaluation of the … (currency)
the revaluation of the … (currency)
the (re-)introduction of exchange controls
a breakdown in telecommunications between our two countries
the world recession
the political unrest in … (place)
the war in … (place)
the unexpectedly severe winter in this country
a drought in … (location)
an earthquake in … (location)
a hurricane in … (location)
a typhoon in … (location)
a forest fire/forest fires in … (location)
(heavy) (widespread) flooding in … (location)
the … (name of river, e.g. the Danube) breaking its banks in … (location)

… it has been impossible to access the necessary data
… we have run into financial difficulties
… we have had administrative difficulties
… we are experiencing (temporary) liquidity problems
… we are owed substantial sums of money
… we ourselves are owed substantial amounts by our own customers
… we are unable to obtain credit from our bankers at the usual rate
… one of our major customers has not yet settled his debts to us
… several of our major customers have not settled their debts to us
… one/several of our major trading partners has/have gone bankrupt
… one/several of our major trading partners has/have filed for bankruptcy
… one/several of our major trading partners has/have become insolvent
… we (currently) have an acute cash-flow problem
… it has been impossible to transfer money from one country to another

	The delay in payment has been caused by The delay in payment has been brought about by This delay in payment has come about because of	… (see list of reasons above)		
– explanations (buyer is not at fault)*	We have not (yet) paid your invoice(s)/statement (of account) because We have withheld payment because Payment has been withheld because	the wrong goods were delivered the wrong quality was supplied you assured us in your telephone call of … (date) that the wrong goods would be collected and replaced. We are still waiting for this to happen , since you delivered the goods late, we will not be paying until 30 days after delivery, as agreed per contract you gave us the wrong bank account number, as a result of which the amount transferred was returned to us the goods arrived damaged so we are not prepared to pay the full price for them the invoice amount does not tally with the amount stated in the sales agreement your statement (of account) contains several inaccuracies (see *Unit 7 "Payment"*, pages 91–92, for further reasons) the wrong price was charged (see *Unit 7 "Payment"*, pages 91–92, for further reasons) we were short-shipped by … (number) units we were under-supplied by … (number) units we were over-supplied by … (number) units and await your instructions as to what to do with the excess goods		
– payment will be late*	Owing to As a result of As a consequence of	unforeseen circumstances circumstances (entirely) beyond our control … (see list of reasons above)	we are sorry to tell you that we regret to inform you that we are (unfortunately) obliged to tell you that	we will be unable we will (unfortunately) not be able it will (unfortunately) not be possible for us
	… to pay … to settle	your invoice(s) no./nos. … (and …) of/dated … for … (amount(s)) your statement (of account) for the quarter ending … (date, e.g. 31 March ..) showing a debit balance of … (amount) your bill(s) no./nos. … (and …) of/dated … for … (amount(s))		on time on schedule as agreed as arranged within the time stipulated by … (+ date) for … (+ period of time, e.g. the next month)
	… to balance … to clear	our account (with you/your company)		

3	Confirmation that payment has been made*	Your invoice(s) Your statement (of account) Your bill(s)	has have	in fact already in actual fact already	been paid been settled	We remitted We transferred We instructed our bankers to transfer We posted you a cheque for/an IMO for/an international banker's draft etc. for	… (amount) the amount due the amount owing the sum in question the sum of … (amount) the first/second/third etc. part-payment of … (amount) the first/second/third etc./final instalment of … (amount)
		Our account	has		been balanced been cleared		
		this morning this afternoon yesterday … on … (date, e.g. 15 January ..)	We enclose We are enclosing We have enclosed Enclosed you will find We are sending you		a copy of the transfer slip a copy of … (document, e.g. the bank statement indicating that payment has been made) a note from our bankers	for your information confirming this by way of confirmation	
		… (amount) The sum of … (amount) The amount in question The above-mentioned sum			was remitted to you was transferred to your bank account was credited to your account	this morning this afternoon yesterday … on … (date, e.g. 15 January ..)	
		A cheque for An International Money Order for An international postal order for A banker's draft for	… (amount) the sum of … (amount) the amount in question the above-mentioned sum		was posted to you was mailed to you was sent to you		

– payment will be made*	We promise to We guarantee to We undertake to You may rest assured that we will	pay remit transfer	the amount due the amount owing the outstanding amount the balance the next instalment all monies owing	by … (+ date) within … (+ period of time, e.g. within the next 7 days)	without fail
	You have our word that we will	pay settle	your invoice(s) no./nos. … (and …) of/dated … for … (amount(s)) your statement (of account) for the quarter ending … (date, e.g. 31 March ..)		
		balance clear	our account (with you/your company)		
– request(s) for concession(s)*	Since our difficulties are through no fault of our own Since our current difficulties are only of a temporary nature In view of the fact that the difficulties we are experiencing will be solved in the near future In view of our long-standing business relationship In view of the large volume of business we have done with your company up to now In view of the fact that we have so far placed orders with you to the value of … (amount, e.g. $100,000) In view of our good payment record up to now Much as we regret having to make this request As our two companies have been doing business with each other for … (no. of years, e.g. 5/a number of/many) years now			please would it be possible to we would ask you to we would request you to we would be grateful if you would we would very much appreciate it if you would	
	… allow us a further two weeks to pay … grant us an extension of 30 days … extend the deadline for payment by 14 days … allow us to pay the sum due on … (date), i.e. two weeks from now … allow us to pay the outstanding amount in … (number, e.g. 3) (equal) instalments of … (amount) at … (time, e.g. two-weekly/monthly) intervals starting on … (date) … draw a draft on us for the outstanding amount (plus interest at the agreed/current rate), which we will accept and honour at maturity … accept that we make a part payment of … (amount/percentage, e.g. $10, 000/33 %) now and remit the balance (of …) on … (date)/by … (+ date)/within … (+ period of time)				

4 Hope that the concession(s) will be granted*

We hope We very much hope that We sincerely hope that	you will you will be able to you will be in a position to it will be possible for you to	allow us extra time allow us the extra time we have requested agree to our suggestion agree to our paying the outstanding amount over a period of … (time, e.g. 3 months) grant us this concession accept our proposition extend the credit period (by … (period of time, e.g. 30 days)) extend the payment period (by … (period of time, e.g. 30 days)) accept a part-payment for the time being allow us to pay in instalments

– second apology for the delay*

… and	as already said please let us once again say that we would like to say once again that as mentioned at the beginning of this letter/message to you	we are sorry about we are very sorry about we apologize for we wish to apologize for we offer you our sincerest apologies for we sincerely regret we most sincerely regret we deeply regret we very much regret	this delay the delay in payment this oversight this error this misunderstanding	, which was due to no fault of our own , which was due to circumstances beyond our control , which was entirely our own fault , which was due to exceptional circumstances , which was due to an unfortunate combination of events , which was due to a(n unfortunate) misunderstanding on our part

We (once again) May we (once again) Please let us (once again)	offer you our sincerest apologies for express our regret about	the oversight on our part the error on our part			
		the fact that our account	has not been was not could not be	balanced settled cleared	on time within the period agreed as stipulated

	We promise that We assure you that We guarantee that You may rest assured that You have our word that You may be sure that We undertake to ensure that We will do our very best to ensure that We will do our utmost to make certain that Everything in our power will be done to ensure that We will take appropriate steps to ensure that	it won't happen again such a thing will not happen again there will be no such delays in future there will be no repetition of this
	We'll make certain that We will ensure that We will do our very best to ensure that We will do our utmost to ensure that Everything in our power will be done to ensure that We will take appropriate steps to ensure that	it doesn't happen again such a thing does not happen again there is no such delay in future there is no repetition of this
5 Polite ending	We hope to hear from you soon We look forward to receiving your comments on this matter We look forward to hearing from you soon We very much hope that future business will not be affected by this unfortunate delay in payment We hope that this delay, due to circumstances beyond our control, will not jeopardize business relations between our two companies Please do not hesitate to contact us should you require any further information	
6 Enclosure(s)	Copy of bank transfer slip Copy of bank statement Banker's letter of confirmation	

Seller's Reply

1 Reference to buyer's letter/fax/e-mail	We refer to With reference to In response to In answer to	your the above-mentioned	letter fax e-mail	dated/of …	regarding in connection with	our invoice(s) … (details) our statement(s) … (details) our statement(s) of account … (details) your account with us showing an outstanding balance of … (amount)
	… in which you	say that tell us that inform us that advise us that explain why	you will not be able to pay on time payment of our invoice(s)/statement (of account) will de delayed you are unable to pay our invoice(s)/statement (of account) as agreed you will not be able to pay on the date agreed you will not be able to balance/settle your account with us on schedule			
		tell us why explain why give us your explanation as to why	the sum of … (amount) is still outstanding we still have not received payment of our invoice(s)/statement (of account) you have not paid our invoice(s)/statement (of account) you have been unable to pay our invoice(s)/statement (of account) payment of our invoice(s)/statement (of account) has been delayed payment of our invoice(s)/statement (of account) was not made • on schedule • by the date agreed our invoice(s)/statement (of account) has/have not been paid to date you are in arrears with payment of our invoice(s)/statement (of account)			
		ask us to request us to	allow you/your company extra time to pay our invoice(s)/statement (of account) agree that the outstanding amount of … (amount) be paid over a period of … (time, e.g. 3 months) extend the credit period (by … (period of time, e.g. 30 days)) extend the payment period (by … (period of time, e.g. 30 days)) accept a part-payment of our invoice(s)/statement (of account) for the time being allow you to pay in (4 equal) instalments (of … (amount, e.g. $1,000) at weekly/monthly intervals) draw a draft on you for the outstanding amount (plus interest at the agreed/current rate), to be accepted and honoured by yourselves at maturity			

2	Grant the concession(s)	Under the circumstances Since this is the first time that payment has been delayed As there has never been a delay in payment on your part before In view of your good payment record up to now In view of our satisfactory (business) relations in the past/up to now As we have now been doing business with each other for a considerable time	we will we are able to we are prepared to we are willing to we will make an exception and	agree to your request allow you extra time allow you the extra time you have requested agree to your suggestion agree to your paying the outstanding amount over a period of … (time, e.g. 3 months) grant you this concession accept your proposition extend the credit period (by … (period of time, e.g. 30 days)) extend the payment period (by … (period of time, e.g. 30 days)) accept a part-payment for the time being allow you to pay in instalments accept an immediate part-payment of … (amount). We enclose our draft at 30 days' sight (30 d/s) for the balance	
		We must point out that We would remind you that	interest at a rate of … % p.a. will be charged	on the outstanding amount on the sum due on the amount owed	together with an administration charge of … (amount, e.g. $50.00) together with an administrative fee of … (amount)
		You will be charged It will be necessary to charge You will incur	interest at a rate of … % p.a. the current rate of interest plus 2 %		
	Refuse the concession(s)	Under the circumstances, however, As you are in breach of contract As prompt payment is a pre-requisite for our exceptionally low prices Since we operate with extremely low profit margins You will appreciate that we, ourselves, must also pay our suppliers, therefore As it is our company's policy not to give credit Since we must meet our own financial commitments As we ourselves have pressing financial obligations Since you have made no attempt up to now to explain the delay		we will not be able to we are not in a position to we are sorry to say that we are unable to we regret to inform you that we will not be able to we regret to inform you that it will be impossible for us to	allow you extra time to pay give you (any more) credit allow you the extra time you have requested agree to your request agree to your suggestion agree to your paying the outstanding amount over a period of … (time, e.g. 3 months) grant you this concession accept your proposition

	As you have disregarded our letters up to now In view of the fact that this is not the first time that payment is late In view of your poor payment habits in the past As we ourselves would be obliged to obtain credit to finance the goods sold to you In view of the fact that we have already been waiting … (time, e.g. 8 weeks) for payment			*(see previous page)*		extend the credit period (by … (period of time, e.g. 30 days)) extend the payment period (by … (period of time, e.g. 30 days)) accept a part-payment for the time being allow you to pay in instalments
				we must we have no choice but to we have no alternative but to	decline	your request for extra time/credit/an extension your request to make a part-payment your request that we draw a draft on you for the outstanding sum your suggestion that the outstanding sum be paid in instalments
	We must therefore insist that	the outstanding amount the invoice amount the entire sum owing	of … (amount)	including interest and our administration fee of … (amount)	be paid be remitted be transferred	in full without any deduction
	by … (+ date) within (+ period of time)	after which we will after which time we will	take the necessary steps to recover	• the sum owing/outstanding • the sum in question • the amount due • all outstanding monies		
			take legal action put the matter in the hands of our solicitors institute legal proceeding turn the matter over to an agent for collection use a collection agency to recover the debt			
3 Polite ending	We hope to hear from you We expect to be hearing from you We trust we will be hearing from you We look forward to receiving your remittance We expect to be receiving your first instalment We expect to be receiving payment of …		soon very soon shortly in the next few days on … (date) by … (+ date) within (+ period time)			

Delay in Payment

Seller

1	**Reference to overdue invoice / account**	***Bezugnahme auf überfällige Rechnung***
	We refer to our invoices nos. 897 and 898 for £1,500.95	*Wir beziehen uns auf unsere Rechnungen Nr. 897 und 898 über 1.500,95 £*
	We are writing in connection with the above-mentioned statement for the sum of £1,500.95	*Wir schreiben Ihnen im Zusammenhang mit dem oben stehenden Kontoauszug für die Summe von 1.500,95 £*
	It has most probably escaped your notice that the above statement of account, showing an outstanding balance of £1,500.95 in our favour, has not been paid yet	*Höchstwahrscheinlich ist es Ihrer Aufmerksamkeit entgangen, dass der obige Kontoauszug, der einen ausstehenden Saldo von 1.500,95 £ zu unseren Gunsten aufweist, noch nicht bezahlt worden ist*
	We are sorry to note that our invoice for £1,000 is still overdue	*Wir bedauern festzustellen, dass unsere Rechnung über 1.000 £ noch überfällig ist*
	This is to inform you that our statement of account for £1,000.95 has now been overdue for 10 days	*Hiermit teilen wir Ihnen mit, dass unser Kontoauszug über 1.00,95 £ jetzt seit 10 Tagen überfällig ist*
	Please note that payment was due on 31 January ..	*Bitte nehmen Sie zur Kenntnis, dass die Zahlung am 31. Januar .. fällig war*
	We wish to point out that our sales agreement provides for payment within 30 days at the latest	*Wir möchten darauf hinweisen, dass unsere Verkaufsvereinbarung eine Zahlung innerhalb von spätestens 30 Tagen vorsieht*
2	**Refer to previous reminder(s) (copy / copies enclosed)***	***Weisen Sie auf frühere Mahnung(en) hin (Kopie(n) als Anlage)****
	We refer to our two previous letters, dated 15 January and 1 February, with regard to our above-mentioned statement of account, showing an outstanding balance of $5,450.87 in our favour, which is still overdue	*Wir beziehen uns auf unsere zwei vorhergehenden Briefe vom 15. Januar und 1. Februar bezüglich unseres obengenannten Kontoauszugs, der einen ausstehenden Saldo von 5.450,87 $ zu unseren Gunsten ausweist und noch offensteht*
	We must point out that this is our third fax to you in this connection	*Wir müssen darauf hinweisen, dass dies unser drittes Fax an Sie in diesem Zusammenhang ist*
	We are sorry to say that this is our second letter with regard to the sum due	*Es tut uns Leid Ihnen mitzuteilen, dass dies unser zweiter Brief bezüglich der fälligen Summe ist*
	We have now been waiting for our invoices to be paid for two months	*Wir warten jetzt seit zwei Monaten auf die Zahlung unserer Rechnungen*
	Our January statement is now 8 weeks overdue	*Unser Januar-Auszug ist jetzt 8 Wochen überfällig*

	– no response to previous correspondence*	***– keine Reaktion auf vorhergehenden Schriftverkehr****
	Although you have already received a reminder we have still heard nothing from you	*Obwohl Sie bereits eine Mahnung erhielten, haben wir immer noch nichts von Ihnen gehört*
	Despite the fact that you have already received several reminders, you have made no attempt whatsoever to contact us	*Trotz der Tatsache, dass Sie schon mehrere Mahnungen erhalten haben, haben Sie noch keinen Versuch unternommen, mit uns Kontakt aufzunehmen*
	As we have received neither an explanation nor a remittance …	*Da wir weder eine Erklärung noch eine Überweisung erhalten haben, …*
	Since you are now 10 days in arrears …	*Da Sie jetzt 10 Tage im Rückstand sind, …*
	In view of the fact that you have sent us neither the amount owing nor an explanation of the delay …	*Angesichts der Tatsache, dass Sie uns weder den geschuldeten Betrag noch eine Erklärung für die Verzögerung geschickt haben, …*
	– promises have not been kept*	***– Versprechen wurden nicht eingehalten****
	Although you assured us that the new draft drawn upon you would be accepted and honoured at maturity, we still have not received it	*Obwohl Sie uns versicherten, dass der neue, auf Sie gezogene Wechsel akzeptiert und bei Fälligkeit eingelöst würde, haben wir ihn noch nicht erhalten*
3	**Express surprise that this should happen***	***Drücken Sie Überraschung aus, dass dies passiert ist****
	As payment has not been delayed before, we have not contacted you until now	*Da die Zahlung bisher noch nie verzögert wurde, haben wir bis jetzt noch nicht mit Ihnen Kontakt aufgenommen*
	In view of the fact that this is the first time that payment has been late, we must assume that there has been a misunderstanding of some sort	*Angesichts der Tatsache, dass dies das erste Mal einer Zahlungsverspätung ist, nehmen wir an, dass es ein Missverständnis irgendeiner Art gegeben hat*
	Given that you have always paid regularly up to now, we can only assume that this is due to an oversight on your part	*Da Sie bisher immer regelmäßig gezahlt haben, können wir nur annehmen, dass es sich um ein Versehen Ihrerseits handelt*
	We can't imagine what has gone wrong	*Wir können uns nicht vorstellen, was falsch gelaufen ist*
	We are at a loss to understand why we have not received your remittance	*Wir können einfach nicht verstehen, warum wir Ihre Überweisung nicht erhalten haben*
4	**Request an explanation**	***Bitten Sie um eine Erklärung***
	Why has our invoice not been paid?	*Warum ist unsere Rechnung nicht bezahlt worden?*

	We would very much welcome an explanation as to why payment is delayed	*Wir würden eine Erklärung, warum die Zahlung verspätet erfolgt, sehr begrüßen*
	If you are unable to pay at least give us your reasons for non-payment	*Wenn Sie nicht in der Lage sind zu zahlen, geben Sie uns wenigstens die Gründe für Ihre Nichtzahlung an*
	It might be possible to agree on new terms if you are experiencing problems of a financial nature	*Es bestünde die Möglichkeit, neue Bedingungen zu vereinbaren, wenn Sie Probleme finanzieller Art haben*
5	**Request payment and set a deadline***	***Erbitten Sie die Zahlung und setzen Sie eine letzte Frist****
	We must therefore request that you pay by June 15 .. at the latest	*Wir müssen Sie deshalb bitten, bis spätestens 15. Juni .. zu zahlen*
	We must therefore insist that you make a minimum payment of $2,000 / 33 % of the sum outstanding within 7 days without fail	*Wir müssen daher darauf bestehen, dass Sie unbedingt eine Mindestzahlung von 2.000 $ / 33 % der ausstehenden Summe innerhalb von 7 Tagen leisten*
	Please make sure that payment is made within 7 days at the very latest	*Bitte stellen Sie sicher, dass die Zahlung spätestens innerhalb von 7 Tagen erfolgt*
	Please transfer $2,000 to our account no. 897655 at the Commerzbank, sorting code 45240056, by June 30 ..	*Bitte überweisen Sie bis 30. Juni .. 2.000 $ auf unser Konto Nr. 897655 bei der Commerzbank, Bankleitzahl 45240056*
	Please remit this amount without delay	*Bitte überweisen Sie diesen Betrag unverzüglich*
	Deadlines	***Fristablauf***
	We will let you have until the end of the month to pay	*Wir geben Ihnen bis zum Monatsende Zeit zu zahlen*
	We are prepared to allow you a further two weeks to pay	*Wir sind bereit, Ihnen weitere zwei Wochen zur Zahlung einzuräumen*
	We are prepared to give you another two weeks	*Wir sind bereit, Ihnen weitere zwei Wochen zu gewähren*
	If we don't receive payment by next Monday ...	*Wenn wir nicht bis nächsten Montag die Zahlung erhalten, ...*
	Should payment not have been made within 7 days ...	*Sollte die Zahlung nicht innerhalb von 7 Tagen erfolgt sein, ...*
	We are setting you a final deadline for payment of 7 days	*Wir setzen Ihnen eine letzte Zahlungsfrist von 7 Tagen*
6	**Consequences of non-payment***	***Folgen der Nichtzahlung****
	If you do not settle our statement of account, we'll re-consider our terms of business with you	*Wenn Sie unseren Kontoauszug nicht begleichen, werden wir unsere Geschäftsbeziehungen mit Ihnen überdenken*

	If we do not receive the amount due on your account, we will be obliged to change the terms on which we are able to do business with you	*Wenn wir den auf Ihrem Konto fälligen Betrag nicht erhalten, werden wir gezwungen sein, die Bedingungen zu ändern, zu denen wir mit Ihnen Geschäfte machen können*
	Should you not settle our statement we will have to deal with your company on a "cash with order" basis	*Wenn Sie unseren Kontoauszug nicht begleichen, müssen wir mit Ihrer Firma auf einer Basis „Barzahlung bei Auftragserteilung" arbeiten*
	Should you fail to pay our invoices we will have no choice but to stop all further deliveries	*Wenn Sie es versäumen, unsere Rechnungen zu bezahlen, werden wir keine andere Wahl haben, als alle weiteren Lieferungen einzustellen*
	Failure to pay our statement may well mean that we will have no alternative but to require you to return the goods for which you have not paid	*Ihr Versäumnis, unseren Kontoauszug zu begleichen, kann bedeuten, dass wir keine andere Wahl haben, als von Ihnen zu verlangen, die von Ihnen nicht bezahlten Waren zurückzugeben*
	... it may well be necessary to change our terms to "cash with order" only	*... möglicherweise ist es erforderlich, unsere Bedingungen in nur „Barzahlung bei Auftragserteilung" umzuändern*
	... we will be obliged to deal with your company on "cash against documents" terms	*... wir werden gezwungen sein, mit Ihrer Firma zu der Bedingung „Kasse gegen Dokumente" zu arbeiten*
	... we will be compelled to take the necessary steps to recover the sum owing, together with interest at a rate of 15 % p. a. and an administration charge of $50.00	*... wir werden gezwungen sein, die nötigen Schritte zu unternehmen, um die geschuldete Summe einzutreiben, zuzüglich Zinsen zu einem Satz von 15 % p. a. und einer Verwaltungsgebühr von 50,00 $*
	... it may well prove necessary to put the matter in the hands of our solicitors	*... es mag sich durchaus als notwendig erweisen, die Angelegenheit unseren Anwälten zu übergeben*
	... we very much hope that it will not be necessary to take steps which might cause your company serious harm	*... wir hoffen sehr, dass es nicht nötig sein wird, Schritte zu unternehmen, die Ihrer Firma ernsthaften Schaden zufügen könnten*
	We would not like to take any action which might endanger your company's reputation	*Wir würden ungern irgendwelche Schritte unternehmen, die den Ruf Ihrer Firma gefährden könnten*
7	**Regret that a reminder is necessary***	***Bedauern Sie, dass eine Mahnung erforderlich ist****
	We regret having to write to you again	*Wir bedauern, dass wir Ihnen erneut schreiben müssen*

	We are sorry that it has proved necessary to write to you once more and feel sure that the delay is as a result of an oversight on your part	*Es tut uns Leid, dass es sich als notwendig erwiesen hat, Ihnen erneut zu schreiben; wir sind sicher, dass die Verzögerung auf ein Versehen Ihrerseits zurückzuführen ist*
	Much as we regret having to contact you again, we must insist on payment by the date stated	*Obwohl wir es sehr bedauern, Sie erneut anzusprechen, müssen wir auf der Zahlung bis zum festgesetzten Datum bestehen*
8	**Polite ending**	***Höflicher Schluss***
	We trust you will be remitting the sum in question in the next few days	*Wir vertrauen darauf, dass Sie die infrage stehende Summe in den nächsten Tagen überweisen werden*
	We are confident that we will shortly be receiving the amount owed	*Wir sind zuversichtlich, dass wir in Kürze den geschuldeten Betrag erhalten werden*
	We very much hope that this matter will be settled swiftly and to the satisfaction of all concerned	*Wir hoffen sehr, dass diese Angelegenheit schnell und zur Zufriedenheit aller Beteiligten erledigt wird*
	In view of our satisfactory business relations in the past, we do not doubt that an amicable solution will be found	*In Anbetracht unserer zufriedenstellenden Geschäftsbeziehungen in der Vergangenheit zweifeln wir nicht daran, dass eine freundschaftliche Lösung gefunden wird*
	If payment has already been made please disregard this letter / fax / e-mail	*Wenn die Zahlung bereits erfolgt ist, betrachten Sie diesen Brief / dieses Fax / diese E-Mail bitte als gegenstandslos*
9	**Enclosure(s)**	***Anlage(n)***
	Invoice(s) Statement of Account Our letters dated … and …	*Rechnung(en)* *Kontoauszug* *Unsere Briefe vom … und …*

Buyer

1	**Reference to overdue invoice / account / reminder(s)**	***Bezugnahme auf überfällige Rechnung / überfälliges Konto / Mahnung(en)***
	We refer to your invoices nos. 897 and 898 dated 15 January and 1 February .. for £1,500.95	*Wir beziehen uns auf Ihre Rechnungen Nr. 897 und 898 vom 15. Januar und 1. Februar .. über 1.500,95 £*
	We are writing in connection with the above-mentioned statement of account, dated 31 March .., showing an outstanding balance of $2,545.89 in your favour	*Wir schreiben Ihnen bezüglich des obengenannten Kontoauszugs vom 31. März .., der einen ausstehenden Saldo von 2.545,89 $ zu Ihren Gunsten aufweist*

	We have received your letter of 10 March .. requesting that we settle our account with you	*Wir haben Ihr Schreiben vom 10. März .. erhalten, in dem Sie uns bitten, unser Konto bei Ihnen auszugleichen*
2	**First apology and explanation why payment is late***	***Erste Entschuldigung und Erklärung, warum die Zahlung verspätet erfolgt****
	We would like to apologise for the delay in settling your invoices	*Wir möchten uns für die Verzögerung in der Begleichung unserer Rechnungen entschuldigen*
	Please accept our apologies for the delay in settling your statement for the period 1 January – 31 March .. amounting to $3,245.75	*Bitte nehmen Sie unsere Entschuldigung für die Verzögerung in der Begleichung Ihres Kontoauszugs für den Zeitraum vom 1. Januar bis 31. März .. in Höhe von 3.245,75 $ entgegen*
	– explanation(s) (buyer is at fault)*	***– Erklärung(en) (Käufer ist Schuld)****
	We have not paid your statement because, owing to a breakdown in our computer system, it has been impossible to access the necessary data	*Wir haben Ihren Kontoauszug nicht bezahlt, weil es wegen eines Versagens unserer Computeranlage unmöglich gewesen ist, Zugang zu den notwendigen Daten zu bekommen*
	Payment has been delayed because, as a result of industrial action by the office workers' union, we have run into financial difficulties	*Die Zahlung ist verzögert worden, weil wir aufgrund von Arbeitskampfmaßnahmen der Gewerkschaft des Büropersonals in finanzielle Schwierigkeiten geraten sind*
	We have not yet paid your invoice because, as a consequence of a clerical error by one of our staff, we have had administrative difficulties	*Wir haben Ihre Rechnung noch nicht bezahlt, weil wir als Folge des Fehlers eines Mitglieds unseres Büropersonals verwaltungstechnische Schwierigkeiten hatten*
	We are in arrears with payment because of a fire on our premises	*Wir sind mit der Zahlung im Verzug, weil wir ein Feuer in unseren Geschäftsräumen hatten*
	... a sudden increase in the price of raw materials	*... eine plötzliche Erhöhung im Preis der Rohstoffe*
	... an unexpected lack of demand for electronic computers	*... eine unerwartete Flaute in der Nachfrage nach elektronischen Rechenanlagen*
	... we are experiencing temporary liquidity problems	*... wir haben zur Zeit vorübergehende Liquiditätsprobleme*
	... one of our major customers has not yet settled his debts to us	*... einer unserer Hauptkunden hat seine Schulden bei uns noch nicht bezahlt*
	... several of our major trading partners have gone bankrupt	*... mehrere unserer wichtigen Handelspartner sind in Konkurs geraten*
	... we currently have an acute cash-flow problem	*... wir haben zur Zeit ein akutes Cashflow-Problem*
	– explanations (buyer is not at fault)*	***– Erklärungen (Käufer ist nicht Schuld)****

	We have not paid your invoice because the wrong goods were delivered	*Wir haben Ihre Rechnung nicht bezahlt, weil die falschen Waren geliefert wurden*
	We have not paid because you assured us in your telephone call of 4 July .. that the wrong goods would be collected and replaced. We are still waiting for this to happen	*Wir haben nicht bezahlt, weil Sie uns in Ihrem Telefongespräch vom 4. Juli .. zusicherten, dass die falschen Waren abgeholt und ersetzt würden. Wir warten immer noch darauf, dass dies geschieht*
	We have withheld payment because, since you delivered the goods late, we will not be paying until 30 days after delivery, as agreed per contract	*Wir haben die Zahlung zurückgehalten, weil, da Sie die Güter zu spät geliefert haben, wir vertragsgemäß erst 30 Tage nach Lieferung zahlen werden*
	Payment has been withheld because we were short-shipped by 100 units	*Die Zahlung ist zurückgehalten worden, weil uns 100 Stück zu wenig geliefert wurden*
	... we were over-supplied by 250 units and await your instructions as to what to do with the excess goods	*... wir 250 Stück zu viel geliefert bekamen und wir Ihre Anweisungen erwarten, was mit den überschüssigen Waren geschehen soll*
	– payment will be late*	***– Zahlung wird verspätet erfolgen****
	Owing to unforeseen circumstances, we are sorry to tell you that we will be unable to pay your invoices nos. 767 and 768 of 15 and 28 June .. for $2,500 and $3,000 on time	*Aufgrund unvorhergesehener Umstände tut es uns Leid Ihnen mitzuteilen, dass wir nicht in der Lage sein werden, Ihre Rechnungen Nr. 767 und 768 vom 15. und 28. Juni .. über 2,.500 $ und 3.000 $ pünktlich zu bezahlen*
	As a result of circumstances entirely beyond our control, we are unfortunately obliged to tell you that we will not be able to settle your statement for the quarter ending 31 March .. showing a debit balance of $2,545.75 on schedule	*Als Ergebnis von Umständen, die völlig außerhalb unserer Kontrolle liegen, sind wir leider gezwungen Ihnen mitzuteilen, dass wir nicht in der Lage sein werden, Ihren Kontoauszug für das am 31. März .. endende Quartal, der einen regulären Sollsaldo von 2.545,75 $ aufweist, zu begleichen*
	Owing to the problems in the retail trade here, we regret to inform you that we will be unable to balance our account with your company within the time stipulated	*Aufgrund von Problemen im hiesigen Einzelhandel bedauern wir Ihnen mitzuteilen, dass wir nicht in der Lage sein werden, unser Konto bei Ihrer Firma innerhalb der festgesetzten Zeit auszugleichen*
3	**Confirmation that payment has been made***	***Bestätigung, dass die Zahlung erfolgt ist****
	Your invoice has in fact already been paid. We remitted the amount due this morning	*Ihre Rechnung ist in der Tat bezahlt worden. Wir haben den fälligen Betrag heute morgen überwiesen*

We enclose a copy of the transfer slip for your information	*Wir fügen zu Ihrer Information eine Kopie des Überweisungsabschnittes bei*
We are sending you a note from our bankers by way of confirmation	*Wir schicken Ihnen als Bestätigung eine Mitteilung unserer Bank zu*
The sum of $5,000 was transferred to your bank account this afternoon	*Die Summe von 5.000 $ wurde heute nachmittag auf Ihr Bankkonto überwiesen*
A banker's draft for $5,000 was mailed to you yesterday	*Ein Bankwechsel über 5.000 $ wurde Ihnen gestern zugestellt*
– payment will be made*	*– Die Zahlung wird erfolgen**
We undertake to remit all monies owing by June 30 .. without fail	*Wir verpflichten uns unbedingt, alle geschuldeten Beträge bis 30. Juni .. zu überweisen*
You have our word that we will settle your statement of account for the quarter ending 31 March .. within the next 7 days	*Sie haben unser Wort, dass wir Ihren Kontoauszug für das Quartal, das am 31. März .. endet, innerhalb der nächsten 7 Tage ausgleichen werden*
– request(s) for concession(s)*	*– Bitte(n) um Konzession(en)**
Since our difficulties are through no fault of our own, please allow us a further two weeks to pay	*Da unsere Schwierigkeiten nicht durch unseren eigenen Fehler entstanden sind, gewähren Sie uns bitte zwei weitere Wochen bis zur Zahlung*
Since our current difficulties are only of a temporary nature, we would ask you to grant us an extension of 30 days	*Da unsere laufenden Schwierigkeiten nur vorübergehender Art sind, möchten wir Sie bitten, uns eine Verlängerung von 30 Tagen zu gewähren*
In view of the large volume of business we have done with your company up to now, we would be grateful if you would extend the deadline for payment by 14 days	*Angesichts des großen Umfangs der Geschäfte, die wir mit Ihrer Firma bisher getätigt haben, wären wir Ihnen dankbar, wenn Sie die Zahlungsfrist um 14 Tage verlängern würden*
In view of our good payment record up to now, we would very much appreciate it if you would draw a draft on us for the outstanding amount (plus interest at the current rate), which we will accept and honour at maturity	*Angesichts unserer bisherigen guten Zahlungsmoral würden wir es sehr begrüßen, wenn Sie für den ausstehenden Betrag (plus Zinsen zum laufenden Satz) einen Wechsel auf uns ziehen würden, den wir akzeptieren und bei Fälligkeit einlösen werden*
4 Hope that the concession(s) will be granted*	*Hoffnung, dass die Konzession(en) gewährt wird (werden)**
We very much hope that you will be able to allow us the extra time we have requested	*Wir hoffen sehr, dass Sie in der Lage sein werden, uns die erbetene Verlängerung zu gewähren*
We sincerely hope that you will be in a position to grant us this concession	*Wir hoffen zuversichtlich, dass Sie in der Lage sein werden, uns diese Konzession zu gewähren*

	– second apology for the delay	*– Zweite Entschuldigung für die Verzögerung*
	... and, as already said, we are sorry about this delay, which was due to no fault of our own	*... und, wie bereits gesagt, tut uns diese Verzögerung Leid, die aber auf kein Verschulden unsererseits zurückzuführen ist*
	Please let us once again say that we offer you our sincerest apologies for the delay in payment, which was due to exceptional circumstances	*Bitte lassen Sie uns noch einmal sagen, dass wir uns für die Verspätung in der Zahlung, die auf außergewöhnliche Umstände zurückzuführen war, sehr entschuldigen*
	We once again offer you our sincerest apologies for the oversight on our part	*Wir entschuldigen uns nochmals außerordentlich für das Versehen unsererseits*
	You may rest assured that there will be no such delays in future	*Sie können versichert sein, dass solche Verzögerungen in Zukunft nicht mehr vorkommen werden*
	We'll make certain that it doesn't happen again	*Wir werden dafür sorgen, dass dies nicht wieder geschieht*
5	Polite ending	*Höflicher Schluss*
	We look forward to receiving your comments on this matter	*Wir freuen uns darauf, Ihre Stellungnahme in dieser Angelegenheit zu erhalten*
	We very much hope that future business will not be affected by this unfortunate delay in payment	*Wir hoffen sehr, dass zukünftige Geschäfte von dieser bedauerlichen Zahlungsverzögerung nicht beeinträchtigt werden*
	We hope that this delay, due to circumstances beyond our control, will not jeopardize business relations between our two companies	*Wir hoffen, dass diese Verzögerung, die auf Umstände ausserhalb unserer Kontrolle zurückzuführen war, die zwischen unseren beiden Gesellschaften bestehenden Geschäftsbeziehungen nicht beeinträchtigen wird*
6	Enclosure(s)	*Anlage(n)*
	Copy of bank transfer slip Copy of bank statement Banker's letter of confirmation	*Kopie des Banküberweisungsabschnitts* *Kopie des Bankauszugs* *Bestätigungsschreiben der Bank*

Seller's Reply

1	Reference to buyer's letter / fax / e-mail	*Bezugnahme auf Brief / Fax / E-Mail des Käufers*
	We refer to your letter dated March 24 .. regarding our invoices	*Wir beziehen uns auf Ihren Brief vom 24. März .. bezüglich unserer Rechnungen*

	... in which you advise us that payment will be delayed	*... in dem Sie uns mitteilen, dass die Zahlung sich verzögern wird*
	... in which you explain why you have been unable to pay our statement	*... in welchem Sie uns erklären, warum Sie nicht in der Lage waren, unseren Kontoauszug zu begleichen*
	... in which you ask us to extend the payment period by 30 days	*... in dem Sie uns bitten, die Zahlungsfrist um 30 Tage zu verlängern*
	... in which you request us to draw a draft on you for the outstanding amount plus interest at the current rate, to be accepted and honoured by yourselves at maturity	*... in dem Sie uns bitten, für den ausstehenden Betrag plus Zinsen zum laufenden Satz einen Wechsel auf Sie zu ziehen, den Sie bei Fälligkeit akzeptieren und einlösen wollen*
2	**Grant the concession(s)**	***Gewähren Sie die Konzession(en)***
	Under the circumstances, we are prepared to agree to your request	*Unter den gegebenen Umständen sind wir bereit, Ihrer Bitte zuzustimmen*
	In view of your good payment record up to now, we are willing to extend the credit period by 30 days	*Angesichts Ihrer bisherigen guten Zahlungsmoral sind wir bereit, den Kreditzeitraum um 30 Tage zu verlängern*
	We must point out that interest at a rate of 20 % p. a. will be charged on the outstanding amount together with an administration charge of $50.00	*Wir müssen darauf hinweisen, dass Zinsen zu einem Satz von 20 % p. a. auf den ausstehenden Betrag zuzüglich einer Verwaltungsgebühr von 50.00 $ berechnet werden*
	Refuse the concession(s)	***Lehnen Sie die Konzession(en) ab***
	Since we operate with extremely low profit margins, we are sorry to say that we are unable to allow you the extra time you have requested	*Da wir mit extrem niedrigen Gewinnmargen arbeiten, müssen wir Ihnen leider mitteilen, dass wir nicht in der Lage sind, die von Ihnen gewünschte Zahlungsverlängerung zu gewähren*
	As it is our company's policy not to give credit, we regret to inform you that it will be impossible for us to grant you this concession	*Da es unsere Unternehmensstrategie ist, keinen Kredit zu gewähren, bedauern wir Ihnen mitteilen zu müssen, dass es uns unmöglich sein wird, Ihnen diese Konzession zu gewähren*
	Since you have made no attempt up to now to explain the delay, we will not be able to allow you extra time to pay	*Da Sie bisher keinen Versuch unternommen haben, die Verzögerung zu erklären, sind wir nicht in der Lage, Ihnen eine zusätzliche Zahlungsfrist einzuräumen*
	In view of your poor payment habits in the past, we will not be able to allow you to pay in instalments	*Angesicht Ihrer schlechten Zahlungsgewohnheiten in der Vergangenheit sind wir nicht in der Lage, Ihnen eine Ratenzahlung zuzugestehen*

	In view of the fact that we have already been waiting 8 weeks for payment, we must decline your request for extra time	*Angesichts der Tatsache, dass wir bereits 8 Wochen auf die Zahlung warten, müssen wir Ihre Bitte um Zahlungsverlängerung ablehnen*
	We must therefore insist that the outstanding amount of $5,000, including interest and our administration fee of $50, be paid in full by 30 September .., after which we will take the necessary steps to recover the sum owing	*Wir müssen deshalb darauf bestehen, dass der ausstehende Betrag von 5.000 $ einschließlich Zinsen und unserer Verwaltungsgebühr von 50 $ bis 30. September .. voll bezahlt wird. Andernfalls werden wir die notwendigen Schritte unternehmen, um die geschuldete Summe einzutreiben*
	... after which time we will put the matter in the hands of our solicitors	*... Nach diesem Zeitraum werden wir die Angelegenheit unseren Anwälten übergeben*
3	Polite ending	*Höflicher Schluss*
	We trust we will be hearing from you shortly	*Wir sind zuversichtlich, dass wir in Kürze von Ihnen hören werden*
	We expect to be receiving your first instalment on 31 August ..	*Wir erwarten den Erhalt Ihrer ersten Rate am 31. August ..*

Unit 11
Agency Agreements

Agent's Application for Agency

1 Source of address + application for agency – solicited application*	With reference to I refer to I am writing in reply to I am writing in connection with	the above-mentioned offer of an agency in … (location) your offer of the post of agent in … (location) as advertised in … 's (day/month etc., e.g. Saturday's) edition of … (publication, e.g. the *Evening Standard*) your advertisement in … (name of publication, e.g. *JobSearch Weekly*) dated/of … (date of publication) regarding the post of agent for your company in … (location, e.g. North Germany) our (pleasant and informative) meeting at … (location)		
	I wish to apply for the post of agent for your company in … (location) I am writing to apply for the position of agent for your company in … (location) I have been informed by … (name of person/company, e.g. Mr Prentice, the Manager of Barclays International in London) that you are looking for an agent in … (location)			
– unsolicited application*	I was most interested to see your company's products I was most impressed by the goods your company exhibited I was able to see your company's wide range of products	at the … (name of fair/exhibition, e.g. the Ideal Home Exhibition in London) at the recent … (name of event)	and feel sure that they would sell well here in … (location, e.g. Germany)	
	Have you considered appointing an agent	to handle your sales to act on your behalf to represent your company's interests	here? in … (location)? in this market?	
	I have obtained your company's address from Your address was given to me by	… (e.g. your local Chamber of Commerce and Industry, Barclays International in … (location))		
	Your local Chamber of Commerce and Industry Barclays International in … (location)	was/were kind enough to give me your (company's) address		
2 Description of yourself/your company: – experience*	I/we know a lot about I/we have considerable experience of I am/we are well acquainted with I am no newcomer to …	this market these products such products … (line of business, e.g. bathroom fittings, precision engineering, interior design)	having worked having been a sales representative having acted as an agent	in the … (name of business/trade, e.g. fashion) trade/business for … (name of company, e.g. Bertolucci Design in Milan)
			having acted on behalf of … (name of company)	
	for 5 years for many years for the last 10 years since … (+ date/month/year) since the company was set up			

	I have I possess	some experience considerable experience several years' experience 5 years' experience many years of experience a wide range of experience	in this field in the field of … (details) in this market in this line (of business)	and	(and so I/we) am/are well acquainted with these products keep up with the latest trends keep abreast of the latest developments
	My company has a staff of … (number)	qualified highly qualified highly successful extremely experienced success-oriented	salesmen saleswomen sales personnel field workers	who	
– sales contacts*	I/we have My company has	excellent/well-established/extensive business contacts a well-established/an extensive sales network sales personnel sales staff facilities a distribution centre (distribution centres) a warehouse (warehouses) a depot (depots)	in … in the local area in the territory you have in mind all over/throughout … (e.g. Germany, Europe, the EU etc.) both in Europe and beyond all over the continent in all major German/European cities in the EU and beyond		
	I have We have My staff has My employees have	(had) an excellent turnover sold a large number of goods (had) good sales figures (always) performed well (always) achieved above-average sales figures (had) good results achieved excellent results broken all records regularly out-sold all our competitors exceeded all expectations	in this field in this line in the local market in … (location)		

– personal qualities*	I am a(n)	young conscientious well-educated dynamic professional experienced outward-going success-oriented	salesman saleswoman freelance salesman/saleswoman freelancer marketing expert	and would very much like to and would welcome the chance to and would welcome the opportunity to and would be delighted to and would be only too pleased to	act on your behalf act on behalf of your company represent your interests boost your sales figures market your goods here open up the market for you here
	We are a(n)	highly motivated flexible versatile dedicated efficient	company marketing company	with a staff of … (number) with … (number) field – workers	
– qualifications/recommendations*	I We All my staff	have possess	a BSc (Bachelor of Science Degree in Business Administration) *(= Betriebswirt)* an MBA (a Masters Degree in Business Administration) *(= Betriebswirt)* a recognised qualification in marketing (see enclosure) a letter/letters of recommendation from a previous client/previous clients (see enclosure(s)) a testimonial/testimonials from a major client/major clients a letter/letters of introduction from … (name) a letter/letters of recommendation from … (name) copies of the sales figures achieved for some of my/our most recent clients		
	I attended the University of … (name, e.g. Tübingen) where I obtained a degree in … (subject(s), e.g. economics) My CV is enclosed I enclose my CV with full details of my educational background and employment up to now				
3 Interest in sole agency/del credere*	I/We would be very interested in		being your sole agent in … (territory) acting as the sole agent for your products in … (territory) being granted the sole agency for … (territory) acquiring the sole agency for … (territory)	and would be prepared to	assume the del credere for my/our customers
	Do you require someone to	be act as	your sole agent for … (territory)	and assume and accept	the del credere for the customers obtained there?

	As my/our customers are reliable companies Given the reliability of the customers I/we have in mind	I we our company	would be willing to would be prepared to would be glad to	assume accept	the del credere for	my/our customers my/our clients the business I/we obtain all contracts obtained
	Since my/our clients here are all reputable firms	I/we would have no hesitation in I/we would have no objection to		accepting assuming		
	... on payment of an appropriate ... if you are able to pay a	del credere commission		of ... % at the standard rate at a suitable rate		
4 Reference(s)	A reference/references can be obtained from ... Should you require references please contact ... , who will be pleased to supply you with any information you may desire ... (name of company, e.g. the Holzmann AG in Berlin) will be happy to provide a reference on us/on our company ... (name of bank/company) will be pleased to supply you with a reference on our company, if required I/We have excellent trade and bank references and enclose a list of our major business partners, who will be pleased to provide you with any information you may require I/We will be happy to provide you with the usual bank and trade references I/We will be pleased to supply you with any further information you may desire on myself/our company					
5 Availability for interview	I am available for interview	on ... (date) from ... (date) to ... (date) at any time during the next ... (period of time, e.g. three weeks) as from ... (date) at any time between ... (time) and ... (time) on ... (date) at a day's notice at 5 days' notice at a week's notice				
	I will be in the ... area (e.g. the London area) I will be visiting ... (details, e.g. Neasden plc) I will be attending the ... (trade fair/exhibition)	on ... (date) from ... (date) to ... (date) in ... (month/season of the year)	and would welcome the chance to and would welcome the opportunity to and would be delighted to	speak to you personally meet you personally call at your office		
			and would be available for interview	at ... (time) at any time between ... (time/date) and ... (time/date) on ... (date) at any time then at any time during that period		

6	Polite ending	Hoping to hear from you soon I/We very much look forward to receiving your reply to my/our application I/We hope to hear from you at your earliest convenience Many thanks in advance for your attention to my application I/We very much hope you will view this application favourably A prompt reply to this application would be most appreciated			
7	Enclosure(s)	CV Qualifications Letter(s) of recommendation Testimonial(s)			

Principal's Offer of Agency

1	Reference to application for agency	Thank you for Many thanks for I refer to In reply to We were delighted to receive	your letter/ fax/ e-mail dated/of …	in which you	apply for the position of agent for our company in … (territory) express an interest in acting as our agent in … (territory) enquire about the post of agent for our company in … (territory) enquire about an agency in … (territory)
		Thank you for the above-mentioned letter/fax/ e-mail			
	– recommendation	Your name has been given to us by … (name), who You have been recommended to us by … (name), who	tells us that has written to tell us that	you are looking for an agency in … (territory) you might be interested in acting on our behalf in … (territory) you wish to market … (products) in the … (location,e. g. London) area you are looking for an agency for … (goods) in the … (location) area	
		… (name of person/company)			
	– source of agent's address	We have seen your advertisement in the … (publication) and note With reference to your advertisement in the … (publication) we note We have learned from … (source, e. g. the a. Chamber of Commerce in Adelaide) We note from the Bayernbank's "Trade Bulletins" When talking to our Ms/Mr … (name) at the (recent) … (event,.e. g. Las Vegas Shoe Convention) you mentioned			that you are looking for a position as agent for a company in the … trade/business that you are interested in obtaining an agency for … (goods/services, e. g. ladies' fashionwear) in … (location) that you might be interested in acting as our agent in … (location)

2	Description of your company	We are a	major leading well-established well-known successful fast-growing	manufacturer of … producer of … distributor of … wholesaler of … supplier of …	and are a household name in the field of … (e.g. machine tools, data-processing equipment etc.) and have an annual turnover well in excess of … (figure, e.g. 5 million euros) and have • an extensive / • a highly efficient / • a highly successful distribution network	
3	Description of the sort of agent you require	We need someone who is We are looking for someone who is		highly motivated conscientious experienced well-mannered well-educated efficient flexible dynamic innovative imaginative reliable honest trustworthy	and knows a lot about and is acquainted with and has a sound knowledge of	the local market local market trends local business practices this type of product our product line our range of products this field this market segment
		The person we have in mind should be The right person for the job would be He or she would need to be			and know a lot about and be (well) acquainted with and have a sound knowledge of	
		This post requires This position pre-supposes		a high degree of a great deal of a great amount of a significant amount of	motivation conscientiousness experience efficiency flexibility dynamism innovation imagination reliability honesty trustworthiness	on the part of the agent

4	Request for (more) information on the agent's market*	We would also like you to provide us with details of Please let us have some information on	your projected sales figures the level of turnover you expect to achieve the amount of business you would expect to do on our behalf		
			the type of goods you would be able to sell the nature of the goods required	Do you require Would you be obtaining orders for Would you be passing on orders for	first-class goods (or) low-priced goods (or) modestly priced goods (or) mass-market articles, etc.?
			potential customers the type of customers you expect to obtain	Would they be	small businesses (or) medium-sized businesses (or) large companies (or) companies employing at least ... (number) people (or) major concerns (or) multinational companies (or) skilled workers (or) manual workers (or) the upper/middle/lower income bracket, professional people, etc.?
		We must also know whether you represent any other companies with similar products/lines			
5	Request for (more) references/ information*	Please let us have the name(s) of	• a/two/three referee(s) • a company that is willing to provide you with a reference		
		We would be grateful if you would also provide us with the names of two companies whose interests you have represented			
		We would like to take up your offer of a list of your most recent major customers and would ask you to send it to us so we can contact them			
		Please let us have the names and addresses of the two major concerns you have been representing for the past few years			
		Before we are able to make you a concrete offer, we would require the names and addresses of two major referees			
		Please let us have authenticated/notarised copies of all your qualifications and certificates			
		We would also require an authenticated/a notarised copy of your ... (document, e.g. engineering qualifications, membership of the Freight Forwarders' Association)			
		Please let us have a more comprehensive CV (without omissions), indicating in more detail what companies you have represented			
		Please fill in the application form enclosed			
		Please let us have your CV and a recent passport photograph			

6 Arrange an interview	We note that you are available for interview on … (date) Would you be able to attend an interview on … (date) at … (time) ? A company representative will be visiting … (location) in the near future and would welcome the opportunity of meeting you personally Our Ms/Mr Brandt will be in the … (location, e. g. Munich) area from … (date) to … (date) and would very much like to meet you Please phone Mr/Ms Bergmann in the Personnel Department on … (telephone number) to arrange an appointment You will appreciate that as there has been more than one application for this post only the successful candidate's expenses will be refunded Any expenses incurred when attending the interview will be refunded by us in full on presentation of the original receipts Our company is willing to cover your expenses for this interview on presentation of the original receipts Your travel and accommodation expenses will be refunded on presentation of the original receipts Only travel to and from the interview and accommodation expenses for one night at the … Hotel will be refunded We enclose directions to … (location, e. g. the hotel, our premises, our office in Berlin) We have booked a room for you at the … Hotel (see hotel map enclosed) for … (date) We enclose a return train/airline ticket from … (location) to … (location). Please take a taxi to our office from the airport/ Our driver will meet you at the airport	
	Please let us know Would you (therefore) please let us know	if this suits you if you can come if you will be available then whether you are able to attend an interview on this date whether you are available for interview at this time whether you will be able to meet our representative then whether this appointment is convenient for you
7 Polite ending	We look forward to hearing from you in the near future We look forward to meeting you personally on … (date) Your application will be progressed as soon as the documents requested have been supplied to us Your application will be progressed as soon as your references have been taken up	
8 Enclosures	Application Form (Hotel) Map Train/Airline ticket	

Agent's Correspondence with Principal

1 Reference to account sales	I enclose my account sales (a/s)	for … (period of time, e.g. January, the quarter ending March 31) for the last month/quarter			
	My account sales				is enclosed together with my latest orders for this period
	I enclose the above-mentioned account sales				
2 Explanation of good sales figures*	… and wish to point out that … and would point out that You will no doubt notice that	the figures my sales figures the results turnover demand	is/are has/have been	good (most) promising above average higher than expected unusually good very good excellent	for this time of year for this type of product for this line under the circumstances in view of the stiff competition
	… because of … as a result of … owing to … as a consequence of	the highly successful advertising campaign the use of telesales to contact potential customers a most successful series of mail shots aimed at prospective buyers the use of the new, highly attractive packaging good after-sales service our good pricing policy			
	because due to the fact that	both the quality and the price are right we have an edge over our competitors as regards • quality • service • advertising • speed of delivery			
– poor sales figures*	… and wish to point out that … and would point out that You will no doubt have noticed that	demand interest in your products turnover sales the sales figures		has/have fallen has/have not increased (significantly) has/have been slack is/are • low • slightly lower • below average • somewhat lower than usual • lower than usual • disappointing	because of … as a result of … owing to … as a consequence of …

	... the recession ... the high level of unemployment in this area ... a general downturn in the business cycle ... a general lack of purchasing power ... a chronic lack of demand for these products ... a lack of advertising ... a number of unfortunate problems with this line ... the poor quality of the last batch of products supplied ... the fact that our competitors have brought out a cheaper product ... the fact that these products are over-priced		which has had a direct effect on sales which has reduced turnover which has made regular customers more cautious than usual which has changed spending habits in this market	
	... the weather ... the ... (details, e.g. rail) strike ... my unfortunate illness/accident ... (details)		which made it difficult for me to visit the same number of customers as usual which made it impossible for me to get any new orders for ... (period of time, e.g. a week)	
3 Reference to customers' praise*	Some customers Several customers A number of my customers	have said that have told me that have commented that have made a point of saying that	they are very pleased with they are most satisfied with they are highly satisfied with they are delighted by	the products supplied your products the quality of service they have received the after-sales service the advice they have received
– complaints*			they are unhappy with they are not happy with they are displeased with they are dissatisfied with they are not satisfied with they are disappointed by	
	I enclose their letters/faxes/e-mails Their letters/faxes/e-mails are enclosed		for your information	
4 Agent's request(s) regarding goods*: – improved product(s)	As regards (the) ... (name of product) As far as the ... (name of product) is concerned	I think we should I think it would be a good idea to I feel it would be advisable to might I suggest that we	improve the quality (of ... (details, e.g. the materials used)) spend more money on ... (details, e.g. the finish) use a better/more powerful/more efficient/quieter ... (details, e.g. motor) pay more attention to (the) quality (of the ... (details, e.g. paintwork) up-date our ... (e.g. teenagers') fashions/range/collection re-think our entire ... (details, e.g. women's fashion) line	

– new product(s)	introduce a new line introduce a new product offer a new range of products in line with current demand bring out an entirely new selection of goods to keep pace with changing market trends				
– lower prices	I recommend I would suggest	lowering reducing decreasing	the price(s) our rates our price(s) our charges	by … % (e. g. 5 %) slightly a little somewhat considerably significantly	in order to win back customers to gain an edge over our competitors if we are to re-establish ourselves in the local market if we are to gain a foothold in the local market
		(that) we	lower reduce decrease		
– fast delivery	We should speed up delivery Deliveries must be carried out more quickly / more speedily / more promptly Every effort must be made to deliver promptly / on schedule / on time / by the date stated without fail / as promised I feel that it is vital for the goods to be delivered within the period stated, since any delay makes a very bad impression upon my customers and may encourage them to go elsewhere				
– larger / smaller quantity of goods required	Please In future I would ask you to Please make sure that you I would be grateful if you would In view of current demand please		send me supply me with	more … (details, e. g. advertising material / spare parts) … (figure, e. g. 1,000) instead of … (figure, e. g. 500) units of … (product / item) a much larger quantity of … (details, e. g. summer lines) less … (details [uncountable noun], e. g. motor oil) fewer … (details [countable noun], e. g. outsize articles) only half / a third of / a quarter of the number of … (details, e. g. conference tables)	
– better packing	Better packing is essential / vital The quality of the packaging material used must be improved In view of the amount of damage to the goods in transit, please make sure that the goods are packed better in future A number of customers have complained about poor packing. Please bear this in mind when attending to my orders in future The packaging used is obviously inadequate so I would urgently request you to use better material(s)				

5 Agent's requests regarding the agency agreement:	On the matter of As regards With reference to May I point out in connection with	our agency agreement … my contract … the terms of the agency agreement … clause … (number of clause, e.g. 12c) of our agency agreement … the clause concerning … (details, e.g. remuneration) in my contract … our arrangements, as stated in the agency agreement, regarding liability in the event of a customer cancelling his order …	
– more commission	In view of my performance to date In view of my sales figures Given the fact that I have out-performed all other agents in this territory As I have increased sales by … % (e.g. 50 %) Since I have doubled/trebled/quadrupled sales Since I have increased sales fourfold/fivefold/sixfold etc.		I feel it is time for us to reconsider my commission rate I believe that I am now entitled to a rise in commission I would like us to review the amount of commission I am to be paid on sales in future I would like … % (e.g. 10 %) more commission on my orders in future
	I think it is now time we reviewed my commission rate I think it is now time my commission rate were reviewed		
– change in territory	As my territory is	very small small small in comparison to those of other agents of only average size of below average size	I feel it should be extended I would like it to be merged with that of … (name of other agent, e.g. Mr Bown's) I would like it to be re-defined I believe the boundaries should be re-drawn I would like the boundaries to be reviewed
		too large for me to handle alone rather large extremely large for one person very extensive one of the biggest in the area	I feel it should be decreased in size I would like it to be split up into 2 (3) smaller units I would like it to be reduced by … % (e.g. 20 %) I would like to pass the … (name of area, e.g. the area beyond the Rhine) on to someone else
	I have now been working this territory for 5 years and feel that I am now entitled to a better/larger one Having made the very best of this thinly populated territory for the past … years I would now like to be given one with more market potential. The one I have in mind is in … (location)		
– improved advertising	I believe I should be given more money for advertising I am not allowed enough money on advertising My advertising budget should/must be increased by … % Far more money should be spent on advertising this product We should be putting as much money into advertising as our competitors Only when (significantly) more money is spent on advertising will there be any improvement in sales		

	An advertising campaign must be launched for this product There will be no major improvement in sales until we have spent a great deal more on advertising I wish to be given permission to commission an advertising agency to market this product in the media Without proper advertising this product will never get off the ground		
– extension of the agreement	In view of the encouraging sales figures As my sales figures have been above average As there is a growing market for these products	I would like my contract to be extended please extend the agency agreement I would request you to extend the agency agreement	for another … (period of time, e.g. two years) for a further … (period of time, e.g. two years) until … (+ date, e.g. 31 December ..) automatically (for a further year) at the end of each year in future
– termination of the agreement	As there is little demand for goods of this nature As demand for these products is now falling In view of the lack of interest in this type of product Since the market has been flooded with similar goods at much lower prices As I will be 65 years old this time next year As I am approaching retirement age	I wish to terminate my contract with you I must terminate our agency agreement I have no alternative but to terminate our agency agreement	as of … (date, e.g. 31 December ..) with effect from … (date) on expiry of the agreed notice period of … months
6 Polite ending	I look forward to hearing from you in the near future I look forward to your comments on this matter I trust I will be hearing from you in the (very) near future May I take this opportunity to express my appreciation of our good business relations over the past (… e.g. five) years I wish you all the best in the future and will most certainly remain in touch I feel that taking this step is the best for all concerned and wish you all the best in the future		
7 Enclosure(s)	Letter(s)/Fax(es)/E-mail(s) from customer(s) etc.		

Principal's Correspondence with Agent

1 Reference to account sales*	Thank you for We have received We are in receipt of With reference to	your account sales	for the quarter ending … (date, e.g. 31 March) for the last quarter for the past month for the period from … (date) to … (date)
		the above-mentioned account sales	

2 Praise*	We are pleased to see that We are most gratified to see that We note with pleasure that We were pleased to note that	our … (product, e.g. DTYD bottle opener) has been selling well there has been considerable interest in our … (product, e.g. TW3 power supply) sales of … (product) have gone up you have obtained a large number of orders for … (product) demand for (the) … (product, e.g. the TW3 power supply) has increased considerably/substantially/significantly you have increased sales of … (product) there has been a significant increase in the number of orders for … (product)	
– criticism*	We were disappointed to note that We find it regrettable that We note with dismay that We fail to understand why We are at a loss to understand why	you have been unable to obtain (m)any orders for (the) … (product) sales of (the) … (product, e.g. the DTYD bottle opener) have decreased/gone down/fallen/dropped sharply no/hardly any orders have been placed for (the) … (product) demand for (the) … (product) has slackened/decreased/has been falling steadily • since + point in time • for + period of time	
	We must tell you that We regret to inform you that	there have been a number of complaints about	the quality of your advice to customers your lack of punctuality your manner with customers your appearance the frequency of your visits to customers the quality of the service offered
		your sales figures for … (period, e.g. the last month) are the volume of orders for the last quarter is	unsatisfactory disappointing unexpectedly low below average … % (e.g. 20 %) lower than last year/than your predecessor's
	We have (now) found out that We have discovered that It has come to our notice that	you are frequently unpunctual you have been impolite to some of our customers you have an abrasive manner with some of our customers you have not been trying hard enough to obtain orders for (the … (product)) you are spending too little time with customers you have not been giving our customers enough information about our latest products your records are not up-to-date your paperwork is inaccurate you have not been up-dating our customer database as agreed you have not been visiting customers in more remote areas frequently enough	

3 Reference to customers' praise*	We were pleased to learn that We were delighted to learn that	(your) customers are pleased with your/our service/your advice/ our products our products have been well received our products are enjoying considerable popularity sales of our … (product, e.g. new teenagers' lines) have been brisk	
– reference to customers' criticisms*	Your/your customers' criticisms regarding … (details) Please tell your customers that their criticisms	have been noted and will be acted upon will be responded to in full • in the near future • in due course will be dealt with as soon as possible have been taken extremely seriously and will be attended to as soon as possible	
4 Principal's comments regarding goods: – improved product(s)	We will be improving (the quality of) the … (details, e.g. materials used)	in the near future in the next production run as from … (date)	
	The budget allocation for … (details, e.g. paintwork)	has been increased has been raised will be increased	significantly considerably substantially
	We will be allocating more resources to … (details, e.g. quality control) We have decided to allocate more resources to … (details)	as from … (date)	Please make sure that your customers are informed of this
	The … (details, e.g. TW3 model) has now been up-dated and will be on the market in the very near future We have now brought out a new, improved version of the … (details, e.g. TW3 power unit), which no longer has any of its predecessor's faults Our entire range of … (details, e.g. sewing machines) has been up-dated and is now better value for money and more competitively priced		
– new product(s)	We will be bringing out a new product … (date/time , e.g. next month) Our new product/model, the 49C Scanner and Plain Paper Copier, will be available as from … (date) We are currently in the process of designing a(n entirely) new model, which will incorporate all the features of its predecessor(s) together with many important new ones		
	We will unfortunately not be able to bring out a(ny) new product(s) this year and would advise you to do your best to sell off old stocks (by offering discounts) Please make sure you sell the TW3 power unit before you tell our customers about the TW4 model		

– change(s) in price	There will be no change in price for the next … (period of time, e.g, 3 months) We anticipate that prices will remain stable for the next … (period of time, e. g. 6 weeks) The new price list will come into effect as from … (date) There will be a 2 % price rise … (date, e. g. in January) Please let your customers know that we will only be able to keep to current prices as long as stocks last As a result of the increase in the price of … (e. g. raw materials, computer chips, labour) we are forced to raise our prices by … % as from … (date) Make sure you encourage your customers to place their orders before … (date/time, e. g. Christmas) because we intend to raise our prices in/on … (period of time/date)			
– delivery	Please make it clear when taking your customers' orders that delivery will take at least … (period, e. g. 6 weeks) Your customers should be told from the start that we require at least … (period, e. g. a month) for delivery We are now using a new freight forwarder/road haulier/shipping company/airline, which should have the effect of cutting down delivery time As we have been flooded/overwhelmed with orders for this product it will take some time to fill customers' orders. Please tell them we are doing our best to catch up on the backlog			
– quantity	In future, please indicate (to the nearest hundred/dozen/ten units) how many … (details, e. g. starter motors) you require We have to send you these goods in batches of … (number, e. g. 20, a dozen) because they are packed in this way Please let us know, when indenting for new stocks, whether you require 5, 10 or 20 litre drums/10, 20 or 50 kilo sacks/large, medium or small sizes In future we will always supply you with the minimum/maximum number of goods it is economic to transport			
– packing	We will ensure that the goods are better packed in future As the goods are well packed in our works we can only assume that the damage you mention must have been caused by rough handling/in transit If we use better packing material this will increase the price by … %. Please make sure your customers are told this before they place their orders If we pack the goods in … (material, e. g. polystyrene, AE: styrofoam) and not … (material, e. g. corrugated cardboard) this will increase the price by … Please explain this to your customers when they order			
5 Principal's comments regarding the agency agreement: – change in commission rate	In view of your (latest) sales figures In view of your improved sales figures for the last … (period of time, e. g. 6 months) On the basis of your recent performance	we are prepared to we are willing to	increase your commission by … % raise your commission rate to … % grant an extra … % commission	if you keep up this level of performance if it/performance is sustained if you keep it up over the next … (period, e. g. 3 months)

<table>
<tr><td></td><td>As sales have remained steady but not improved
Since there has been no noticeable improvement in your sales figures for the last … (period , e.g. 3 months)
In view of your disappointing sales figures for our … (details, e.g. new line(s))</td><td>we are unable to increase your commission rate
there can be no question of raising your commission for the time being/at present
we must delay any review of your commission rate until there has been a noticeable improvement</td></tr>
<tr><td></td><td colspan="2">All commission rates are reviewed once a year. We would ask you, therefore, to wait until next January
The agency agreement clearly states that the commission rate is fixed for an initial period of… (period). It can only be reviewed after this time has elapsed</td></tr>
<tr><td>– change in territory</td><td>We have re-examined your territory as requested and
We have studied your request regarding a change in the boundaries of your territory and
As far as re-drawing your territory is concerned we
As regards your request for a new territory we</td><td>have decided that
are of the opinion that
have come to the conclusion that</td></tr>
<tr><td></td><td colspan="2">… there is no reason to re-define it
… there is no reason to change it
… it should/must be made smaller/larger
… it should be downsized/extended
… it should be scaled down
… it would be a good idea to include/exclude the … area (details, e.g. the area to the north of the Thames)
… it should be merged/amalgamated with the adjacent territory, which will become vacant in … (time, e.g. 6 months') time
… it should be increased/reduced by (approximately) … (amount, e.g. 25 %, a quarter, a third)
… it must/should be divided up into/split into … (number, e.g. two) parts (of equal size)
… you should now be given a larger/more challenging/new/different one (territory)</td></tr>
<tr><td>– change in advertising allowance</td><td>Your request for a larger advertising allowance
Your application for an increase in your advertising budget
Your request for extra funds for advertising purposes
Your application for a rise in commission to cover expenditure on advertising</td><td>has been/is being considered
has been given consideration
will be reviewed in due course/in the near future
will be considered as soon as possible</td></tr>
<tr><td></td><td>We feel that
We have decided that
We are of the opinion that
We have come to the conclusion that</td><td>an extra … (amount) should be enough
an increase of … (amount, e.g. 10 %, $1,000) (to the amount already allocated) should/will be sufficient
an(y) increase in your advertising budget will not be possible
• before … (date, e.g. 1 January)
• for … (period, e.g. the next 3 months)</td></tr>
</table>

– extension of the agreement	As Since	we are pleased with your work/performance/ sales figures (your) sales (figures) are/have been encouraging your sales figures are/have been above average there is a growing market for these products your performance during the trial period has been (highly) satisfactory	we are prepared to we are willing to we intend to	extend your contract extend the agency agreement	by + period of time (e.g. one year) until + date (e.g. December 31)
– termination of the agreement	As Since In view of the fact that	sales have been poor your sales figures are (most) disappointing you have managed to sell very little over the past … (period of time, e.g. 3 months) you have had little success with our lines/products/ goods you have rendered a disappointing account sales (for the second/third etc. time) you will be 65 years old on … (date)		we must we feel it is in our mutual interest to we have no alternative but to	
	terminate your contract terminate the agency agreement		as of … (date, e.g. 31 December ..) with effect from … (date) on expiry of the agreed notice period of … months		
6 Polite ending	Your contribution to our company's success in your market has most certainly not gone unnoticed. Well done and keep up the good work! We are grateful for the hard work you have put in for our company and look forward to the pleasure of working with you in the future May we take this opportunity to express our appreciation of our enjoyable and mutually rewarding business relations over the past (… e.g. five) years We wish you all the best in the future and most certainly hope that you will remain in touch We feel that taking this step is the best for all concerned and wish you all the best in the future We are certain that you will be successful again in the future and wish you all the very best				
7 Enclosure(s)	Letter(s)/Fax(es)/E-mail(s) from customer(s)				

Application for Agency

1	Source of address + application for agency	*Anschriftenquelle + Bewerbung um Vertretung*
	– solicited application*	*– verlangte Bewerbung**
	I am writing in reply to your advertisement in *JobSearch Weekly* dated 1 February .. regarding the post of agent for your company in Northern Germany	*Ich schreibe in Beantwortung Ihrer Anzeige im* JobSearch Weekly *vom 1. Februar .. bezüglich der Stelle des Vertreters / der Vertreterin für Ihre Firma in Norddeutschland*
	I am writing in connection with the above-mentioned offer of an agency in Northern Germany	*Ich schreibe in Verbindung mit dem obengenannten Angebot einer Vertretung in Norddeutschland*
	I wish to apply for the post of agent for your company in North-Rhine Westphalia	*Ich möchte mich um die Stelle als Vertreter / Vertreterin für Ihre Firma in Nordrhein-Westfalen bewerben*
	– unsolicited application*	*– unverlangte Bewerbung**
	I was most interested to see your company's products at the Ideal Home Exhibition in London and feel sure that they would sell well here in Germany	*Ich habe die Produkte Ihrer Firma auf der Ideal Home-Ausstellung in London mit großem Interesse angesehen und bin sicher, dass sie sich hier in Deutschland gut verkaufen würden*
	Have you considered appointing an agent to handle your sales here?	*Haben Sie schon in Betracht gezogen, einen Vertreter / eine Vertreterin zu ernennen, um Ihre Verkäufe hier durchzuführen?*
	Have you considered appointing an agent to act on your behalf in Bavaria?	*Haben Sie schon darüber nachgedacht, einen Vertreter / eine Vertreterin zu ernennen, die für Sie in Bayern tätig ist?*
2	Description of yourself / your company	*Beschreibung Ihrer Person / Gesellschaft*
	– experience*	*– Erfahrung**
	I have considerable experience of this market having worked in the fashion trade for the last 10 years	*Ich habe beträchtliche Erfahrung in diesem Markt, da ich in den letzten 10 Jahren in der Modebranche tätig gewesen bin*
	I have 5 years' experience in the field of mechanical engineering so I am well acquainted with these products	*Ich habe 5 Jahre Erfahrung auf dem Gebiet des Maschinenbaus, so dass ich mit diesen Produkten gut vertraut bin*
	My company has a staff of 12 highly qualified sales personnel who keep abreast of the latest developments	*Meine Firma verfügt über eine Belegschaft von 12 hochqualifizierten Verkäufer/innen, die mit den letzten Entwicklungen auf dem Laufenden sind*

	– sales contacts*	*– Verkaufskontakte**
	We have extensive business contacts in the territory you have in mind	*Wir haben umfangreiche Geschäftskontakte in dem Gebiet, an das Sie denken*
	My company has distribution centres in all the major German cities	*Meine Firma unterhält Vertriebszentren in allen größeren deutschen Städten*
	We have sold a large number of goods in this field	*Wir haben eine große Menge Waren in diesem Bereich verkauft*
	My employees have always achieved above-average sales figures in the local market	*Meine Angestellten haben auf dem örtlichen Markt stets überdurchschnittliche Verkaufszahlen erreicht*
	– personal qualities*	*– persönliche Eigenschaften**
	I am a success-oriented marketing expert and would welcome the chance to represent your interests	*Ich bin ein erfolgsorientierter Marketingexperte und würde die Gelegenheit begrüßen, Ihre Interessen zu vertreten*
	We are a dedicated company with a staff of 15 and would be only too pleased to open up the market for you here	*Wir sind eine engagierte Firma mit einer Belegschaft von 15 Leuten und würden uns sehr freuen, hier den Markt für Sie zu erschliessen*
	– qualifications / recommendations*	*– Qualifikationen / Empfehlungen**
	All my staff have a recognised qualification in marketing (see enclosures)	*Mein gesamtes Personal hat eine anerkannte Marketingqualifikation (siehe Anlagen)*
	I attended the University of Tübingen where I obtained a degree in economics	*Ich habe an der Universität Tübingen studiert, wo ich das Examen in Wirtschaftswissenschaften ablegte*
	My CV is enclosed	*Mein Lebenslauf ist beigefügt*
3	Interest in sole agency / del credere*	*Interesse an Allein- / Delkredere-Vertretung**
	I would be very interested in being your sole agent in Lower Saxony and would be prepared to assume the del credere for my customers	*Ich wäre sehr daran interessiert, Ihr/e Alleinvertreter/in in Niedersachsen zu werden und wäre bereit, das Delkredere für meine Kunden zu übernehmen*
	Do you require someone to be your sole agent for Lower Saxony and assume the del credere for the customers obtained there?	*Brauchen Sie jemanden als Alleinvertreter/in für Niedersachsen, der/die das Delkredere für die dort erworbenen Kunden übernimmt?*
	As my customers are reliable companies I would be glad to assume the del credere for all contracts obtained	*Da meine Kunden verlässliche Firmen sind, wäre ich gern bereit, das Delkredere für alle erworbenen Verträge zu übernehmen*
	… if you are able to pay a del credere commission at a suitable rate	*… wenn Sie in der Lage sind, eine Delkredere-Provision zu einem geeigneten Satz zu zahlen*

4	**Reference(s)**	***Referenz(en)***
	Should you require references please contact Designer Mode GmbH in Gelsenkirchen, who will be pleased to supply you with any information you may desire	*Sollten Sie Referenzen benötigen, treten Sie bitte mit der Designer Mode GmbH in Gelsenkirchen in Verbindung, die Ihnen gern jede Information, die Sie möglicherweise wünschen, zur Verfügung stellen wird*
	We will be happy to provide you with the usual bank and trade references	*Wir geben Ihnen gern die üblichen Bank- und Handelsreferenzen*
5	**Availability for interview**	***Für ein Gespräch zur Verfügung stehen***
	I am available for interview at any time during the next three weeks	*Ich stehen Ihnen jederzeit während der nächsten drei Wochen für ein Vorstellungsgespräch zur Verfügung*
	I am available for interview at a week's notice	*Ich stehe Ihnen für ein Vorstellungsgespräch gerne zur Verfügung, wenn Sie mich den Termin eine Woche vorher wissen lassen*
	I will be visiting Neasden plc on February 28 .. and would welcome the chance to speak to you personally	*Ich werde am 28. Februar .. die Neasden plc besuchen und würde die Gelegenheit begrüßen, mit Ihnen persönlich zu sprechen*
	I will be attending the Birmingham Car Show in the spring and would welcome the opportunity of meeting you personally	*Ich werde im Frühling die Autoausstellung in Birmingham besuchen und würde Sie bei dieser Gelegenheit gerne persönlich treffen*
6	**Polite ending**	***Höflicher Schluss***
	I very much look forward to receiving your reply to my application	*Ich freue mich darauf, von Ihnen eine Antwort auf meine Bewerbung zu erhalten*
	I very much hope you will view this application favourably	*Ich hoffe sehr, dass Sie diese Bewerbung wohlwollend prüfen*
7	**Enclosure(s)**	***Anlage(n)***
	CV	*Lebenslauf*
	Qualifications	*Qualifikationen*
	Letter(s) of recommendation	*Empfehlungsschreiben*
	Testimonial(s)	*Zeugnis(se)*

Principal's Offer of Agency

1	Reference to application for agency	*Bezugnahme auf Bewerbung um eine Vertretung*
	Thank your for your letter of 28 January .., in which you apply for the position of agent for our company in Baden-Württemberg	*Vielen Dank für Ihren Brief vom 28. Januar .., in dem Sie sich um die Stelle eines Vertreters / einer Vertreterin für unsere Gesellschaft in Baden-Württemberg bewerben*
	Thank you for the above-mentioned fax in which you express an interest in acting as our agent in south Germany	*Vielen Dank für das oben erwähnte Fax, in welchem Sie Interesse daran bekunden, als unsere Vertreter/in in Süddeutschland tätig zu sein*
	– recommendation	*– Empfehlung*
	You have been recommended to us by Herr Heinrich Schulz, who has written to tell us that you are looking for an agency in the Berlin area	*Sie wurden uns von Herrn Heinrich Schulz empfohlen, der uns schriftlich mitgeteilt hat, dass Sie eine Vertretung im Raum Berlin suchen*
	– source of agent's address	*– Quelle der Anschrift des Vertreters / der Vertreterin*
	We have seen your advertisement in the *Marketing Weekly* and note that you are looking for a position as agent for a company in the sportswear business	*Wir haben Ihre Anzeige im* Marketing Weekly *gesehen und stellen fest, dass Sie eine Stelle als Vertreter/in für eine Firma im Sportbekleidungsgeschäft suchen*
	We have learned from the Chamber of Commerce in Adelaide that you might be interested in acting as our agent in South Australia	*Wir haben von der Handelskammer in Adelaide erfahren, dass Sie vielleicht daran interessiert sind, als unser/e Vertreter/in in Südaustralien tätig zu werden*
2	Description of your company	*Beschreibung Ihrer Gesellschaft*
	We are a major manufacturer of water filters and are a household name in the field of biological appliances	*Wir sind ein größerer Hersteller von Wasserfiltern und auf dem Gebiet biologischer Geräte ein Begriff*
	We are a well-known wholesaler of food processors and have an extensive distribution network with agents throughout Northern Europe	*Wir sind ein bekannter Großhändler für Küchenmaschinen und verfügen über ein weitreichendes Vertriebsnetz mit Vertretern in ganz Nordeuropa*
3	Description of the sort of agent you require	*Beschreibung der Art des/der von Ihnen benötigten Vertreters / Vertreterin*
	We are looking for someone who is highly motivated and has a sound knowledge of the local market	*Wir suchen nach jemandem, der hoch motiviert ist und über eine fundierte Kenntnis des örtlichen Marktes verfügt*

	The person we have in mind should be flexible and know a lot about our range of products	*Die Person, an die wir denken, sollte flexibel sein und eine Menge über unsere Produktpalette wissen*
	This post requires a great amount of experience on the part of the agent	*Diese Stelle erfordert eine große Menge Erfahrung seitens des Vertreters / der Vertreterin*
4	**Request for (more) information on the agent's market***	***Bitte um (mehr) Informationen über den Markt des Vertreters / der Vertreterin****
	We would also like you to provide us with details of your projected sales figures	*Wir möchten auch, dass Sie uns Einzelheiten Ihrer geplanten Verkaufszahlen liefern*
	Please let us have information on the type of goods you would be able to sell	*Bitte lassen Sie uns Informationen über die Art der Waren, die Sie verkaufen könnten, zukommen*
	Would you be obtaining orders for first-class goods or mass-market articles?	*Würden Sie Aufträge für erstklassige Güter oder Massenartikel einholen?*
	Please let us have some information on the type of customers you expect to obtain	*Bitte lassen Sie uns Informationen über die Art der Kunden zukommen, die Sie gewinnen wollen*
	Would they be small businesses or major concerns?	*Würden dies kleine Geschäfte oder größere Konzerne sein?*
	We must also know whether you represent any other companies with similar lines	*Wir müssen auch wissen, ob Sie irgendwelche andere Firmen mit ähnlichen Produktserien vertreten*
5	**Request for references / information***	***Bitte um Referenzen / Informationen****
	We would be grateful if you would also provide us with the names of two companies whose interests you have represented	*Wir wären Ihnen dankbar, wenn Sie uns auch Namen von zwei Firmen zukommen ließen, deren Interessen Sie vertreten haben*
	Please let us have your CV and a recent passport photograph	*Bitte schicken Sie uns Ihren Lebenslauf und ein neueres Passfoto*
6	**Arrange an interview**	***Vereinbaren Sie ein Vorstellungsgespräch***
	We note that you are available for interview on 28 February ..	*Wir entnehmen Ihrem Brief, dass Sie am 28. Februar .. für ein Vorstellungsgespräch zur Verfügung stehen*
	A company representative will be visiting Brighton in the near future and would welcome the opportunity of meeting you personally	*Ein Firmenvertreter wird in nächster Zeit nach Brighton kommen und würde Sie bei dieser Gelegenheit gerne persönlich kennenlernen*
	Please phone Ms Bergmann in the Personnel Department on +49 201 9270756 to arrange an appointment	*Bitte rufen Sie Frau Bergmann in der Personalabteilung unter +49-2 01-9 27 07 56 an, um einen Termin zu vereinbaren*

	Your travel and accommodation expenses will be refunded on presentation of the original receipts	*Ihre Reise- und Unterbringungskosten werden bei Vorlage der Original-quittungen erstattet*
	Please let us know whether you are able to attend an interview on this date	*Bitte teilen Sie uns mit, ob Sie an diesem Tag zu einem Vorstellungsgespräch kommen können*
7	Polite ending	*Höflicher Schluss*
	We look forward to hearing from you in the near future	*Wir freuen uns darauf, bald von Ihnen zu hören*
	Your application will be progressed as soon as your references have been taken up	*Ihre Bewerbung wird bearbeitet, sobald wir Ihre Referenzen eingeholt haben*
8	Enclosure(s)	*Anlage(n)*
	Application Form Hotel Map, Map Train / Airline Ticket	*Bewerbungsformular* *Hotelplan, Stadtplan* *Zugfahrkarte / Flugticket*

Agent's Correspondence with Principal

1	Reference to account sales*	*Bezugnahme auf Verkaufsabrechnung**
	I enclose my account sales (a/s) for the quarter ending March 31 ..	*Ich füge meine Verkaufsabrechnung für das am 31. März .. endende Quartal bei*
2	Explanation of good sales figures*	*Erklärung für gute Verkaufszahlen**
	... and wish to point out that the figures are good for this time of year	*... und möchte darauf hinweisen, dass die Zahlen für diese Jahreszeit gut sind*
	You will no doubt notice that turnover has been above average in view of the stiff competition	*Sie werden zweifellos feststellen, dass der Umsatz angesichts der starken Konkur-renz überdurchschnittlich gewesen ist*
	... because of the highly successful advertising campaign	*... wegen der höchst erfolgreichen Werbekampagne*
	... as a result of the use of telesales to contact potential customers	*... als Ergebnis des Einsatzes des Tele-verkaufs, um potentielle Kunden zu kontaktieren*
	... owing to a most successful series of mail shots aimed at prospective buyers	*... auf Grund einer höchst erfolgreichen Serie von Postwurfsendungen, die auf potentielle Kunden abzielten*
	... due to the fact that we have an edge over our competitors as regards service	*... auf Grund der Tatsache, dass wir unseren Konkurrenten im Hinblick auf den Service voraus sind*

	– poor sales figures*	– *schlechte Verkaufszahlen**
	... and wish to point out that the sales figures are somewhat lower than usual as a consequence of the poor quality of the last batch of products supplied	*... und möchte darauf hinweisen, dass die Umsatzzahlen als Folge der schlechten Qualität der letzten Partie gelieferter Waren etwas niedriger waren als gewöhnlich*
	... and would point out that demand has fallen because of the recession which has had a direct effect on sales	*... und würde Sie gern darauf aufmerksam machen, dass die Nachfrage wegen der Rezession, die eine direkte Auswirkung auf den Umsatz hatte, zurückgegangen ist*
	You will no doubt have noticed that interest in your products has been slack as a result of a general downturn in the business cycle, which has reduced turnover	*Sie werden zweifellos festgestellt haben, dass das Interesse an Ihren Produkten schwach war; dies ist das Ergebnis eines allgemeinen Abschwungs in der Konjunktur, welcher den Umsatz reduziert hat*
3	Reference to customers' praise*	*Bezugnahme auf Lob der Kunden**
	Some customers have said that they are very pleased with the products supplied	*Einige Kunden haben gesagt, dass sie mit den gelieferten Produkten sehr zufrieden sind*
	A number of my customers have commented that they are highly satisfied with the quality of service they have received	*Mehrere meiner Kunden haben sich dahingehend geäußert, dass sie mit der Qualität des erhaltenen Service außerordentlich zufrieden sind*
	– complaints*	– *Beschwerden**
	Several customers have told me that they are dissatisfied with the after-sales service	*Mehrere Kunden haben mir mitgeteilt, dass sie mit dem Kundendienstservice unzufrieden sind*
	I enclose their letters for your information	*Ich füge ihre Briefe zu Ihrer Information bei*
4	Agent's request(s) regarding goods*	*Bitte(n) des Vertreters / der Vertreterin bezüglich der Waren**
	– improved product(s)	– *verbessertes Produkt / verbesserte Produkte*
	As far as the H49 car mats are concerned I think we should improve the quality of the materials used	*Was die H49 Automatten betrifft, glaube ich, dass wir die Qualität der benutzten Materialien verbessern sollten*
	I think it would be a good idea to up-date our teenagers' fashionwear collection	*Ich denke, es wäre eine gute Idee, unsere Teenager-Modekollektion auf den neuesten Stand zu bringen*
	– new product(s)	– *neues Produkt / neue Produkte*
	Might I suggest that we offer a new range of products in line with current demand?	*Dürfte ich vorschlagen, dass wir eine neue Produktserie, die der aktuellen Nachfrage entspricht, anbieten?*

	– lower prices	*– niedrigere Preise*
	I recommend lowering the price by 5 % in order to win back customers	*Ich empfehle, den Preis um 5 % zu senken, um Kunden zurückzugewinnen*
	I would suggest reducing our charges somewhat to gain an edge over our competitors	*Ich würde vorschlagen, die Kosten etwas zu senken, um einen Vorteil gegenüber unseren Konkurrenten zu haben*
	– fast delivery	*– schnelle Lieferung*
	We should speed up delivery	*Wir sollten die Lieferung beschleunigen*
	Every effort must be made to deliver on schedule	*Jede Anstrengung muss unternommen werden, um planmäßig zu liefern*
	– larger / smaller quantity of goods required	*– größere / kleinere Menge der gewünschten Waren*
	Please send me fewer / more outsize articles	*Bitte schicken Sie mir weniger / mehr Artikel in Übergröße(n)*
	In future I would ask you to supply me with 1,000 instead of 500 units of article no. A77	*In Zukunft bitte ich Sie, mir 1.000 statt 500 Stück des Artikels Nr. A77 zu liefern*
	– better packing	*– bessere Verpackung*
	Better packing is vital	*Bessere Verpackung ist unbedingt erforderlich*
	In view of the amount of damage caused to the goods in transit, please make sure that the goods are packed better in future	*Angesichts der Menge von Beschädigungen an den Waren während des Transports stellen Sie bitte sicher, dass die Waren in Zukunft besser verpackt werden*
	The packaging used is obviously inadequate, so I would urgently request you to use better materials	*Die benutzte Verpackung ist offensichtlich unzureichend, so dass ich Sie dringend bitte, bessere Materialien zu verwenden*
5	Agent's requests regarding the agency agreement	*Bitten des Vertreters / der Vertreterin bezüglich des Vertretervertrages*
	On the matter of our agency agreement …	*Was unseren Vertretervertrag betrifft …*
	May I point out in connection with clause 12c of our agency agreement that …	*Darf ich im Zusammenhang mit Klausel 12c unseres Vertretervertrages darauf hinweisen, dass …*
	– more commission	*– mehr Provision*
	In view of my performance to date, I feel it is time for us to reconsider my commission rate	*Im Hinblick auf meine Leistung bis heute denke ich, ist es an der Zeit, dass wir meinen Provisionssatz überprüfen*
	Given the fact that I have outperformed all other agents in this territory, I would like us to review the amount of commission I am to be paid on sales in future	*Wenn man die Tatsache bedenkt, dass ich alle anderen Vertreter in diesem Gebiet übertroffen habe, würde ich gern die Höhe der Provision, die ich in Zukunft auf den Umsatz ausbezahlt bekomme, revidieren*

	I think it is now time we reviewed my commission rate	*Ich denke, es ist jetzt an der Zeit, dass wir meinen Provisionssatz neu festsetzen*
	– change in territory	***– Änderung im Gebiet***
	As my territory is small in comparison to those of other agents I would like it to be re-defined	*Da mein Gebiet im Vergleich zu dem anderer Vertreter klein ist, möchte ich, dass es neu festgesetzt wird*
	As my territory is too large for me to handle alone I would like it to be split up into two smaller units	*Da mein Gebiet zu groß ist, als dass ich es allein bewältigen könnte, wäre es besser, wenn es in zwei kleinere Einheiten aufgeteilt würde*
	I have now been working this territory for 5 years and feel that I am now entitled to a better one	*Ich bearbeite dieses Gebiet seit nunmehr 5 Jahren und glaube, dass ich jetzt Anspruch auf ein besseres habe*
	– improved advertising	***– verbesserte Werbung***
	My advertising budget should be increased by 25 %	*Mein Werbebudget sollte um 25 % erhöht werden*
	We should be putting as much money into advertising as our competitors	*Wir sollten so viel Geld in die Werbung stecken wie unsere Konkurrenten*
	An advertising campaign must be launched for this product	*Für dieses Produkt muss eine Werbekampagne gestartet werden*
	Without proper advertising this product will never get off the ground	*Ohne geeignete Werbung wird dieses Produkt niemals in Gang kommen*
	– extension of the agreement	***– Vertragsverlängerung***
	As my sales figures have been above average, I would request you to extend the agency agreement for a further two years	*Da meine Umsatzzahlen überdurchschnittlich waren, bitte ich, den Vertretervertrag um weitere zwei Jahre zu verlängern*
	– termination of the agreement	***– Beendigung des Vertrages***
	As demand for these products is now falling I wish to terminate my contract with you as of 31 December ..	*Da die Nachfrage nach diesen Produkten jetzt zurückgeht, möchte ich meinen Vertrag mit Ihnen zum 31. Dezember .. beenden*
	As I am approaching retirement age I must terminate our agency agreement on expiry of the agreed notice period of three months	*Da ich mich dem Rentenalter nähere, muss ich unseren Vertretervertrag nach Ablauf der vereinbarten Kündigungszeit von drei Monaten beenden*
6	**Polite ending**	***Höflicher Schluss***
	I look forward to your comments on this matter	*Ich sehe Ihrer Stellungnahme in dieser Angelegenheit gern entgegen*
	I wish you all the best in the future and will most certainly remain in touch	*Ich wünsche Ihnen in Zukunft alles Gute und werde sicherlich in Kontakt bleiben*

7	Enclosure(s)	*Anlage(n)*
	Letter(s)	*Brief(e)*
	Fax(es)	*Fax(e)*
	E-mail(s) from customer(s)	*E-Mail(s) vom (von den) Kunden*

Principal's Correspondence with Agent

1	Reference to account sales*	*Bezugnahme auf Verkaufsabrechnung**
	Thank you for your account sales for the quarter ending 31 March	*Vielen Dank für Ihre Verkaufsabrechnung für das am 31. März endende Quartal*
	We have received the above-mentioned account sales	*Wir haben die oben erwähnte Verkaufsabrechnung erhalten*
2	Praise*	*Lob**
	We are pleased to see that our DTYD bottle opener has been selling well	*Wir freuen uns festzustellen, dass unser DTYD-Flaschenöffner sich gut verkauft*
	We are most gratified to see that there has been considerable interest in our TW3 power supply	*Wir sind höchst erfreut zu sehen, dass erhebliches Interesse für unseren TW3-Netzanschluss besteht*
	We were pleased to note that you have obtained a large number of orders for our DH33 hair spray	*Wir waren erfreut festzustellen, dass Sie eine große Anzahl von Aufträgen für unser DH33-Haarspray erhalten haben*
	– criticism*	*– Kritik**
	We were disappointed to note that sales of the DTYD bottle opener have dropped sharply	*Wir waren enttäuscht festzustellen, dass die Verkäufe für den DTYD-Flaschenöffner stark gefallen sind*
	We note with dismay that hardly any orders have been placed for the DH44 hair spray	*Wir stellen mit Bestürzung fest, dass für das DH44-Haarspray kaum Aufträge erteilt worden sind*
	We regret to inform you that there have been a number of complaints about your manner with customers	*Wir bedauern Ihnen mitzuteilen, dass wir eine Anzahl von Beschwerden über Ihr Verhalten gegenüber Kunden erhalten haben*
	We regret to inform you that your sales figures for the last month are unexpectedly low	*Wir bedauern Ihnen mitzuteilen, dass Ihre Verkaufszahlen für letzten Monat unerwartet niedrig sind*
	We have now found out that you have not been trying hard enough to obtain orders for DH44 hair spray	*Wir haben nun herausgefunden, dass Sie sich nicht intensiv genug bemüht haben, Aufträge für das DH44-Haarspray zu bekommen*
	We have discovered that you have not been up-dating our customer database as agreed	*Wir haben festgestellt, dass Sie unsere Kunden-Datenbank nicht wie vereinbart auf den neuesten Stand gebracht haben*

	It has come to our notice that you have not been giving our customers enough information about our latest products	*Es ist uns mitgeteilt worden, dass Sie unseren Kunden nicht genügend Informationen über unsere neuesten Produkte gegeben haben*
3	**Reference to customers' praise***	***Bezugnahme auf Lob der Kunden****
	We were glad to learn that your customers are pleased with our service	*Es hat uns gefreut zu hören, dass Ihre Kunden mit unserem Service zufrieden sind*
	We were delighted to learn that our products are enjoying considerable popularity	*Wir haben uns gefreut zu erfahren, dass unsere Produkte sich erheblicher Popularität erfreuen*
	– reference to customers' criticisms*	***– Bezugnahme auf Kritik der Kunden****
	Your customers' criticisms regarding after-sales service have been taken extremely seriously and will be attended to as soon as possible	*Die Kritik Ihrer Kunden bezüglich des Kundendienstes ist außerordentlich ernst genommen worden; wir werden uns so bald wie möglich darum kümmern*
	Please tell your customers that their criticisms will be responded to in full in the near future	*Bitte teilen Sie Ihren Kunden mit, dass wir uns mit ihrer Kritik in nächster Zukunft intensiv beschäftigen werden*
4	**Principal's comments regarding goods**	***Stellungnahme des Prinzipals bezüglich der Waren***
	– improved product(s)	***– verbessertes Produkt / verbesserte Produkte***
	We will be improving the quality of the materials used in the next production run	*Wir werden die Qualität der benutzten Materialien im nächsten Produktionsgang verbessern*
	We will be allocating more resources to quality control as from June 30 .. . Please make sure that your customers are informed of this	*Wir werden der Qualitätskontrolle ab 30. Juni .. mehr Mittel zuteilen. Bitte stellen Sie sicher, dass Ihre Kunden hierüber informiert werden*
	We have now brought out a new, improved version of the TW3 power unit which no longer has any of its predecessor's faults	*Wir haben jetzt eine neue, verbesserte Version des TW3-Netzgerätes herausgebracht, das nicht mehr die Fehler seines Vorgängers aufweist*
	– new product(s)	***– neues Produkt / neue Produkte***
	Our new model, the 49C Scanner and Plain Paper Copier, will be available as from August 1 ..	*Unser neues Modell, der 49C Scanner und Normalpapierkopierer, wird ab 1. August .. erhältlich sein*
	We are currently in the process of designing an entirely new model which will incorporate all the features of its predecessor together with many important new ones	*Wir sind im Augenblick im Begriff, ein vollständig neues Modell zu entwerfen, das alle Merkmale seines Vorgängers zusammen mit vielen wichtigen neuen Eigenschaften beinhalten wird*

	– change(s) in price	*– Änderung(en) im Preis*
	We anticipate that prices will remain stable for the next six weeks	*Wir gehen davon aus, dass die Preise in den nächsten sechs Wochen stabil bleiben werden*
	Please let your customers know that we will only be able to keep to current prices as long as stocks last	*Bitte lassen Sie unsere Kunden wissen, dass wir die laufenden Preise nur aufrechterhalten können, solange der Vorrat reicht*
	– delivery	*– Lieferung*
	Please make it clear, when taking your customers' orders, that delivery will take at least six weeks	*Wenn Sie die Aufträge Ihrer Kunden entgengennehmen, stellen Sie bitte klar, dass die Lieferung mindestens sechs Wochen dauern wird*
	We are now using a new road haulier, which should have the effect of cutting down delivery time	*Wir benutzen jetzt einen neuen Lkw-Spediteur, was eine Verkürzung der Lieferzeit zur Folge haben sollte*
	– quantity	*– Menge*
	In future, please indicate to the nearest ten units how many starter motors you require	*Bitte geben Sie in Zukunft an, wie viele Anlassermotoren Sie in auf- oder abgerundeten Einheiten von zehn Stück benötigen*
	Please let us know when indenting for new stocks whether you require 5, 10 or 20 litre drums	*Bitte teilen Sie uns bei Bestellung neuer Lagerbestände mit, ob Sie 5, 10 oder 20-Liter-Tonnen benötigen*
	– packing	*– Verpackung*
	We will ensure that the goods are better packed in future	*Wir werden sicherstellen, dass die Waren in Zukunft besser verpackt sind*
	If we use better packing material this will increase the price by 10 %. Please make sure your customers are told this before they place their orders	*Wenn wir besseres Verpackungsmaterial verwenden, wird dies den Preis um 10 % erhöhen. Bitte stellen Sie sicher, dass Ihre Kunden dies erfahren, bevor sie ihre Bestellungen aufgeben*
	If we pack the goods in polystyrene (AE: styrofoam) and not corrugated cardboard this will increase the price by $5 per unit	*Wenn die Waren in Styropor und nicht in Wellpappe verpackt werden, wird dies den Preis um 5 $ pro Stück erhöhen*
5	**Principal's comments regarding the agency agreement**	*Stellungnahme des Prinzipals bezüglich des Vertretervertrages*
	– change in commission rate	*– Änderung des Provisionssatzes*
	In view of your latest sales figures, we are prepared to increase your commission by 10 % if you keep up this level of performance	*Angesichts Ihrer letzten Verkaufszahlen sind wir bereit, Ihre Provision um 10 % zu erhöhen, wenn Sie diesen Leistungsstand beibehalten*

On the basis of your recent performance we are willing to raise your commission rate to 20 %, if it is sustained	*Auf der Basis Ihrer Leistungen der letzten Zeit sind wir bereit, Ihren Provisionssatz auf 20 % zu erhöhen, sofern diese anhalten*
As sales have remained steady but not improved, we are unable to increase your commission rate	*Da der Umsatz gleichbleibend war, sich aber nicht verbesserte, sind wir nicht in der Lage, Ihren Provisionssatz zu erhöhen*
Since there has been no noticeable improvement in your sales figures for the last three months, there can be no question of raising your commission for the time being	*Da in den letzten drei Monaten keine sichtbare Verbesserung in Ihren Verkaufszahlen eingetreten ist, steht eine Erhöhung Ihrer Provision zur Zeit nicht zur Debatte*
All commission rates are reviewed once a year. We would ask you, therefore, to wait until next January	*Alle Provisionssätze werden einmal im Jahr überprüft. Wir möchten Sie deshalb bitten, bis nächsten Januar zu warten*
– change in territory	***– Änderung im Gebiet***
We have re-examined your territory as requested and have decided that there is no reason to re-define it	*Wir haben Ihr Gebiet wie gewünscht überprüft und beschlossen, dass es keinen Grund gibt, es neu festzusetzen*
We have studied your request regarding a change in the boundaries of your territory and are of the opinion that it should be downsized	*Wir haben Ihre Bitte bezüglich einer Änderung in den Grenzen Ihres Gebiets geprüft und sind der Meinung, dass es verkleinert werden sollte*
As regards your request for a new territory, we have come to the conclusion that you should now be given a more challenging one	*Was Ihre Bitte bezüglich eines neuen Gebiets betrifft, sind wir zu dem Schluss gelangt, dass Sie jetzt eines bekommen sollten, das Sie mehr herausfordert*
– change in advertising allowance	***– Änderung im Werbezuschuss***
Your request for a larger advertising allowance is being considered	*Ihre Bitte bezüglich eines höheren Werbezuschusses wird zur Zeit geprüft*
We feel that an extra $1,000 should be enough	*Wir sind der Meinung, dass zusätzliche 1.000 $ genügen sollten*
We have come to the conclusion that any increase in your advertising budget will not be possible before 1 January ..	*Wir sind zu dem Schluss gekommen, dass eine Erhöhung Ihres Werbebudgets vor dem 1. Januar .. nicht möglich sein wird*
– extension of the agreement	***– Vertragsverlängerung***
As we are pleased with your sales figures we are prepared to extend your contract by one year	*Da wir mit Ihren Umsatzzahlen zufrieden sind, sind wir bereit, Ihren Vertrag um ein Jahr zu verlängern*

	Since your sales figures have been above average we intend to extend the agency agreement until December 31 ..	*Da Ihre Umsatzzahlen überdurchschnittlich waren, haben wir vor, Ihren Vertretervertrag bis zum 31. Dezember .. zu verlängern*
	– termination of the agreement	***– Beendigung des Vertrages***
	Since sales have been poor we must terminate your contract as of 31 December ..	*Da der Umsatz schlecht war, müssen wir Ihren Vertrag zum 31. Dezember .. beenden*
	In view of the fact that you have had little success with our lines, we feel it is in our mutual interest to terminate the agency agreement on expiry of the agreed notice period of three months	*Angesichts der Tatsache, dass Sie wenig Erfolg mit unseren Produktlinien hatten, sind wir der Meinung, dass es in unserem beiderseitigen Interesse liegt, den Vertretervertrag bei Ablauf der vereinbarten Kündigungsfrist von drei Monaten zu beenden*
6	**Polite ending**	***Höflicher Schluss***
	Your contribution to our company's success in your market has most certainly not gone unnoticed. Well done and keep up the good work!	*Ihr Beitrag zum Erfolg unseres Unternehmens in Ihrem Markt ist selbstverständlich nicht unbeachtet geblieben. Sie haben gute Arbeit geleistet, machen Sie weiter so!*
	May we take this opportunity to express our appreciation of our enjoyable and mutually rewarding business relations over the past five years	*Wir möchten diese Gelegenheit wahrnehmen und unsere Anerkennung unserer erfreulichen und gegenseitig einträglichen Geschäftsbeziehungen in den vergangenen fünf Jahren zum Ausdruck bringen*
	We feel that taking this step is the best for all concerned and wish you all the best in the future	*Wir denken, dass es das Beste für alle Beteiligten ist, diesen Schritt zu unternehmen, und wir wünschen Ihnen in Zukunft alles Gute*
	We are certain that you will be successful again in the future and wish you all the very best	*Wir sind sicher, dass Sie in Zukunft wieder erfolgreich sein werden und wünschen Ihnen alles Gute*
7	**Enclosure(s)**	***Anlage(n)***
	Letter(s) Fax(es) E-mail(s) from customer(s)	*Brief(e)* *Fax(e)* *E-Mail(s) vom (von den) Kunden*

Unit 12
Credit Enquiries

Standard Expressions

Credit Enquiries

1 Direct / indirect reference to the company for which a credit reference is required*	The Metal Box Company Ltd Rutland Enterprises plc Messrs Pollock, Pratt and Pumphrey Mr / Miss / Mrs / Ms Leslie Crowther	in … (location)	has have	named given	you your company your firm	as a reference				
	The company / person named on the enclosed slip (has)	told informed	me us	that	you your company your firm	are is	willing to prepared to	provide supply	me us	with a reference
	I / We understand from	the Metal Box Company Ltd Rutland Enterprises plc Messrs Pollock, Pratt and Pumphrey Mr / Miss / Mrs / Ms Leslie Crowther the company / person named on the enclosed slip				have / has kindly offered to act as a referee				
	Your company has been You have been	named given	as a reference	by	the Metal Box Company Ltd Rutland Enterprises plc Messrs Pollock, Pratt and Pumphrey Mr / Miss / Mrs / Ms Leslie Crowther the company named on the enclosed slip	in … (location)				
	BE: Your credit reference agency AE: Your credit bureau	has been recommended to us by			a business partner a business associate the Chamber of Commerce and Industry in … (location) … (name of person / company) in … (location)					
	We have been given your company's name by We have obtained your company's name from Your company's name was passed on to us by									
	We found your company's name and address	in a commercial directory on the Internet			and would be most grateful if you would provide us with a credit report on … and would like to order a "snapshot report" / a full report on …					

2 The sort of information required	As we have not done business with this company before … Since this firm is unknown to us … In view of the fact that we have had no dealings with this firm before …
– snapshot* – full reference*	I / We | would | be glad / be pleased / be grateful / very much appreciate it | if you would | let me/us have | details of / an indication of / any relevant information you may have as regards / some information regarding / a snapshot reference on / a full reference on | this company's / this firm's / this business's / his / her / their financial standing/reputation/directors/volume of business/profitability/payment habits/(business) operation
– financial standing/ reputation	What is the company's financial standing? What sort of a reputation has the company got? Does the company enjoy a good reputation? Would you describe this company as reputable?
– directors	Are you in a position to let us have any information on the company's (managing) director(s)/the company secretary/ Mr/Mrs/Ms … (name)?
– volume of business	How much business has the company done with you? We would appreciate details of the company's volume of business with you
– profitability	How would you assess the company's performance currently? Is the company solvent/making a profit/thriving/just breaking even/just keeping its head above water?
– payment habits	We are particularly interested in knowing | if they/he/she/it/the company pay(s) on time / whether its/his/her/their debts are paid promptly/on time/on schedule / whether the company is prompt in paying its invoices / how quickly the company settles its debts / how promptly the company meets its financial obligations / whether the company is (frequently/ever/sometimes) in arrears with its payments
– credit line	… (name of company) / The firm in question / The company in question / The firm we refer to / The company named on the enclosed slip | has / have | asked for / requested / applied for / submitted an application for / asked us to grant it/them | a(n unsecured) monthly / a(n unsecured) quarterly | credit line of / credit facility of a credit in the sum of | … (amount, e.g. $75,000)

– advisability of granting this amount of credit	Please tell us if (whether) Please let us know if (whether)				you think it a good idea you think it advisable	to grant this line of credit to offer this much credit to the company to let the company have this amount of credit to offer credit facilities of this nature to the company
	We would be most grateful We would very much appreciate it	if you would let us know if (whether) if you would indicate to us if (whether)				
	Please advise us as to whether We would be grateful if you could let us have your opinion as to whether					
	We would (therefore) very much welcome an indication of this company's credit rating					
– recommended credit line	… and, should you feel that this is too much … and, if you feel that this is excessive	how much would you grant them/the company? what would be a reasonable figure in this case? how much credit would you say the company is good for? how much credit would you advise granting the company? what line of credit would you recommend for this company?				
– request for any other relevant information (e.g. from a credit reference agency)	Please also let us have We would also be grateful to receive	any further details you may have any other relevant information you may have			on the company on the person	mentioned referred to in question
					on … (name) on them/him/her	
	… such as details of its balance sheet, profit and loss account, any county court judgements, bankruptcy filings etc. … including a copy of the company's accounts as submitted to Companies House (UK)					
3 Promise to treat all information confidentially and without obligation	We assure you that You have our word that You may rest assured that It goes without saying that You may rely on the fact that	any all	information data	given supplied provided made available	will remain confidential will be treated in the strictest confidence will be treated with the utmost discretion	and without (any) obligation (at all) on your part with no obligation on your part whatsoever without any liability on your part whatsoever and that we will not hold you responsible for it in any way whatsoever

4	Polite ending – offer of reciprocation	We will, of course, be pleased to Please let us know if you would like us to	reciprocate return the favour offer you assistance of a similar nature provide you with any information you yourself/yourselves may require		
		If we can If ever you want us to If you would like us to Should you wish us to			please let us know don't hesitate to tell us do not hesitate to contact us we will be pleased to help
		I/We enclose an international reply coupon for your convenience			
5	Enclosure(s)	Name and address of company International reply coupon			

Credit Reference

1	Direct/indirect reference to the company for which a credit reference is required*	In reply to In answer to With reference to We have received Thank you for	your enquiry your letter	dated/of …	regarding as regards in connection with	… (name of company/person) the company you name
			the above-mentioned enquiry your request for a reference			
2	Information on the company / individual	… we can give you … we are pleased to let you have … we can let you have … we can only let you have			the following information: the following data: the little information (on … (name)) that is available to us	
		… we are able to … we are pleased to … we are unfortunately only able to … we are, regrettably, only in a position to		supply you with provide you with		

	We have been doing business with this company We have been trading with … (name) We have (only) had business dealings with this company We have only had dealings with this company	for (the past) … months/years… since … (date, e.g. January ..)		
	We started doing business with this company … months/years ago (Although) we only started doing business with them/the company 6 months ago According to publicly available records (BE: filed at Companies House) …			
– favourable impression	… (and) (we) have seen for ourselves that the company … (and) (we) have come to the conclusion that it … (and) (we) have had no reason to doubt that it … (and) (we) have had every reason to believe that the company	is	well run healthy reputable reliable shrewdly run well managed (financially) sound financially secure on a secure financial footing not over-ambitious not likely to commit itself beyond its means not likely to take on more business than it can handle a well-respected firm with a good track record (over the past … years) a well-established (family) business with an excellent reputation both at home and abroad	
		has	a sound financial base enough capital to meet its commitments (and expand) enough resources (and potential) to achieve its goals	
	Its director(s) Mr/Mrs/Ms/Miss … (name) and … (name)	is are	well-known well-liked well-respected	over here locally in the local community in the area in business circles in this market
		has/have a good name enjoy(s) an excellent reputation		

– non-committal	… so it's too early to tell … so we can't really tell you very much about them … and for this reason we are unable to give you any information on them at present … so it is too early to tell whether the company is/they are reliable or not … and it has only placed a few orders with us, only amounting to … (amount, e.g. $5,000) … and our terms have been "cash on receipt of invoice" so far … and we have dealt with them on a strictly cash basis … and our terms have (always) been "cash with order" … and we have only had a small volume of business with them on a cash basis		
– unfavourable impression	… (but) we have gained the impression that … (but) our impression is (nevertheless) that … (but) we have come to the conclusion that … (but) it would seem that	it is the company is	badly run in poor shape unreliable badly managed (financially) unsound financially insecure not on a secure financial footing over-ambitious likely to commit itself beyond its means prone to taking on more business than it can handle
		it does not have the company does not have	a sound financial base enough capital to meet its commitments (and expand) enough resources (and potential) to achieve its goals
	We have heard that It has come to our notice that A reliable business partner has informed us that		the company has recently incurred heavy losses the company is seriously under-capitalized the company is (currently) experiencing serious financial difficulties one/some of the company's major trading partners has/have recently gone bankrupt the firm is virtually insolvent the firm is on the verge of bankruptcy the firm is barely managing to stay afloat

	Its director(s) Mr/Mrs/Ms/Miss … (name) and … (name)		is not are not	known liked respected	locally in the local community in the area in local business circles
			is/are unknown does/do not have a good name does/do not enjoy a good reputation		
	This company This business This firm Mr/Ms/Mrs/Miss …		pays irregularly rarely pays on time has irregular payment habits has poor payment habits cannot be relied on to pay on schedule is frequently (up to 21 days) in arrears with payments often defaults on its payments seldom meets its financial obligations on time		
3 Recommended terms of business with the company/individual in question – good risk	Therefore, Consequently, For this reason For these reasons … and so	it is our opinion that we believe that	… (name of company) the company in question the company named the firm you refer to the firm referred to in your letter	is (undoubtedly) good for your figures is good for a credit line of … (amount, e.g. $50,000) per month/per quarter should have no difficulty in handling a credit facility of … (amount) per month/quarter should have no difficulty in meeting obligations of up to … (amount) per month/quarter is well-placed to handle a credit in the sum you mention should/would have no difficulty in keeping to a credit line/facility of …	
	We would (therefore) recommend We would (therefore) suggest		granting allowing	a credit line of … (amount) a credit facility of … (amount)	per month per quarter on a monthly basis on a quarterly basis
			that you grant that you allow		
	We therefore have no hesitation in		suggesting recommending		

– non-committal	For this reason we are not in a position to comment on this company's financial standing or future prospects We are, therefore, unfortunately unable to offer an opinion as regards the advisability of granting this company the credit line you refer to					
– poor risk	In view of the firm's/the director's Given the firm's/ Mr/Ms … 's	(poor) credit record to date current financial predicament unsatisfactory record poor track record poor performance proven record of unreliability recent county court judgement(s) poor payment habits unpredictable payment habits recent bankruptcy chronic unreliability as regards its financial commitments	we would (strongly) recommend that you we would suggest that you		proceed with caution refuse the company a credit facility delay any decision regarding the granting of credit facilities until further data is available only have dealings with this company on a secured basis avoid all dealings with this company on an unsecured basis require collateral before granting any credit insist that collateral be provided require the company to provide collateral before allowing it (any) credit	
			we would not advise you to	grant this company allow this company	a credit facility credit facilities any credit	for the time being in the near future
			we would advise against	granting this firm allowing this business		
	We recommend that you We would advise you to	deal with them deal with this company insist, when dealing with this company, that all transactions be		on a "cash with order" basis on strictly cash terms on a cash basis only		
4 Reminder that you are only expressing an opinion*	Please note We would point out It goes without saying	that any view expressed by us is that any recommendation expressed here is	entirely subjective, no more than an opinion,		wholly based upon our own personal experience of this company and is not necessarily valid under different circumstances and will not apply under all circumstances	

		We would ask you to bear this in mind when coming to your own decision about Please take this into consideration when taking your decision on		... (name of company) this company the company in question the firm you refer to	
		The views expressed here are entirely subjective and only based upon our own personal experience of the company in question The information and views contained in this letter/fax/e-mail are an entirely subjective expression of personal opinion with no claim to objectivity. We would request you treat them as such			
5	Reminder that the information is confidential	This information This data The above details Any facts and/or opinion(s) expressed in this reference	is/are supplied is/are provided is/are made available	on condition that	it/they be treated in the strictest confidence it/they remain strictly confidential it/they be treated with the utmost discretion and are not divulged to any third parties
				in the strictest confidence on the assumption that it/they will be treated confidentially and not be divulged to anyone else	
		Please treat this information confidentially This information is, of course, confidential and intended for your use only We would ask you to exercise the utmost discretion when using this information			
6	Reminder that no responsibility will be accepted for it	... and is made available without (any) obligation (whatsoever) on our part This information is provided without responsibility on our part We would remind you that we do not take any responsibility for the information supplied and the views expressed here We would expressly point out that no obligation or liability is accepted for the views expressed			
7	Polite ending	We hope this information will help you to come to a decision We hope the information provided will be of use to you We very much hope we have been able to provide you with the information you require Please do not hesitate to get in touch with us, should any of the points mentioned above require clarification			

Credit Enquiries

1	Direct / indirect reference to the company for which a credit reference is required*	*Direkte / indirekte Bezugnahme auf die Gesellschaft, für die eine Kreditreferenz gewünscht wird**
	The Metal Box Company Ltd in Glasgow has named you as a reference	*Die Metal Box Company Ltd. in Glasgow hat Sie als Referenz benannt*
	The company named on the enclosed slip has told us that you are prepared to supply us with a reference	*Die auf dem beigefügten Zettel genannte Firma hat uns mitgeteilt, dass Sie bereit sind, uns eine Referenz zu geben*
	We understand from Ms Leslie Crowther that your firm has kindly offered to act as a referee	*Wie wir von Frau Leslie Crowther erfahren, hat sich Ihre Firma netterweise bereit erklärt, eine Auskunft zu erteilen*
	BE: Your credit reference agency (AE: credit bureau) has been recommended to us by a business partner	*Ihre Auskunftei ist uns von einem Geschäftspartner empfohlen worden*
	We have been given your company's name by the Chamber of Commerce and Industry in New York	*Wir erhielten den Namen Ihrer Gesellschaft von der Industrie- und Handelskammer in New York*
2	The sort of information required	*Art der gewünschten Informationen*
	As we have not done business with this company before, we would be glad if you would provide us with any relevant information you may have as regards this company's financial standing	*Da wir mit dieser Firma noch keine Geschäfte getätigt haben, wären wir froh, wenn Sie uns alle wichtigen Informationen liefern könnten, die Sie möglicherweise bezüglich der finanziellen Lage dieser Gesellschaft haben*
	We require a snapshot reference / a full reference*	*Wir benötigen eine Kurzreferenz / eine vollständige Referenz**
	Are you in a position to let us have any information on the company's managing director and the company secretary?	*Sind Sie in der Lage, uns Informationen über den Geschäftsführer und den Company Secretary der Gesellschaft zukommen zu lassen?*
	– volume of business	*– Umfang des Geschäfts*
	How much business has the company done with you?	*Wie viele Geschäfte hat die Firma mit Ihnen getätigt?*
	– profitability	*– Rentabilität*
	How would you assess the company's performance currently?	*Wie würden Sie die Leistung der Firma zur Zeit bewerten?*
	– payment habits	*– Zahlungsgewohnheiten / -moral*
	We are particularly interested in knowing whether its debts are paid promptly	*Wir sind besonders daran interessiert zu erfahren, ob ihre Schulden prompt bezahlt werden*

	– credit line	– *Kreditlinie*
	The firm we refer to has asked for an unsecured monthly credit line of $75,000	*Die Firma, auf die wir uns beziehen, hat uns um eine monatliche ungesicherte Kreditlinie von 75.000 $ gebeten*
	– advisability of granting this amount of credit	– *Ratsamkeit der Gewährung eines Kredits in dieser Höhe*
	Please tell us if you think it advisable to grant this line of credit	*Bitte teilen Sie uns mit, ob Sie es für ratsam halten, diese Kreditlinie zu gewähren*
	We would very much welcome an indication of this company's credit rating	*Wir würden einen Hinweis auf die Beurteilung der Kreditwürdigkeit dieser Gesellschaft sehr begrüßen*
	– recommended credit line	– *empfohlene Kreditlinie*
	... and, if you feel that this is excessive, how much credit would you say the company is good for?	*... und, wenn Sie glauben, dass dies zu viel ist, wieviel Kredit würden Sie sagen, kann diese Firma verkraften?*
	– request for any other relevant information (e.g. from a credit reference agency)	– *Bitte um jede andere wichtige Information (z. B. von einer Auskunftei)*
	Please also let us have any other relevant information you may have on the company mentioned, including a copy of the company's accounts as submitted to Companies House (UK)	*Bitte lassen Sie uns auch jegliche andere wichtige Information zukommen, die Sie möglicherweise über die erwähnte Firma haben, einschließlich einer Kopie der Bilanzen der Firma, wie Sie dem Companies House (GB) vorgelegt wurde*
3	**Promise to treat all information confidentially and without obligation**	*Versprechen, sämtliche Informationen vertraulich und unverbindlich zu behandeln*
	We assure you that any information given will remain confidential and without any obligation at all on your part	*Wir versichern Ihnen, dass alle erteilten Informationen vertraulich und vollkommen unverbindlich für Sie bleiben werden*
	You may rest assured that all data provided will be treated with the utmost discretion without any liability on your part whatsoever	*Sie können versichert sein, dass alle gelieferten Daten mit der größten Diskretion und ohne jegliche Haftung Ihrerseits behandelt werden*
4	**Polite ending**	*Höflicher Schluss*
	– offer of reciprocation	– *Angebot der Erwiderung*
	We will, of course, be pleased to reciprocate	*Wir werden natürlich gern Ihre Hilfe erwidern*
	Please let us know if you would like us to return the favour	*Bitte lassen Sie uns wissen, ob Sie wünschen, dass wir die Gefälligkeit erwidern*
5	**Enclosure(s)**	*Anlage(n)*
	Name and address of company International reply coupon	*Name und Anschrift der Firma* *Internationaler Antwortschein*

Credit Reference

1	**Direct / indirect reference to the company for which a credit reference is required***	***Direkte / indirekte Bezugnahme auf die Gesellschaft, über die eine Kreditauskunft gewünscht wird****
	In reply to your enquiry dated 15 January .. regarding Wilmotts Computer GmbH	*In Beantwortung Ihrer Anfrage vom 15. Januar .. bezüglich der Wilmotts Computer GmbH*
	Thank you for your letter of 15 January .. as regards the company you name	*Vielen Dank für Ihren Brief vom 15. Januar .. bezüglich der von Ihnen genannten Firma*
2	**Information on the company / individual**	***Informationen über die Firma / Person***
	– favourable impression	***– günstiger Eindruck***
	We have seen for ourselves that the company is well run	*Wir haben uns selbst davon überzeugt, dass die Firma gut geführt wird*
	We have had every reason to believe that the company is on a secure financial footing	*Wir hatten jeden Grund anzunehmen, dass die Firma auf einer sicheren finanziellen Grundlage steht*
	Its directors, Herr Martin Bergmann and Frau Sabine Schulz, are well-respected in business circles	*Ihre Direktoren, Herr Martin Bergmann und Frau Sabine Schulz, sind in Geschäftskreisen gut angesehen*
	– non-committal	***– neutral***
	We are unfortunately only able to supply you with the little information on Gebrüder Meier that is available to us	*Wir sind leider nur in der Lage, Ihnen die wenigen uns über Gebrüder Meier zur Verfügung stehenden Informationen zu geben*
	It has placed a few orders with us, only amounting to $5,000	*Sie hat uns einige Aufträge erteilt, die sich nur auf 5.000 $ beliefen*
	We have only had a small volume of business with them on a cash basis	*Wir hatten nur einen geringen Geschäftsumfang mit ihnen auf Barzahlungsbasis*
	– unfavourable impression	***– ungünstiger Eindruck***
	We are, regrettably, only in a position to provide you with the little information on Gebrüder Meier that is available to us	*Wir sind bedauerlicherweise nur in der Lage, Ihnen die wenigen uns über Gebrüder Meier zur Verfügung stehenden Informationen zu geben*
	Our impression is, nevertheless, that the company is financially insecure	*Trotz allem ist unser Eindruck, dass die Firma finanziell unsicher ist*
	It would seem that the company is prone to taking on more business than it can handle	*Es scheint, dass die Firma dazu neigt, mehr Geschäfte anzunehmen, als sie bewältigen kann*
	It has come to our notice that the firm is on the verge of bankruptcy	*Es ist uns zur Kenntnis gelangt, dass die Firma kurz vor dem Konkurs steht*

	Its directors, Frau Germaine Altmeier and Dr Mario Sabrinski, are not respected in the local community	*Ihre Direktoren, Frau Germaine Altmeier und Dr. Mario Sabrinski, genießen am Ort kein hohes Ansehen*
	This company pays irregularly	*Dieses Gesellschaft zahlt unregelmäßig*
	This firm has poor payment habits	*Diese Firma hat schlechte Zahlungsgewohnheiten / eine schlechte Zahlungsmoral*
3	**Recommended terms of business with the company / individual in question**	***Empfohlene Geschäftsbedingungen mit der in Frage stehenden Gesellschaft / Person***
	– good risk	***– geringes Risiko***
	For this reason it is our opinion that the company in question is, undoubtedly, good for your figures	*Aus diesem Grund ist unsere Meinung, dass die in Frage stehende Firma zweifellos gut für Ihre Zahlen ist*
	Therefore, we believe that the firm you refer to should have no difficulty in meeting obligations of up to $50,000 per quarter	*Daher glauben wir, dass die Firma, auf die Sie sich beziehen, keine Schwierigkeiten haben sollte, Verpflichtungen bis zu 50.000 $ pro Quartal zu erfüllen*
	We would, therefore, recommend granting a credit line of $10,000 per quarter	*Wir würden daher empfehlen, pro Quartal eine Kreditlinie von 10.000 $ zu gewähren*
	We therefore have no hesitation in recommending a credit facility of $25,000 on a quarterly basis	*Wir würden daher nicht zögern, eine Kreditmöglichkeit von 25.000 $ auf Quartalsbasis zu empfehlen*
	– non-committal	***– neutral***
	We are, therefore, unfortunately unable to offer an opinion as regards the advisability of granting this company the credit line you refer to	*Wir sind daher leider nicht in der Lage, eine Meinung hinsichtlich der Ratsamkeit, dieser Firma die von Ihnen angegebene Kreditlinie zu gewähren, zu äußern*
	– poor risk	***– hohes Risiko***
	In view of the firm's poor credit record to date, we would strongly recommend that you proceed with caution	*Angesichts der schlechten Kreditsituation der Firma bis heute würden wir dringend empfehlen, dass Sie mit Vorsicht verfahren*
	Given Dr Sabrinski's proven record of unreliability, we would suggest that you require collateral before granting any credit	*Auf Grund der nachgewiesenen Unzuverlässigkeitsquote von Dr. Sabrinski würden wir vorschlagen, dass Sie Sicherheiten verlangen, bevor Sie einen Kredit gewähren*
	We recommend that you deal with them on a cash basis only	*Wir empfehlen, dass Sie nur auf Barzahlungsbasis mit ihnen handeln*

4	**Reminder that you are only expressing an opinion***	***Erinnerung daran, dass Sie nur eine Meinung äußern****
	We would point out that any view expressed by us is entirely subjective, wholly based upon our own personal experience of this company	*Wir möchten darauf hinweisen, dass jede von uns geäußerte Ansicht absolut subjektiv ist und voll und ganz auf unseren eigenen persönlichen Erfahrungen mit dieser Firma beruht*
	The information and views contained in this letter are an entirely subjective expression of personal opinion with no claim to objectivity. We would request you treat them as such	*Die in diesem Brief enthaltenen Informationen und Ansichten sind ein vollständig subjektiver Ausdruck unserer persönlichen Meinung und erheben keinen Anspruch auf Objektivität. Wir bitten Sie daher, sie als solche zu behandeln*
5	**Reminder that the information is confidential**	***Erinnerung daran, dass die Informationen vertraulich sind***
	Please treat this information confidentially	*Bitte behandeln Sie diese Information vertraulich*
	This information is made available on condition that it be treated with the utmost discretion and is not divulged to any third parties	*Diese Informationen sind unter der Bedingung zur Verfügung gestellt worden, dass sie mit der äußersten Diskretion behandelt und nicht an Dritte weitergegeben werden*
6	**Reminder that no responsibility will be accepted for it**	***Erinnerung daran, dass keine Verantwortung dafür übernommen wird***
	This information is supplied without any obligation or liability on our part whatsoever	*Diese Informationen werden ohne jegliche Verpflichtung oder Haftung unsererseits zur Verfügung gestellt*
7	**Polite ending**	***Höflicher Schluss***
	We hope this information will help you to come to a decision	*Wir hoffen, dass diese Informationen Ihnen helfen werden, eine Entscheidung zu treffen*
	Please do not hesitate to get in touch with us, should any of the points mentioned above require clarification	*Bitte zögern Sie nicht, mit uns Verbindung aufzunehmen, falls einer der oben erwähnten Punkte einer Erklärung bedarf*

Unit 13

Job Applications

Applicant's Accompanying Letter

1 Source of employer's address* – solicited application	I have seen I refer to I am writing with reference to	your advertisement the above-mentioned advertisement		in the … (name of publication, e.g. *Evening News*)	of … (date)
				in last … (day, e.g. Friday's) edition of the … (name of publication) on the Internet	
	… and am most interested in applying for the post	of … (name of job) in question you offer			
– unsolicited application	I have been given the address of your company	by … (name and address of company or person), who tell(s) me … by my local employment exchange in … (location), which has told me… by … (name of company, e.g. the JobSearch Employment Agency) in … (location) which has told me …			
	… that you have a vacancy for the post of … (name of job, e.g. Assistant to the Personnel Manager) … that your company wishes to fill the post of … (name of job)				
	I am interested in applying for the post of … (details) I would be grateful if you would consider my application for the post of … as		advertised	in yesterday's … (name of publication, e.g. *Daily Telegraph*) in (the) … (name of publication, e.g. *Daily Telegraph*) of … (date)	
	I am writing to enquire whether you might have a vacancy for a(n) … (name of post, e.g. foreign-language correspondent with German as mother tongue) I would be most grateful if you would let me know whether you have a vacancy for a(n) … (name of post)				
2 Present situation – employment/ training course	As you can see from my enclosed CV/ resume	I work for I am currently employed by my current employer is	… (name of present employer)	, where I have been working	as a(n) … (name of position, e.g. a (trainee) business administration clerk)
		I have my own business I am a sole trader I am a sole proprietor I am currently self-employed	and have been	working in this capacity running my own company operating independently	
	… for … (the past) + length of time (e.g. the past 2 years) … since … + date (e.g. September 15 ..)			My training course there ends on (date, e.g. 30 June ..) My contract expires on … (date)	

– responsibilities/ duties	At present At the present time At the moment	I've got a job in I am working in I am employed in I am in charge of	... (name of department, branch etc., e.g. the Export Sales Section)	in ... (location, e.g. Düsseldorf) at ... (branch/office), e.g. our Hamburg office)	
		... and ... where	I am responsible for my duties include	processing ... (e.g. orders) dealing with ... (e.g. complaints) carrying out ... (e.g. maintenance work) supervising ... (e.g. our technical staff) drawing up ... (e.g. contracts) implementing ... (e.g. quality control standards) co-ordinating ... (e.g. work carried out by subcontractors)	
	My current My present	post position	is that of ... (name of position, e.g. Sales Manager)	at ... (name of company)	in ... (location)
	I am currently employed		as a(n) ... (name of position)		
– promotion/ progress within the company	I have held this	post position	for + period of time since + date	... having started in ... (date) as a(n) ... (original position, e.g. sales assistant/office junior)	
	I joined my present company		in ... (month/year)	as a(n) ... (position, e.g. junior administrator) and	after ... (period of time , e.g. a year)
	I was (subsequently)	made promoted to the position of transferred to ... (location) to become		... (name of post, e.g. Head of Export Sales) European Sales Manager Personal Assistant to the M.D./ CEO in ... (location)	having started as a(n) ... (original post)
	I have occupied this post		for + period of time (e.g. the past five years) since + date/event (e.g. since the company was taken over by Trondheim AG in 1996)		
– unemployed	I'm between jobs at the moment I'm out of work (at present) I am currently unemployed		and have been so	for ... + length of time (e.g. 2 years) since ... + date (e.g. September ..)	
	I was made redundant I was one of the 400 employees to be made redundant		in ... (month/year)	when ... (name of company, e.g. Trondheim AG) closed down/ was wound up/ceased trading	
	My last employer was ... (name)		where for whom	I worked for ... (period of time, e.g. 5 years)	as a ... (position) in ... (name of department etc., the Sales Department)

3 Reason(s) for leaving current job*	Even though Although Despite the fact that	I am successful I have been successful I have had considerable success	in my current position in my present post	I now wish to I now feel the time is right to I now feel I have gained enough experience to	move on move on to a post with more responsibility take up a new challenge work abroad for a period of time look for something new (and exciting/challenging) put my knowledge of … (skill) to good use
	After … (length of time, e.g. 3 years)				
– prospects	As I am employed in a family business, Since there will be no suitable vacancy for me here for the time being, In view of the fact that there are no promotion prospects for the time being where I am employed,		I want to find a job I am looking for a position	which will	stretch me challenge me offer me a new challenge give me a chance to develop new skills open up new horizons enable me to use all my skills/abilities/potential
	As my present employer is unable to offer me a permanent post on completion of my training course,			I am looking for a suitable vacancy with another employer	
	As the company at which I am presently employed		is in financial difficulties is going through a bad patch is declining is being downsized (to a significant degree) will be making a large number of its staff redundant in the near future is shortly to be divided up and sold is unable to renew my contract because its prospects are uncertain		
			has told its staff that one in two/three etc.	will be made redundant will be laid off will have to seek alternative employment cannot be employed after … (date, e.g. December ..)	
	I am seeking alternative employment I am looking for a suitable post with another employer I am currently investigating alternative sources of employment				

	My present employer would like me to stay on but Although I could stay on at my present firm if I wished, Despite the fact that the company at which I am training has offered me a permanent post		I'd like a change I'm looking for something new I wish to broaden my experience (in this field) and take up a permanent post elsewhere
	This is why I'd like to work for For this reason I would very much welcome the opportunity to work for	a firm a company an organisation	at which I would be able to put the knowledge and skills I have obtained to good use specialising in … (name of field, e.g. fashionwear) working in/involved in … (name of field, e.g. (the field of) marketing/the wholesale/retail trade, import (and export))

– salary	My current salary	is (unfortunately) the same as it was … years ago has remained unchanged	• for + period of time (e.g. the past five years) • since + date/event (e.g. since I was first employed)		with little hope of review with no prospect of improvement and is not up for review until … (date)
		is … (details of salary, e.g. $50,000) p.a.	and is (not) performance-related and includes commission on … (details, e.g. sales) including an annual Christmas bonus of … (details, e.g. a full month's pay) excluding an annual bonus of … (details, e.g. a month's/two months' salary)		
		amounts to … (details)	including and includes This includes In addition, there is	a marriage allowance a child allowance for … child/children a … (name of city, e.g. Munich) weighting allowance a rent allowance a company car an interest-free car loan a car allowance private medical insurance assistance with relocation costs assistance with school fees a performance-related bonus (a … %) commission on sales/all contracts concluded an entitlement to purchase shares in the company a 20 % discount on all goods manufactured by the company a profit-sharing scheme based on the company's annual performance	

	Reason(s) for seeking new activity	As my business is now As the market for … (product/service, e. g. software applications) is Since demand for … (product/service) is	growing expanding flourishing	fast rapidly faster than ever before beyond all expectations	I would like to	expand into a new area widen my range of products open up a new market /new markets
4	Request to be considered for the post	I very much hope that you will I (very much) hope it will be possible for you to				grant me an interview consider me for the post advertised consider my application put me on your waiting list allow me to take the aptitude test
		I feel sure that your company has the opening I am looking for	and would therefore be most grateful if you would and would therefore very much appreciate it if you could			
	– availability for interview/to take aptitude test	I am I will be	available for interview able to attend an interview	at short notice at … (period of time, e. g. a week's, two weeks' notice) in a week's/two/three etc. weeks' time		
		I will call you next … (day/time, e. g. Wednesday morning) to see if we can set up an appointment at your convenience I will call you next week to see if we can meet I will call you on … (date) for further details				
		I will be pleased to take the aptitude test on … (date)				
		I am (unfortunately) unable to take the aptitude test on … (date) I will unfortunately be unable to take/attend the aptitude test on … (date)	for personal reasons owing to illness because of a pressing prior appointment as I will be on holiday on that date since I will be on a business trip at that time	… but am able to attend at any time on or after … (date)		
5	Reference(s)/testimonial(s)	I enclose … and enclose	my CV/resume (and) copies of my qualifications (and) a testimonial/testimonials from my previous employer(s)			
		Should you require	a reference, references,	the referee(s) named in the enclosed CV/resume … (name of person/position/company, e. g. Herr Wilhelm Storch, the Managing Director of Uniplex GmbH, in Essen, Germany) and … (name of person/company)	will be pleased to provide you with any information you may need	

	For a reference For references If a reference is required If references are	please contact please get in touch with	… , who has/have agreed to … , who will be pleased to	act as a referee/act as referees supply you with any information you may require corroborate this information and provide you with any further details needed
	References are available on request			
6 Polite ending	Hoping to hear from you soon I hope to hear from you at your earliest convenience I very much look forward to receiving your reply to my application (and hope it will be viewed favourably) I look forward to hearing from you at your earliest convenience Many thanks (in advance) for your attention to my application I very much hope you will view this application favourably			
7 Enclosures	CV/Resume Qualifications Testimonial(s) Letter(s) of recommendation			

Curriculum Vitae

1 Name*:	Christine Meyer Christine Katharina Meyer Frank Schmidt Frank Heribert Schmidt
First name(s) (forename(s)/ Christian name(s))*:	Maren Banu Stiliani Helge
Surname (family name/ last name)*:	John Julius Yildirim Chalkiadaki

2	Address:	Sachsenstr. 22 41528 Essen Germany	
	Telephone number:	+49 (0)201 333828	
	Fax number:	+49 (0)201 333900	
	E-mail address:	Johanna.Meyer@t-online.de	
	Internet (Home page):	http://home.t-online.de/home/joh.meyer	
3	Date of birth: (see *Unit 1 "Layouts"* for more detail)	28 December 1961 December 28, 1961 December 28th 1961	
4	Marital status:	Single Married Divorced Widow Widower Single parent	with 1 child with 2/3/4 children with 1 child aged 12 with 1 son/daughter aged 15 with 3 children aged 19, 17 and 9
5	Nationality*:	German/Turkish/Italian/Portuguese/Spanish/Greek/Croatian/Serbian/Bosnian etc.	
	Immigration status*:	Entry Clearance (UK) Business Visa (UK, senior level posts) Green Card (USA) Employment First Preference Visa (USA) Employment Second/Third/Fourth/Fifth Preference Visa (USA) Nonimmigrant Visa/Visitor Visa (USA)	
6	Driving licence(s):	BE: Full driving licence (i. e. motor car licence) AE: Driver's license (i. e. motor car licence) BE: Motor cycle licence/AE: Motor cycle license BE: HGV Licence (Heavy Goods Vehicle Licence, i. e. lorry/truck licence) AE: Commercial Vehicle License BE: Large Passenger Vehicle Licence (i. e. bus/coach driver's licence) AE: Bus Driver's License	

7 Objective*	To obtain a position To obtain a post To secure a post	with more scope for personal initiative with greater responsibility with more flexibility with new challenges with good promotion prospects in which I will be able to put my knowledge of … (field / skill, e. g. Chinese, foreign languages, marketing, accountancy) to good use
	To seek a more challenging appointment To use my knowledge of … (field / skill) To use my … (details, e. g. accountancy, organisational, marketing, programming) skills To make use of my skills in the field of … (details, e. g. personnel management, computer programming) To secure a part-time position	
8 Education and Qualifications – primary* / secondary school	– *name and address of school, with English / American equivalent in brackets:* Grundschule = (UK) primary school, (USA) elementary school Hauptschule = (no exact English equivalent in the UK) secondary school, (no exact equivalent in the USA) middle school Realschule = (no exact English equivalent in the UK) secondary school, (no exact equivalent in the USA) middle school Gesamtschule = (UK) comprehensive school, (no exact equivalent in the USA) middle and high school Gymnasium = (UK) grammar school, (no exact equivalent in the USA) middle and high school – *description of qualifications obtained:* FOR = GCSE equivalents in … (number, e. g. 8) subjects, including … (names of important subjects, e. g. mathematics and English) FHR = German higher education entrance qualifications Abitur = (UK) German university entrance qualifications specialising in … *(give the names of the main "Leistungskurse", e. g., "English and mathematics",)* Abitur = (USA) High School Diploma – *state average grade with English equivalent in brackets:* Average grade: 1.9 (merit)	
– higher education	Universität = (UK) university, (USA) college / university Technische Hochschule = technical / technological university Fachhochschule = university (polytechnic) / institute of higher education Gesamthochschule = (integrated) university / institute of higher education Fernuniversität = Distance Learning (Course at the) University of … (name) (also in the UK: The Open University) Lehrerbildungsanstalt / Pädagogische Hochschule = teacher training college (UK), teachers college (USA)	

– vocational training course(s)	– *name and address of vocational training college / vocational school at which you did your training course:* Berufsschule = vocational training college (UK) / vocational school (USA) Europäisches Berufskolleg der Stadt Essen (Essen College / School of Vocational Training) Sachsenstr. 27 41528 Essen Germany Tel. … Fax … E-mail: … Internet: …
	– *name and address of company at which you are doing or did your training:* Eurostahl AG, Essen, Germany – *description or name of qualification, e. g.:* A recognised qualification in business administration / office administration / business communication / retailing / wholesaling / export sales / freight forwarding A recognised qualification as a plumber, electrician, hotelier, cook, air traffic controller, business administration clerk, office administration clerk, foreign-language correspondent, etc. A 2-year / 3-year full-time vocational course at … (name of institution) (for students with / without university entrance qualifications) to become a state-qualified commercial assistant with languages (English / French / Spanish etc.) – *state final result or expected final result with English equivalent in brackets:* Final result / Average grade: 1.9 (merit) – *or:* Final result expected: 1/2 (distinction / merit) in December ..
– other vocational skills	Typing (60 w. p. m. (= words per minute)) Shorthand (100 w. p. m.) Conversant with Windows / Microsoft Word for Windows / Microsoft Word for the Mackintosh / Excel / WordPerfect for Windows etc. Conversant with all / most / a large number of major software packages Conversant with Internet applications including e-mail

9	Employment – temporary work	Temporary work:	as a(n) (guide and) interpreter at … (event, e.g. the IGEDO Fashion Show in Düsseldorf) as a clerical assistant at … (name of company) a shop assistant at … (name of shop) as a waiter/waitress as a bartender		
			with the "Zeit-Share" employment agency in … (location)	as a typist as an office clerk as a sales assistant as personal secretary to … (person, e.g. the Chief Executive Officer)	at … (company)
	– permanent post(s)	Company:	… (name and address of firm/company/organisation)		
		Position:	Secretary to the Managing Director Employee in the Export Sales Department Marketing Executive Head of the … Department Head of Exports/Imports/Advertising/Marketing Assistant Manager (of …) Manager (of …) Team Leader in the … Section/Department Deputy Team Leader in the … Section/Department etc.		
		Responsibilities:	Dealing with In charge of Responsible for I dealt with I was in charge of I was responsible for	filing correspondence (with foreign (overseas) customers) documentation shipping documents incoming/outgoing orders export sales maintaining the company's data-base customer complaints customer services placing orders with suppliers/contractors/overseas agents co-ordinating vehicle movements in the EU all correspondence for the Managing Director/Chief Executive Officer/Head of Sales etc. making appointments/making travel arrangements all sales transactions with foreign companies	

	Achievements*:	I increased … (details, e.g. sales, productivity) by … % I decreased/eliminated … (details, e.g. customer complaints) I designed … (details, e.g. a highly successful new order-processing procedure/system, which widely reduced human error) I negotiated … (details, e.g. a new agreement with the works council/union resulting in an increase in productivity of 25 %) I improved … (details, e.g. performance, the employees' readiness to cooperate, productivity, morale etc.) I implemented the new EU guidelines on … (details, e.g. safety at work) I was promoted to the position of … (details, e.g. Head of the Export Department) in recognition of my performance	
		During the time when I was responsible for … (details, e.g. exports) Under my leadership In the course of my three years in charge of the … Section Whilst I was in charge of … (details, e.g. negotiations with financial institutions) While I was running the … Department	we won … (number, e.g. 20) new sales contracts operating procedures were tightened up significantly there was a noticeable improvement in the company's performance working procedures were streamlined and rationalised our relations with … (e.g. our major suppliers) improved significantly a large number of major contracts were negotiated there was a significant increase in sales/exports/business productivity rose by … % productivity doubled/trebled/quadrupled/increased fourfold/fivefold etc. I was instrumental in launching … (new product/service, e.g. the new Alpha Delivery Service)
– reason(s) for leaving*	Expiry of employment contract The department in which I was working was rationalised/cut/closed down Redundancy (brought about by the company's financial difficulties) One of 500 employees to be made redundant as from … (date) Lack of promotion prospects in my current position Lack of opportunity to use my abilities in the field of … (details, e.g. overseas/foreign trade) Desire to move on (to a post with more responsibility)		

		I wish to take up a new challenge I now want to look for something new (and exciting/challenging) I have recently obtained a qualification in … (skill, e.g. translating and interpreting, advertising) and now wish to make (full) use of it My current employer is unable to provide me with the opportunity I am seeking (to take on more responsibility/operate more independently etc.) I have reached the top of the ladder at my present company and now wish to take up a new challenge elsewhere Despite my considerable success my employer is unwilling to pay me on a performance-related basis and has no suitable new opening for me My current employer has no suitable new opening for me I now wish to work abroad in an English-speaking country 30 % of the employees in my section/department/at my branch are being made redundant in the near future. As I am single/unmarried/have no children I have opted to look for alternative employment Birth of my first/second/third etc. child
10	National (Military) Service*	Military/National service in … (the army/the navy/the air force) in … (location) as a(n) … (rank/position)
	Community (Social) Service*	As I am a conscientious objector / As I am a pacifist — I did / I opted to do / I chose to do — community (social) service in … (name of institution, e.g. an old peoples' home, a hospice) in … (location) — instead of national service / as a substitute for national service
11	Community Work*/ Other skills and Experience* – community work	I am a member of the Red Cross I am a member of Amnesty International I am a voluntary social worker for the Church etc. I look after … (details, e.g. the homeless, refugees, asylum-seekers etc.) I run an adult literacy course I am a member of the Salvation Army I am a(n active) member of (a(n)/the) … (name of charity, e.g. an SOS Kinderdorf organisation, Brot für die Welt, i.e. Food for the World)
	– other skills*	I speak some … (language, e.g. Russian) I have a working knowledge of … (language) I have a fair command of (both written and spoken) … (language) I speak (and write) … (language) fluently I am bi-lingual in … and … (e.g. Turkish and German) I have a pilot's licence (AE: license) Yachting Certificate Sailing Certificate Certified/Licensed sailing instructor

	Lifeguard qualification Swimming Instructor Tennis instructor Ski instructor Amateur footballer (AE: soccer player)/handball player/ice-hockey player for ... (name of club, e.g. Langendreer 04) I train a football team for the under 8s/9s/10s etc. I co-ordinate fund-raising for our local church/school/old people's home etc. I am the secretary of the local Arts Society/Drama Society/Chess Club	
– experience*	I have lived in I have travelled widely in I regularly spend my holidays in	... (name of country, e.g. the USA) Europe and North America Eastern Europe Africa South America the tropics hot countries Arab countries Islamic countries the Middle East the Far East
	I have worked as a crew member	on board a yacht on board a steamship on board a sailing ship on board a cross-channel ferry
12 Interests	Sports: aerobics, athletics (discus, high-jump, hurdles, javelin, long-jump, marathon, pole vault, shot-putting, sprinting, triple-jump), badminton, canoeing, climbing, cricket, dancing, diving, fencing, football (AE: soccer), fox-hunting, gliding, gymnastics, handball, hang gliding, hiking, hockey, hunting, ice hockey, jazz dance, jogging, motor-racing, mountaineering, pot-holing, riding, rock-climbing, rowing, rugby, shooting, skating, skiing, snowboarding, squash, surfing, swimming, table tennis, tennis, volleyball, windsurfing	
	Other activities: basket-making, chess, clay-modelling, computers, dress-making, foreign countries, jazz, music, painting, photography, playing the guitar/violin/trumpet/piano/cello, reading, restoring works of art, sculpture, sewing, travel, walking etc.	

13 References	References are available on request			
	References:/Referees: 1 (Name) … (Position) … (Company) … (Address of company) … Tel.: … Fax: … E-mail: … 2 (Name) … (Position) … (Company) … (Address of company) … Tel.: … Fax: … E-mail: …			

Employer's Reply

1 Reference to application	Thank you for Many thanks for We have received	your application for your letter dated/of … (date), in which you apply for the above-mentioned letter with your application for	the post of … (details) the position of … a job as a(n) … a post as a(n) … the above-mentioned post	
	I/We refer to our telephone conversation of … (date, e.g. today/this morning/10 December ..) I am writing in connection with our telephone conversation of … (date) I am writing with reference to your visit to our company on … (date)		regarding in connection with in which we spoke about	a post with us as a(n) … (details) a job at our company as a(n) …

2 Invitation to an aptitude test*	We would like you to You are among the candidates who have been selected to	take take part in	an aptitude test an initial test	as part of our selection procedure as the first stage of our selection procedure
	The test will take place at … (time, e.g. 3 pm) on … (date)			at our Head Office in … (location) at our … (location, e.g. Essen) branch at the … (name of hotel, e.g. Hotel Pacific) in Würzburg
	The test will be marked immediately and Your result will be made available to you the same day and	successful candidates will be interviewed successful candidates will then be invited to an initial interview		on the same day that afternoon the next day in due course a short time later
– an initial interview*	We wish to / We are pleased to — invite you to attend We would like you to attend You are among the candidates who have been selected to attend You are one of the candidates who are being invited to attend	an interview an initial interview		
	Directions are enclosed for your convenience For the exact location please refer to the enclosed directions … which can be reached easily by car/by public transport (see map/directions enclosed)			
– the final interview*	Short-listed candidates will (later) be invited to attend We would (now) like you to attend We now wish to invite you to attend Having successfully completed the first part of our selection procedure, you are now invited to attend We are now able to inform you that you have passed the first stage of our interview procedure and are now invited to attend			the final interview, which will take place …
	We are pleased to inform you that	you are one of the (two/three/four) candidates who are being invited to attend		

	... at ... (time) on ... (date)	at our Head Office in ... (location) at our ... (location, e.g. Essen) branch at the ...(name of hotel, e.g. Hotel Pacific) in Würzburg	Directions are enclosed for your convenience For the exact location please refer to the enclosed directions ... which can be reached easily by car/by public transport You will be met at the ... (railway station/airport) by our driver Our Ms/Mr ... will meet you at the station in ... (location)/... airport at ... (time) on ... (date)
3 Conditions*: – qualifications	This post is only open to We are only able to consider applications from	fully qualified candidates candidates with a(n) ... (details, e.g. recognised qualification as a foreign-language correspondent) candidates with appropriate qualifications candidates with a BSc (Bachelor of Science Degree in Business Administration) *(= Betriebswirt)* candidates with an MBA (a Masters Degree in Business Administration) candidates possessing a recognised qualification in ... (name of field, e.g. marketing) who have completed a recognised training course to become a(n) ... (occupation, e.g. business administration clerk) or possess a similar qualification	
	Please note that We must point out that You will appreciate that	only candidates with ... (details of qualifications, e.g. a university degree in marketing)	will be considered are eligible for this post can be considered for this position
– experience		only candidates: with considerable experience in this field with at least a year's/... (number) years' experience in this field with a record of successful ... (activity, e.g. advertising) with a successful sales record	
		we are only able to consider candidates	with (considerable) experience of this type of work who are able to provide evidence of having worked in this field • for at least ... (time) • for a number of years

– references	Please note that it will take some time to deal with your application Your application will take several days to process. We will be contacting you again in due course We are now in the process of taking up your references and will be contacting you in due course We note that you have only given the name of one referee. As two referees are required for this post we would ask you to name another person willing to provide you with a reference We now require you to give us the names of two referees to enable us to progress your application We note that one of your testimonials is over five years old. Would you please arrange to have it up-dated or send us a more recent one?		
– nationality/ immigration status	Should you require assistance with applying for	a visa an entry visa a work permit a residence permit permission to enter the country/ Germany etc.	we will be pleased to help you do not hesitate to contact us we would ask you to contact … (name of employee) on … (tel.) please get in touch with Ms/Mr … in our Personnel Department
	By law For administrative reasons For technical reasons In conformity with current immigration laws In conformity with the EU's directive in this connection	we are only able to offer this job to this post can only be offered to this position is only open to	German/British/French etc. nationals citizens of the EU applicants already holding a work permit/ residence permit
– probationary period	There is a probationary period of … (time, e.g. three months) The candidate chosen will initially be employed for a trial period of … (time)	, after which (time) his/her/your contract will be reviewed , after successful completion of which he/she/you will be eligible for a permanent post	
	All new staff are initially employed for a trial period of … (time) Newly recruited members of staff are first employed for a trial period of … (time)	, after which (time) their contracts are reviewed Contracts are then renewed or terminated by mutual consent	
– salary	Please refer to the enclosure	for further information on our pay scales for details of our salary scales	
	The successful candidate will receive a starting salary of … (amount, e.g. $50,000) p.a.	to be reviewed yearly/every two years etc. … with yearly/two-yearly increments of … (amount, e.g. $500) …	
	… depending on … subject to	performance sales figures	

The successful applicant	will receive an initial salary at will initially be remunerated at will initially qualify for remuneration at	point 1/2/3 etc. level 1/2/3 etc. grade 1/2/3 etc.	on our company's pay scale (see enclosure)	subject to annual review subject to status
Your initial salary will be at				

The successful candidate You	may also qualify for may also be eligible for	a marriage allowance a child allowance for … (number) child/children a … (name of city, e.g. Munich) weighting allowance a rent allowance a company car an interest-free car loan a car allowance private medical insurance assistance with relocation costs assistance with school fees a performance-related bonus (a … %) commission on sales/all contracts concluded an entitlement to purchase shares in the company a 20 % discount on all goods manufactured by the company a profit-sharing scheme based on the company's annual performance further allowances	subject to status on a discretionary basis in certain cases under exceptional circumstances on completion of his/her/your probationary period

Please let us know what salary you would expect
Please let us have an indication of the salary expected
The salary for this post is subject to negotiation (and thereafter performance-related)
As you have not indicated what salary you expect, we would ask you to do so to enable us to progress your application
We guarantee to match your current salary
We guarantee to exceed your current salary

– expenses	Please note that We wish to point out that It is our company's policy that You will appreciate that	expenses will (only) be only the successful candidate's expenses will be only short-listed candidates' expenses will be only the expenses incurred when attending the final interview will be	paid reimbursed refunded	on presentation of	appropriate receipts the original receipts
	Your travel and accommodation expenses will be Any expenses incurred when attending the interview will be Only travel to and from the interview and accommodation expenses for one night at the … Hotel will be				
	Our company is willing to cover your expenses for this interview				
	No expenses will be refunded We are unfortunately unable to refund your expenses for this interview				
	We have booked a room for you at the … Hotel (see hotel map enclosed) for … (date) We enclose a return train/airline ticket from … (location) to … (location). Please take a taxi to our office from the airport/ Our driver will meet you at the airport				
– accommodation	You will be accommodated at … (address) Candidates for this post are being accommodated at … We have reserved a room for you at … Should you require accommodation, please telephone Frau Bergmann on … (telephone number), or send her a fax/e-mail at … (fax number/e-mail address)				
4 Rejection – reasons	We are sorry to tell you that We regret to inform you that	… (see "3 Conditions: – qualifications/– experience" for reasons for rejecting an application)			
		this post the post in question	is taken is no longer available has been filled has now been occupied		
		we have no vacancy for a(n) … (job, e.g. a European Sales Clerk) at present we have no jobs of this nature we have no vacancies of the nature you describe all our posts are currently filled your application reached us after the post had been filled we (unfortunately) received your application after the deadline of … (date) we are fully staffed at present			

	We have considered your application and Having considered your application we	are sorry to tell you that regret to inform you that have come to the conclusion that	we are unable to offer you the post in question we are unable to offer you the above-mentioned post we require someone with more experience we need someone with a different background we would be unable to pay the salary indicated you are over-qualified / under-qualified for this post you do not have the language skills necessary for this position the position advertised requires someone with a greater knowledge of … (details, e. g. foreign trade)	
	The position advertised is intended for someone starting out on a career in … (field, e. g. foreign trade) The post in question would be suitable for someone well-versed in the field of … (field, e. g. business finance)			and, judging by your CV, would consequently be unsuitable for you
– waiting list	We have noted your particulars and will get in touch with you if we have a suitable vacancy at a later date Your application has (however) been filed and will be used at a later date if a suitable post becomes vacant Your name has been placed on a waiting list and you will be contacted (immediately) should a suitable vacancy arise			
– referral to another employer	If you wish Should you so wish If you would like us to do so With your consent	your name your application your particulars	can be given to can be sent to can be passed on to can be made available to	… (name of company), with whom we work closely our business partners, … (name of company) our Head Office in … (location) our subsidiary in … (location) our local Chamber of Commerce and Industry in … (location) … (name of trade association, e. g. The German Shoe Association) of which we are members
– reference to return of application documents	We are returning	your application documents your certificate(s) your portfolio the sample(s) of your work sent to us		with this letter under separate cover by separate post
	We will be returning You will be receiving			in the next few days in due course under separate cover by separate post
	Your application documents Your certificate(s) Your portfolio The sample(s) of your work sent to us		will be sent to you will be returned to you	

5	Polite ending	We look forward to your reply We look forward to hearing from you in the near future Please let us have your comments (on this) to enable us to continue processing your application Your application will be progressed as soon as the documents requested have been supplied to us As soon as we have received this information/your comments we will be able to let you have our decision Your application will be progressed as soon as your references have been taken up Please do not hesitate to contact us by telephone or in writing, should any of the points mentioned here require further clarification We look forward to meeting you personally in … (location)/on … (date) We enclose directions to … (location, e.g. the hotel, our premises, our office in Berlin) We regret that we are unable to help you (this time) and wish you every success in the future Despite the fact that this vacancy has been filled we will bear your application in mind should a similar post become available
6	Enclosure(s)	Map Directions Train ticket Airline ticket Application documents Certificate(s) Portfolio Pay scale

Writing a Reference / Testimonial

1	Date/Salutation	28 December .. December 28 .. Dear + Name
2	Reference Testimonial	To Whom it May Concern
3	Subject line	Sabine Schmidt/Thorsten Lubowski/Dr Heribert Hermanns

4	Reference to request for reference	I refer to our (telephone) conversation (on ...) regarding ... Mr/Mrs/Ms/Dr ... (name) I have received your letter/fax/e-mail (dated ...) requesting a reference on ...	in connection with his/her application for the post of ...	and am pleased to supply you with and am able to provide you with	the reference requested a brief reference the following information the following details no more than a brief impression of ... (name) as a(n) employee /colleague/business associate
		In reply to your request for a reference on Mr/Mrs/Ms/Dr ... (name) (dated ...) With regard to your request for a reference on Mr/Mrs/Ms/Dr ... (name) (dated ...)		I am pleased to provide you with I am (only) able to supply you with	
		I refer to our telephone conversation of ... (e.g. today, this morning/afternoon, 28 December) regarding Mr/Mrs/Ms/Dr ... (name) and am (as I said) (unfortunately) (only) able to supply you with the following information			
5	How well you know the candidate	I have known Mr/Mrs/Ms/Dr ... (name) Mr/Mrs/Ms/Dr ... (name) has been known to me		for + period of time (e.g. six months) since + date (e.g. 1995)	
		Mr/Mrs/Ms/Dr ... (name) has worked for me Mr/Mrs/Ms/Dr ... (name) has been a colleague of mine			
		I was acquainted with ... (name) I worked with ... (name) I had the pleasure of working with ... (name)	for + period of time (e.g. five years) for a short time only, i.e. ... (time, e.g. six months) for a number of years from ... (date) – (date) (e.g. from 1990–1993)		during which time he/she worked as a(n) ... (see below "6 The candidate's work/position")
		Mr/Mrs/Ms/Dr ... (name) and I have (now) been	colleagues working together working in the same department working in the same office working for the same organisation/company		for + period of time (e.g. six months) since + date (e.g. 1995)
		Mr/Mrs/Ms/Dr ... (name) (only)	worked for me worked in my department worked in the ... (name, e.g. Sales) Department worked for my company had a job at my company as a(n) ... (see 5)		for ... (period of time, e.g. nine months) in ... (year, e.g. 1997) from ... (date) – (date) (e.g. from 1990–1993) for a short time in ... (year, month) for a short period of time some years ago

			was (only) with my company was (only) employed by me as a(n) … *(see previous page)* was (only) an employee at my company was (only) in my employ was one of my employees			
6	The candidate's work/position	… as a(n)	office junior typist shorthand typist secretary personal assistant receptionist salesman agent overseas agent overseas representative administrator accountant advertising manager	in the … (e.g. Sales/Export) Department	with responsibility for in charge of mainly concerned with	filing incoming orders outgoing orders overseas orders orders form abroad imports exports importing … (goods) from … (location) exporting … (goods) to … (location) customer accounts customer services the granting of credit dealing with complaints maintenance contracts service contracts rationalising our operation in … (location) dealing with (foreign) visitors
		He She	works as a(n) worked as a(n) is employed as a(n) was employed as a(n)			
		His Her	position is that of position was that of			

– quality of work	His work	has (always) been			acceptable
	Her work	was (always)			satisfactory
					above average
					excellent
					exceptional
					to good standard
					of a satisfactory standard
					of a high standard
					of an exceptionally high standard
					of exceptional quality
					beyond reproach
	He has (always)	performed his/her		duties	satisfactorily
	She (always)	carried out his/her		work	reliably
					efficiently
					competently
					conscientiously
					diligently
					meticulously
					impeccably
					intelligently
					in a satisfactory manner
					in the manner expected (of him/her)
					to my/our (complete/entire) satisfaction
					in a (highly professional) manner
					in a manner beyond reproach
					with meticulous attention to detail
					with imagination and intelligence
	He/She has (always) done his/her work				to a high degree of accuracy
	He/She (always) did her work				in a manner entirely befitting the responsibility with which he/she has been/was entrusted
	His/Her work was	always	–	done	
	His/Her work has	normally	been	carried out	
		mostly		performed	
				completed	
				executed	

	He/She	speaks some … (language, e.g. Russian)	
		has a working knowledge of … (language)	
		has a fair command of (both written and spoken) … (language)	
		speaks (and writes) … (language) fluently	
		is (perfectly) bi-lingual in … and … (e.g. Turkish and German)	
		has good typing skills	
		can take shorthand (at 100 w.p.m. (= words per minute))	
		is always at pains to keep up with recent developments in his/her field	
7 The candidate's nature (manner)	Mr/Mrs/Ms/Dr … (name)	is	cheerful
			well-mannered
			even-tempered
			poised
			of a friendly disposition
			of a sunny disposition
			outward-going
			charming
			sensible
			highly personable
			good with people
			a natural leader
			an individualist
			a team player
			a self-starter
			a good organiser
			flexible
			versatile
			dynamic
			efficient
			thoughtful
			resourceful
			unflappable
			a cautious individual
			impeccably dressed
			known for his/her natural leadership qualities
			known for his/her eloquence and persuasiveness

		has	charm a charming manner charisma initiative a good manner with people a natural skill with people a good sense of humour considerable social skills impeccable manners a friendly nature a naturally confident manner	
	He/She	pays great attention to detail can be left to get on with the job without supervision concentrates wholly on the task at hand spares no effort to deal with the task at hand is prepared to work late to meet a deadline is willing to do more than the minimum to achieve a goal		
8 The candidate's character	He/She is	totally entirely	honest trustworthy reliable dedicated loyal	and does not shirk responsibility and can be entrusted with duties/responsibilities requiring a high degree of personal integrity
		usually mostly always invariably		punctual and reliable
		discreet self-effacing modest a caring individual sensitive to other people's needs the last to complain (if things go wrong/if the going is tough)		
	His/Her	honesty is beyond reproach integrity is exemplary loyalty is unquestioning as is his/her commitment to the task at hand		

	He/She has	a strong sense of responsibility a sense of duty		
	His/Her time-keeping	has always been has, for the most part, been was always was, for the most part,		satisfactory punctual excellent exemplary as expected
9 Reason(s) for leaving*	He/She	left the company terminated his/her contract opted not to extend his/her contract	of his/her own accord in order to take up a post elsewhere in order to try out another line of business in order to start his/her own business for personal reasons because she was expecting her first/second/third etc. child for reasons unknown to me because his wife/her husband took up employment elsewhere, thus making it necessary for them to move	
10 Suitability for the position in question (reference)	I would (therefore) recommend Mr/Mrs/Ms/Dr … (name)	for this post for this position	whole-heartedly without reservation	
	I (therefore) have no hesitation	in recommending Mr/Mrs/Ms/Dr … (name) for this post in supporting Mr/Mrs/Ms/Dr … (name)'s application for this post		
	I (therefore) feel that I would therefore say that	Mr/Mrs/Ms/Dr … (name) would be	ideally suited to this type of work wholly suitable for the post in question entirely suited for this position the right person for the job	
		… (name) he she	would be suitable for this post after appropriate training would be able to manage the job advertised in the long run would be able to handle this type of work after having acquired the necessary experience in this field may well be suited for this position at a later date in his/her career	
	I am (therefore) (unfortunately) unable to say For this reason, I am not in a position to say In view of my brief acquaintance with … I cannot say		whether he/she/Mr/Mrs/Ms/Dr … (name) is suited for the post in question or not whether he/she/Mr/Mrs/Ms/Dr … (name) would be suitable for this position or not	

	– recommendation for further employment (testimonial)	I have no hesitation in recommending him/her for employment I have no hesitation in recommending him/her to any future employee I feel sure he/she will be an asset to any future employee
11	Complimentary close (reference)	Yours sincerely (after salutation with "Dear + name") Yours faithfully (after salutation with "Dear Sir (or Madam)")
	Signature, name and position of person (testimonial)	Sabine Hinze Sabine Hinze (Ms) Personnel Officer

Applicant's Accompanying Letter

1	**Source of employer's address***	***Quelle der Adresse des Arbeitgebers****
	– solicited application	***– verlangte Bewerbung***
	I have seen your advertisement in the *Evening News* of 24 March ..	*Ich habe Ihre Anzeige in der* Evening News *vom 24. März .. gesehen*
	… and am most interested in applying for the post of European Sales Clerk	*… und bin sehr daran interessiert, mich um die Stelle des (der) europäischen Verkaufssachbearbeiters (-sachbearbeiterin) zu bewerben*
	– unsolicited application	***– unverlangte Bewerbung***
	I have been given the address of your company by Meier GmbH in Münster, who tell me that you have a vacancy for the post of Assistant to the Personnel Manager	*Ich erhielt die Adresse Ihrer Firma von Meier GmbH in Münster, die mir sagten, dass Sie eine Vakanz für die Stelle des Assistenten / der Assistentin des Personalschefs haben*
	I am writing to enquire whether you might have a vacancy for a foreign-language correspondent with German as mother tongue	*Ich schreibe Ihnen um anzufragen, ob Sie vielleicht eine Vakanz für eine Fremdsprachenkorrespondentin mit Deutsch als Muttersprache haben*
2	**Present situation**	***Gegenwärtige Lage***
	– employment / training course	***– Anstellung / Ausbildung***
	As you can see from my enclosed CV / resume, I am currently employed by Lorenz GmbH in Essen, where I have been working as a business administration clerk for the past 2 years	*Wie Sie aus meinem beigefügten (tabellarischen) Lebenslauf ersehen können, bin ich gegenwärtig bei der Lorenz GmbH in Essen angestellt, wo ich in den vergangenen 2 Jahren als Industriekaufmann/frau gearbeitet habe*
	My training course there ends on 31 April ..	*Meine Ausbildung dort endet am 31. April ..*
	At present I am working in the Export Sales Section in Düsseldorf	*Zur Zeit arbeite ich im Verkaufsbereich Export in Düsseldorf*
	– responsibilities / duties	***– Aufgaben / Obliegenheiten***
	… and my duties include implementing quality control standards	*… und meine Aufgaben schließen die Einführung der Qualitäts-Kontrollnormen ein*
	My current post is that of Sales Manager at Konrad Software AG in Dortmund	*Ich bin zur Zeit Verkaufsmanager bei der Konrad Software AG in Dortmund*
	– promotion / progress within the company	***– Beförderung / Werdegang innerhalb der Firma***
	I have held this post for three years, having started in .. as an office junior	*Ich habe diese Stelle seit drei Jahren inne. Angefangen habe ich .. als Büroangestellte(r) / Bürohilfe*

	I have occupied this post since the company was taken over by Trondheim AG in ..	*Ich habe diese Stelle inne, seit die Firma von der Trondheim AG .. übernommen wurde*
	– unemployed	*– arbeitslos*
	I am currently unemployed and have been so since September ..	*Ich bin zur Zeit arbeitslos und dies seit September ..*
	I was one of the 400 employees to be made redundant in January .. when Trondheim AG closed down	*Ich war einer der 400 Angestellten, denen im Januar .. betriebsbedingt gekündigt wurde, als die Trondheim AG ihre Tätigkeit einstellte*
3	Reason(s) for leaving current job*	*Grund (Gründe) für den beruflichen Wechsel**
	Even though I am successful in my current position, I now wish to move on to a post with more responsibility	*Obwohl ich in meiner gegenwärtigen Stelle erfolgreich bin, möchte ich jetzt einen Posten mit mehr Verantwortung übernehmen*
	... I wish to look for something new (and exciting / challenging)	*... Ich suche etwas Neues (und Aufregendes / mit einer Herausforderung)*
	– prospects	*– Aussichten*
	In view of the fact that there are no promotion prospects for the time being where I am employed, I am looking for a position which will offer me a new challenge	*Angesichts der Tatsache, dass zur Zeit dort wo ich angestellt bin, keine Beförderungsaussichten bestehen, suche ich eine Position, die mir eine neue Herausforderung bietet*
	As the company at which I am presently employed is being downsized to a significant degree, I am seeking alternative employment	*Da die Firma, bei der ich im Moment beschäftigt bin, in bedeutendem Maße verkleinert wird, suche ich eine andere Stelle*
	– salary	*– Gehalt*
	My current salary is $50,000 p. a., including an annual Christmas bonus of a full month's pay	*Mein jetziges Gehalt beträgt 50.000 $ pro Jahr einschließlich einer jährlichen Weihnachtsgratifikation in Höhe eines ganzen Monatsgehalts*
	Reason(s) for seeking new activity	*Grund (Gründe) für die Suche nach einer neuen Tätigkeit*
	As my business is now growing fast I would like to open up a new market	*Da mein Geschäft jetzt schnell wächst, möchte ich gern einen neuen Markt erschließen*
4	Request to be considered for the post	*Bitte, für die Stelle in Betracht gezogen zu werden*
	I very much hope that you will grant me an interview	*Ich hoffe sehr, dass Sie mir ein Vorstellungsgespräch ermöglichen*

	I feel sure that your company has the opening I am looking for and would, therefore, be most grateful if you would consider my application	*Ich glaube sicher, dass Ihre Firma die Stelle hat, nach der ich suche, und ich wäre Ihnen daher sehr dankbar, wenn Sie meine Bewerbung berücksichtigen würden*
	– availability for interview / to take aptitude test	***– Verfügbarkeit für ein Vorstellungsgespräch / für einen Eignungstest***
	I am available for interview at short notice	*Ich stehe für ein Vorstellungsgespräch kurzfristig zur Verfügung*
	I will be pleased to take the aptitude test on 15 June ..	*Ich werde den Eignungstest am 15. Juni .. gern ablegen*
5	**Reference(s) / testimonial(s)**	***Referenz(en) / Zeugnis(se)***
	I enclose my CV / resume and copies of my qualifications and testimonials from my previous employers	*Ich füge meinen (tabellarischen) Lebenslauf und Kopien meiner Qualifikationen und Zeugnisse der früheren Arbeitgeber bei*
	Should you require references, the referees named in the enclosed CV / resume will be pleased to provide you with any information you may need	*Sollten Sie Referenzen benötigen, werden die im beigefügten Lebenslauf / tabellarischen Lebenslauf genannten Auskunftgeber Ihnen gern alle Informationen, die Sie möglicherweise brauchen, zukommen lassen*
	References are available on request	*Referenzen sind auf Wunsch verfügbar*
6	**Polite ending**	***Höflicher Schluss***
	Many thanks in advance for your attention to my application	*Vielen Dank im Voraus für die meiner Bewerbung gewidmete Aufmerksamkeit*
7	**Enclosure(s)**	***Anlage(n)***
	CV / Resume Qualifications Testimonial(s) Letter(s) of recommendation	*(tabellarischer) Lebenslauf* *Qualifikationen* *Zeugnis(se)* *Empfehlungsschreiben*

Curriculum Vitae / Resume (Extracts)

7	**Objective***	***Ziel****
	To obtain a position with more scope for personal initiative	*Eine Stelle mit mehr Raum für persönliche Initiative zu bekommen*
	… with greater responsibility	*… mit mehr Verantwortung*
	… with more flexibility	*… mit mehr Flexibilität*
	… with new challenges	*… mit neuen Herausforderungen*
	… with good promotion prospects	*… mit guten Beförderungsaussichten*
	… in which I will be able to put my knowledge of foreign languages to good use	*… in der ich in der Lage bin, meine Fremdsprachenkenntnisse erfolgreich einzusetzen*

8	**Education / Qualifications**	***Ausbildung/Qualifikationen***
	See "CURRICULUM VITAE Standard Expressions" (page 257)	*Siehe „CURRICULUM VITAE Standard Expressions" (Seite 257)*
	– vocational training course(s)	***– Berufsausbildungskurs(e)***
	A recognised qualification in business administration	*Eine anerkannte Qualifikation als Industriekaufmann/frau*
	office administration	*Bürokaufmann/frau*
	retailing	*Einzelhandelskaufmann/frau*
	wholesaling	*Großhandelskaufmann/frau*
	freight forwarding	*Speditionskaufmann/frau*
	– other vocational skills	***– weitere berufliche Kenntnisse***
	Typing (60 w.p.m. (= words per minute)	*Schreibmaschine (60 Wörter pro Minute)*
	Shorthand (100 w.p.m.)	*Kurzschrift (100 Wörter pro Minute)*
	Conversant with Windows / Microsoft Word for Windows / Microsoft Word for the Mackintosh / Excel / WordPerfect for Windows etc.	*Vertraut mit Windows / Microsoft Word for Windows / Microsoft Word for the Mackintosh / Excel / WordPerfect for Windows etc.*
	Conversant with all / most / a large number of major software packages	*Vertraut mit allen / den meisten / einer großen Anzahl von größeren Software-Programmen*
	Conversant with Internet applications including e-mail	*Vertraut mit Internet-Anwendungen einschließlich E-Mail*
9	**Employment**	***Berufstätigkeit***
	– temporary work	***– Zeitarbeit***
	Temporary work with the "Zeit-Share" employment agency in Essen as a sales assistant	*Zeitarbeit mit der „Zeit-Share" Vermittlungsfirma in Essen als Verkäufer/in*
	– permanent post(s)	***– feste Arbeitsstelle(n)***
	Position	***Position***
	Secretary to the Managing Director / Marketing Executive	*Sekretärin des geschäftsführenden Direktors / Marketingleiters*
	Responsibilities	***Verantwortungsbereich***
	Dealing with incoming / outgoing orders	*Handhabung von eingehenden / ausgehenden Aufträgen*
	Responsible for documentation	*Verantwortlich für die Dokumentation*
	I was in charge of correspondence with foreign customers	*Ich war verantwortlich für die Korrespondenz mit ausländischen Kunden*
	Achievements*	***Leistungen****
	I increased sales by 20 %	*Ich habe den Umsatz um 20 % erhöht*
	I negotiated a new agreement with the union resulting in an increase in productivity of 25 %	*Ich habe eine neue Vereinbarung mit der Gewerkschaft ausgehandelt, wodurch eine Produktivitätserhöhung von 25 % erreicht wurde*

	I was promoted to the position of Head of the Export Department in recognition of my performance	*Ich wurde in Anerkennung meiner Leistung zum Leiter / zur Leiterin der Exportabteilung befördert*
	In the course of my three years in charge of the European Sales Section there was a noticeable improvement in the company's performance	*Im Verlauf der drei Jahre, die ich Leiter/in der Verkaufsabteilung Europa war, verbesserte sich die Produktivität / Leistung der Firma erheblich*
	Whilst I was in charge of negotiations with financial institutions, productivity rose by 15 %	*Während ich die Verhandlungen mit Finanzinstituten leitete, stieg die Produktivität um 15 %*
	– reason(s) for leaving*	***– Grund (Gründe) für den Weggang****
	Expiry of employment contract	*Ablauf des Arbeitsvertrages*
	Redundancy brought about by the company's financial difficulties	*Freistellung / Betriebsbedingte Kündigung auf Grund der finanziellen Schwierigkeiten des Unternehmens*
	Lack of promotion prospects in my current position	*Mangel an Beförderungsaussichten in meiner gegenwärtigen Position*
	I have recently obtained a qualification in translating and interpreting in German and English and now wish to make full use of it	*Ich habe kürzlich die Übersetzer- und Dolmetscher-Qualifikation in Deutsch und Englisch erworben und möchte diese jetzt voll nutzen*
	Despite my considerable success my employer is unwilling to pay me on a performance-related basis and has no suitable new opening for me	*Trotz meines erheblichen Erfolgs ist mein Arbeitgeber nicht bereit, mich auf einer leistungsbezogenen Basis zu bezahlen und hat auch keine geeignete neue Stelle für mich*
	Birth of my first / second / third etc. child	*Geburt meines ersten / zweiten / dritten usw. Kindes*
13	**References**	***Referenzen***
	References are available on request	*Referenzen sind auf Wunsch erhältlich*

Employer's Reply

1	**Reference to application**	***Bezugnahme auf Bewerbung***
	Thank you for your application for the post of European Sales Clerk	*Vielen Dank für Ihre Bewerbung um die Stelle des / der Verkaufssachbearbeiters / -sachbearbeiterin Europa*
	I refer to our telephone conversation of today regarding a post with us as a European Sales Clerk	*Ich beziehe mich auf unser Telefongespräch von heute bezüglich einer Stelle bei uns als Verkaufssachbearbeiter/in Europa*

2	**Invitation to an aptitude test***	***Einladung zu einem Eignungstest****
	We would like you to take an aptitude test as part of our selection procedure	*Wir möchten, dass Sie als Teil unseres Auswahlverfahrens an einem Eignungstest teilnehmen*
	Your result will be made available to you the same day and successful candidates will then be invited to an initial interview the next day	*Ihr Ergebnis wird Ihnen am gleichen Tag zugänglich gemacht, und erfolgreiche Kandidaten werden dann am nächsten Tag zu einem 1. Vorstellungsgespräch eingeladen*
	– an initial interview*	***– erstes Vorstellungsgespräch****
	We wish to invite you to attend an initial interview	*Wir möchten Sie zu einem ersten Vorstellungsgespräch einladen*
	Directions are enclosed for your convenience	*Nähere Beschreibungen für Sie fügen wir bei*
	– the final interview*	***– Bewerbungsgespräch****
	Short-listed candidates will later be invited to attend the final interview	*Kandidaten, die in die engere Wahl kommen, werden später zu einem (endgültigen) Vorstellungsgespräch / Bewerbungsgespräch eingeladen*
	Having successfully completed the first part of our selection procedure, you are now invited to attend the final interview, which will take place on 15 June .. in Munich	*Nachdem Sie mit Erfolg den ersten Teil unseres Auswahlverfahrens durchlaufen haben, werden Sie jetzt eingeladen, am Bewerbungsgespräch teilzunehmen, das am 15. Juni .. in München stattfinden wird*
3	**Conditions***	***Bedingungen****
	– qualifications	***– Qualifikationen***
	We are only able to consider applications from candidates possessing a recognised qualification in marketing	*Wir sind nur in der Lage, Bewerbungen von Kandidaten und Kandidatinnen zu berücksichtigen, die eine anerkannte Marketing-Qualifikation besitzen*
	– experience	***– Erfahrung***
	We must point out that we are only able to consider candidates with considerable experience of this type of work	*Wir müssen darauf hinweisen, dass wir nur Kandidaten und Kandidatinnen berücksichtigen können, die erhebliche Erfahrung in diesem Arbeitsbereich haben*
	– references	***– Referenzen***
	We are now in the process of taking up your references and will be contacting you in due course	*Wir sind jetzt dabei, Ihre Referenzen einzuholen und werden uns zu gegebener Zeit mit Ihnen in Verbindung setzen*
	– nationality / immigration status	***– Nationalität / Einwanderungsstatus***
	Should you require assistance with applying for a work permit, do not hesitate to contact us	*Sollten Sie Hilfe bei der Beantragung einer Arbeitserlaubnis benötigen, zögern Sie nicht, sich an uns zu wenden*

	In conformity with current immigration laws, we are only able to offer this job to citizens of the EU	*In Übereinstimmung mit den gegenwärtigen Einwanderungsgesetzen sind wir nur in der Lage, diese Stelle Bürgern der EU anzubieten*
	– probationary period	***– Probezeit***
	There is a probationary period of three months, after which time your contract will be reviewed	*Die Probezeit beträgt drei Monate. Nach dieser Zeit wird Ihr Vertrag überprüft*
	– salary	***– Gehalt***
	Please refer to the enclosure for details of our salary scales	*Bitte entnehmen Sie Einzelheiten unserer Gehaltsskala der beigefügten Anlage*
	The successful candidate will receive a starting salary of $50,000 p. a., to be reviewed yearly	*Der erfolgreiche Bewerber erhält ein Anfangsgehalt von 50.000 $ pro Jahr, das jährlich überprüft wird*
	The successful applicant will receive an initial salary at point 3 on our company's pay scale (see enclosure), subject to annual review	*Die erfolgreiche Bewerberin erhält ein Anfangsgehalt nach Punkt 3 der Gehaltsskala unseres Unternehmens (siehe Anlage), das jährlich überprüft wird*
	You may also be eligible for further allowances on a discretionary basis	*Möglicherweise werden Ihnen weitere Vergütungen auf Diskretionsbasis gewährt*
	Please let us have an indication of the salary expected	*Bitte geben Sie uns einen Hinweis bezüglich Ihrer Gehaltsvorstellungen*
	We guarantee to match your current salary	*Wir geben Ihnen die Garantie, dass wir Ihrem laufenden Gehalt entsprechend zahlen*
	We guarantee to exceed your current salary	*Wir geben Ihnen die Garantie, dass Sie mehr als Ihr laufendes Gehalt erhalten werden*
	– expenses	***– Ausgaben***
	We wish to point out that only the successful candidate's expenses will be refunded on presentation of appropriate receipts	*Wir möchten darauf hinweisen, dass nur die Ausgaben des erfolgreichen Bewerbers gegen Vorlage der entsprechenden Belege erstattet werden*
	No expenses will be refunded	*Ausgaben werden nicht erstattet*
	– accommodation	***– Unterbringung***
	Candidates for this post are being accommodated at the Hotel Pacific in Hamburg	*Bewerber/innen für diese Stelle werden im Hotel Pacific in Hamburg untergebracht*
4	**Rejection**	***Ablehnung***
	– reasons	***– Gründe***
	We are sorry to tell you that this post is taken	*Wir bedauern, Ihnen mitzuteilen, dass diese Stelle bereits besetzt ist*

	We regret to inform you that we have no vacancy for a European Sales Clerk at present	*Wir bedauern, Ihnen mitzuteilen, dass wir zur Zeit keine freie Stelle für eine Verkaufssachbearbeiterin Europa haben*
	We have considered your application and are sorry to tell you that we are unable to offer you the post in question	*Wir haben Ihre Bewerbung in Betracht gezogen und bedauern, Ihnen mitzuteilen, dass wir Ihnen die infrage stehende Position nicht anbieten können*
	– waiting list	*– Warteliste*
	We have noted your particulars and will get in touch with you if we have a suitable vacancy at a later date	*Wir haben Ihre Personalien notiert und werden mit Ihnen in Verbindung treten, wenn wir zu einem späteren Zeitpunkt eine geeignete Vakanz haben*
	– referral to another employer	*– Verweisung an einen anderen Arbeitgeber*
	If you wish, your personal data can be given to Möbeldesign Havekamp GmbH, with whom we work closely	*Wenn Sie wünschen, können wir Ihre Personalien der Möbeldesign Havekamp GmbH geben, mit der wir eng zusammenarbeiten*
	– reference to return of application documents	*– Bezugnahme auf Rücksendung der Bewerbungsunterlagen*
	We are returning your application documents with this letter	*Wir schicken Ihnen die Bewerbungsunterlagen mit diesem Brief wieder zurück*
5	Polite ending	*Höflicher Schluss*
	We look forward to hearing from you in the near future	*Wir freuen uns, in Kürze wieder von Ihnen zu hören*
	We look forward to meeting you personally in Düsseldorf on 1 August ..	*Wir freuen uns, Sie persönlich am 1. August .. in Düsseldorf zu treffen*
	We regret that we are unable to help you this time and wish you every success in the future	*Wir bedauern, dass wir Ihnen dieses Mal nicht helfen können und wünschen Ihnen für die Zukunft viel Erfolg*
6	Enclosure(s)	*Anlage(n)*
	Application documents	*Bewerbungsunterlagen*
	Certificate(s)	*Bescheinigung(en)*
	Pay scale	*Lohn- und Gehaltsskala*

Writing a Reference / Testimonial (Extracts)

4	**Reference to request for reference**	***Bezugnahme auf Bitte um Referenz***
	I refer to our (telephone) conversation on 15 January .. regarding Dr Büdenbender, in connection with her application for the post of European Sales Director and am pleased to supply you with the reference requested	*Ich beziehe mich auf unser (Telefon-) Gespräch vom 15. Januar .. über Frau Dr. Büdenbender im Zusammenhang mit ihrer Bewerbung für die Stelle der Europäischen Verkaufsdirektorin und bin erfreut, Ihnen die erbetene Referenz zu geben*
	I am only able to supply you with a brief reference	*Ich kann Ihnen nur eine kurze Referenz zur Verfügung stellen*
	I refer to our telephone conversation of this morning regarding Dr Büdenbender and am, as I said, unfortunately only able to supply you with the following information	*Ich beziehe mich auf unser Telefongespräch von heute morgen über Frau Dr. Büdenbender und bin, wie ich sagte, leider nur in der Lage, Ihnen die folgenden Informationen zu geben*
5	**How well you know the candidate**	***Wie gut Sie den Kandidaten / die Kandidatin kennen***
	I have known Dr Büdenbender for six years / since ..	*Ich kenne Frau Dr. Büdenbender seit sechs Jahren / seit ..*
	I worked with Frau Henrietta Stratmann for five years, during which time she worked as a sales representative	*Ich habe fünf Jahre lang mit Frau Henrietta Stratmann zusammengearbeitet. Während dieser Zeit war sie als Verkaufsvertreterin beschäftigt*
	Dr Büdenbender and I have now been colleagues for six years / since ..	*Frau Dr. Büdenbender und ich sind jetzt seit sechs Jahren / seit .. Kollegen / Kolleginnen*
	Dr Büdenbender only worked for me for nine months in ..	*Frau Dr. Büdenbender hat im Jahr .. nur neun Monate lang für mich gearbeitet*
6	**The candidate's work**	***Die Arbeit des Bewerbers / der Bewerberin***
	... as a personal assistant in the Sales Department, with responsibility for incoming and outgoing orders	*... als persönlicher Assistent / persönliche Assistentin in der Verkaufsabteilung, verantwortlich für hereinkommende und ausgehende Aufträge*
	... as a salesman, mainly concerned with exporting goods to Sri Lanka	*als Verkäufer, hauptsächlich verantwortlich für den Export von Waren nach Sri Lanka*
	– quality of work	***– Qualität der Arbeit***
	Her work has always been acceptable / satisfactory / above average / excellent	*Ihre Arbeit war immer akzeptabel / zufriedenstellend / überdurchschnittlich / ausgezeichnet*
	She has always performed her duties efficiently / competently / conscientiously	*Sie hat ihre Aufgaben immer effizient / kompetent / gewissenhaft ausgeführt*
	She speaks some Russian	*Sie spricht etwas Russisch*

	She has a working knowledge of Chinese	*Sie hat chinesische Grundkenntnisse*
	She has a fair command of both written and spoken Italian	*Sie beherrscht Italienisch recht gut in Wort und Schrift*
	She speaks and writes Spanish fluently	*Sie spricht und schreibt Spanisch fließend*
	She is (perfectly) bi-lingual in Turkish and German	*Sie ist (perfekt) zweisprachig in Türkisch und Deutsch*
	She has good typing skills	*Sie hat gute Schreibmaschinenkenntnisse*
	She can take shorthand at 100 w. p. m. (= words per minute)	*Sie beherrscht Stenografie mit 100 Wörtern pro Minute*
7	**The candidate's nature (manner)**	***Die Art (das Auftreten) des Bewerbers / der Bewerberin***
	Dr Büdenbender is cheerful / even-tempered / outward-going / highly personable	*Frau Dr. Büdenbender ist freundlich / ausgeglichen / offen / sehr sympathisch*
	She can be left to get on with the job without supervision	*Man kann ihr die Arbeit ohne Überwachung anvertrauen*
	She spares no effort to deal with the task at hand	*Sie scheut bei der Bewältigung einer anstehenden Aufgabe keine Mühe*
8	**The candidate's character**	***Der Charakter des Bewerbers / der Bewerberin***
	She is totally honest and does not shirk responsibility	*Sie ist völlig ehrlich und drückt sich nicht vor der Verantwortung*
	She is entirely reliable and can be entrusted with duties requiring a high degree of personal integrity	*Sie ist voll zuverlässig, und man kann ihr Aufgaben anvertrauen, die einen hohen Grad persönlicher Integrität verlangen*
	She is usually punctual and reliable	*Sie ist gewöhnlich pünktlich und zuverlässig*
9	**Reason(s) for leaving***	***Grund (Gründe) für den Weggang****
	She left the company of her own accord	*Sie hat auf eigenen Wunsch die Firma verlassen*
	She opted not to extend her contract for personal reasons	*Sie hat sich dafür entschieden, ihren Vertrag aus persönlichen Gründen nicht zu verlängern*
10	**Suitability for the position in question (reference)**	***Eignung für die infrage stehende Position (Referenz)***
	I would therefore recommend Dr Büdenbender for this post whole-heartedly	*Ich würde daher Frau Dr. Büdenbender für diese Stelle aufrichtig empfehlen*
	I therefore have no hesitation in recommending Dr Büdenbender for this post	*Ich habe daher keine Bedenken, Frau Dr. Büdenbender für diese Stelle zu empfehlen*
	I therefore feel that Frau Felicitas Szepanski would be suitable for this post after appropriate training	*Ich glaube deshalb, dass Frau Felicitas Szepanski nach geeigneter Einarbeitung für diese Stelle geeignet wäre*

I am, therefore, unfortunately unable to say whether she is suited for the post in question or not	*Ich bin daher leider nicht in der Lage zu sagen, ob sie für den infrage stehenden Posten geeignet ist oder nicht*
In view of my brief acquaintance with Frau Szepanski, I cannot say whether she would be suitable for this position or not	*In Anbetracht meiner kurzen Bekanntschaft mit Frau Szepanski kann ich nicht sagen, ob sie für diese Position geeignet wäre oder nicht*
– recommendation for further employment (testimonial)	*– Empfehlung für weitere Beschäftigung (Zeugnis)*
I have no hesitation in recommending her for employment	*Ich habe keine Bedenken, sie für eine Beschäftigung zu empfehlen*
I feel sure she will be an asset to any future employer	*Ich bin sicher, dass sie für jeden zukünftigen Arbeitgeber eine wertvolle Kraft ist*

Unit 14
Forwarding and Insurance

Customer's Enquiry about Freight Forwarding Services

1 Source of address*	We have seen your advertisement			in the … (name of publication) of … (date) in last week's/month's … (name of publication) on the Internet	
	We have been given your (company's) name by We have obtained your company's name from You have been recommended to us by			… (name of person/company) a business associate the … (name of town/city, e. g. Essen) Chamber of Commerce the … (nationality, e. g. Japanese) Embassy/Consulate	
2 Request for quotation* – single/regular shipments – bulk rates	Please quote us your	best lowest most favourable most competitive	(bulk) rates for all-inclusive rates for FOB rates for CIF rates for	a (single) shipment of regular shipments of	… (goods) (see below "3. Details of goods to be transported")
	How much would it cost for How much would you charge for What is/are your tariff(s) for What do you charge for What is your CIF/FOB etc. for				
– Incoterm – groupage rates	… to be transported	separately in a separate container in separate containers as a separate unit as group freight as a groupage consignment as a consolidated shipment		and delivered	… (Incoterm + destination) FOB … (named destination) CIF … (named destination)
– insurance	The goods are The consignment is	to be insured		against all risks (including particular average and force majeure) warehouse-to-warehouse in transit in accordance with Institute Cargo Clauses A (B,C) with general average (WGA) with particular average (WPA) with general but excluding particular average free of particular average (FPA) free of particular average under 10 % (FPA 10 %) free of all averages	

– charter rates	We wish to charter We are interested in chartering Please let us know how much it would cost to charter We would be grateful if you would let us have details of your tariffs to charter Please let us know what (shipping/airline) company/companies would be prepared to let us charter			a ship of approx. 10,000 GRT a ship with a (cargo) capacity of 4,000 tonnes/metric tons a plane with a (cargo) capacity of 900 cbm a plane with a (cargo) capacity of 150 tonnes/metric tons		
	Please let us know whether you are able to arrange a time charter for a suitable vessel to ship … (goods + further details)					
3 Details of goods to be transported – quantity	We wish to We intend to	send ship transport forward	… (quantity, e.g. 100) one dozen (12) two/three dozen (24/36) one/two gross of (144/288) a cargo of … (quantity) a shipment of … (quantity) a consignment of … (quantity) a load of … (quantity)	(boxes of) (crates of) (chests of) (cases of) (carboys of) (bags of) (sacks of) (tins of) (barrels of) (drums of) (bundles of) (bales of) (container(s) of) (pallet(s) of)	… (goods)	in (cardboard/fibreglass) boxes in (plywood) boxes in foam-lined boxes in collapsible cardboard boxes in (generously padded/wooden) boxes in (sturdy) (reinforced) (strongly boarded) crates in (tea) chests (lined with silver paper) in (solid wooden) (damp-proof) (nailed/battened) cases in polystyrene packing material in (100-litre) carboys in (canvas/paper/3-ply reinforced paper) bags in (50 kg) sacks in (securely sealed) (air-tight) tins in (1,000 l) barrels in (sturdy/stout/sealed) (fibre) drums in bundles in bales (2 m × 5 m) in a container/in containers on a pallet/on pallets

– weight	*(see previous page)*	... (weight) *Metric* 100 kg 1,000 kg / 1 tonne 1,500 kg / 1.5 tonnes 2,000 kg / 2 tonnes *Avoirdupois Weight (BE)* 112 lbs / 1 hundredweight / 1 cwt 20 cwt / 1 (long) ton 2240 lbs / 1 long ton	of	*(see previous page)*
– volume		... (volume) *Cubic Measure* 1 cubic foot 100 cu feet cft 100 cu yards 100 cu metres (cbm) *Cubic Capacity* 1 British pint (i. e. 0.568 litres) 1 US pint (i. e. 0.473 litres) 1 gal / 1 British gallon (i. e. 4.546 litres) 1 gal / 1 US gallon (i. e. 3.785 litres) 1,000 gals 1 litre 1,000 litres		
	The shipment consists of The consignment is (made up of) The load in question is The consignment to be shipped is The load we have in mind consists of			
	We wish to ship a consignment of livestock (consisting of ... e. g. 200 dairy cows)		by articulated lorry to ... (destination) in a semi-trailer ... (destination)	via the Channel Tunnel through the Brenner Pass over the Pyrenees

	We would require you to	crate and ship collect and forward collect, pack and forward	a machine weighing … (weight, e. g. 500 kg, 2,000 lbs) a • piece • length • section of (metal/ceramic/concrete) piping weighing … and measuring …		
– dimensions			a(n)/2/3 • vehicle(s) • object(s) • article(s)	measuring the dimensions of which are	1 m × 2.5 m × 2 m (length, width, height) 1' × 8'6" × 6' (length, width, height)
				which is (are) 2.5 metres long by 1 metre wide by 2 metres high (each) which is (are) 8 foot 6 inches long by 1 foot wide by 6 foot high which measure(s) 2.5 metres by 1 metre by 2 metres in length, width and height respectively which measure(s) 1 foot in length by 8 foot 6 inches in width by 6 foot in height	
– nature	This consignment is These goods are This material is This substance is This liquid is This fluid is This gas is The consignment in question is The goods in question are We must point out that goods of this nature are Please bear in mind that products of this nature are		fragile perishable (extremely) valuable of great sentimental value to its/their owner hazardous highly dangerous explosive poisonous caustic corrosive flammable (highly) inflammable radioactive infectious potentially harmful to human beings and animals highly susceptible to fading when exposed to direct sunlight	and must be handled accordingly and should be handled with (extreme) caution and should therefore be handled with appropriate care and may, under no circumstances, be handled roughly	

4 Mode of transport required	We wish to send the goods We require the goods to be shipped Transport would be We require transport The goods must be shipped The goods would need to be sent	by road/lorry/truck/van by rail by sea/ship by conference ship by tramp steamer by cargo liner by ro-ro vessel by (ro-ro) ferry by air by inland waterway by (river) barge by multi-modal transport in a container as a groupage consignment as bulk cargo as package freight using a suitable haulier (haulage contractor) door-to-door using a ship chartered for this purpose	from … (location) to … (location) via … (location)	with delivery to …

5 Location(s)/Date(s) – collection/ delivery	The goods The load The consignment The machine(s) The material(s)	is/are to be would be would have to be would need to be	picked up collected	from our premises from our warehouse from our storage plant from our depot from our plant from our factory from our office from our company's headquarters	in … (location)	on … (date) by … (date) within … (period of time)	at … (time) between … (time) and … (time)
	We would require you to collect We would require collection of	the goods the load the consignment the machine(s) the material(s)					
	… and deliver it/them to … (location) … with delivery to … (location)						

	Please let us know the latest dates for shipment of … (goods) from … (port of shipment, e.g. Southampton) … to … (port of destination, e.g. Durban)		
	We wish to know the names of vessels sailing from … (port) to … (port) Which vessels will be sailing to … (port)		on … (date) as from … (date) next month after … (date) in the next 3 months
	Is it necessary to Must we Are you able to	reserve cargo space? have the goods loaded by a certain date? specify which vessel the goods are to be shipped on?	
	Do ships sailing from … (port of shipment) and docking at … (port of destination) also call at … (name of port)? Please let us have the vessel's sailing card when making your quotation		
– storage	The goods must be kept The goods must be stored We would require the goods to be stored	indoors separately from other goods in an open air storage space in a (locked) warehouse in a guarded warehouse (as the goods are (highly) explosive) in a completely dry (air-conditioned) warehouse in a refrigerated warehouse in a heated warehouse on pallets in a warehouse (with a rail link) in a bonded warehouse	
6 Documentation	Do you provide Does your service include the provision of	shipping documents? the requisite documentation? (all) the necessary documentation?	
	As payment has been agreed by documentary credit	we would require you to provide	the necessary documentation a full set of 3 clean, on-board Bs/L
	Are you able to	obtain certificates of origin obtain consular invoices have invoices legalised/consularised	if necessary? should this be necessary? if specified by certain countries?
	Does your service include	the legalisation and consularisation of documentation?	

7 Other formalities – packing	We would need you to pack the goods We would require the goods to be packed by you Please include in your quotation the charges for packing the goods	on our premises in our warehouse in our depot in our factory at our storage plant at our plant	in (cardboard / fibreglass) boxes in (plywood) boxes in foam-lined boxes in collapsible cardboard boxes in (generously padded / wooden) boxes in (sturdy) (reinforced) (strongly boarded) crates in (steel-strapped) wooden boxes in (tea) chests (lined with silver paper) in (solid wooden) (damp-proof) (nailed / battened) cases in polystyrene packing material in (100 litre) carboys in (canvas / paper / 3-ply reinforced paper) bags in (50 kg) sacks in (securely sealed) (air-tight) tins in (1,000 l) barrels in (sturdy / stout / sealed) (fibre) drums in bundles in bales (2 m × 5 m) in a container / in containers on a pallet / on pallets
– customs clearance	Does your service include customs clearance? Are you also able to arrange for shipments to be cleared through customs? Are you able to deal with all the necessary customs formalities for a load of this nature? We would also require you to attend to all other import and export formalities, including customs clearance		
– collection service	Does your service include COD delivery? Do you also offer a collection service? Are you also able to arrange for payment of the goods on delivery?		If so, please let us have your rates If so, please send us details of your charges Should this be the case, please send us your tariff If you are able to offer this service please let us know how much you would charge (for … + details, e. g. seaworthy packing and customs clearance)
8 Polite ending	Hoping to hear from you soon We look forward to your early reply We hope to hear from you shortly We look forward to your reply with interest Please let us have your offer as soon as possible Many thanks in advance for your attention to our enquiry		

A prompt reply to this enquiry would be most appreciated
If your rates are competitive we will place a trial order with you
Provided you are able to offer us the all-inclusive service we require, we will be pleased to commission you to forward this (and other) shipment(s)
If you are able to offer the service we require, we will be pleased to entrust you with shipping the goods described above

Freight Forwarder's Offer

1 Reference to enquiry	Thank you for Many thanks for With reference to In reply to	your letter/fax/telex/e-mail/ communication dated/of … the above-mentioned enquiry your telephone enquiry the phone call from your agent/ representative Mr/Ms … on … (date)	enquiring about … (details) asking for a quotation for… (details) requesting us to quote you for … (details) about … (details) regarding … (details)		We are …
	I refer to				and am …
	… pleased to let you have the following information/quotation				
2 Request for further information*	Before we can send you our (detailed) quotation Before sending you our (detailed) quotation	we must ask you to we would request you	tell us the (approximate) let us know the (approximate) specify the give us exact information as to the	size weight dimensions	of the load of the consignment of the … (details)
				nature of this properties of this particular	material substance liquid fluid gas
3 Mode of transport	For transporting For shipping For delivering	… (details)	by road/lorry/truck/van by rail by sea/ship by conference ship by tramp steamer by cargo liner by ro-ro vessel	from … (location) to … (location) via … (location)	

	(see previous page)		by (ro-ro) ferry by air by inland waterway by (river) barge by multi-modal transport in a container as a groupage consignment as bulk cargo as package freight using a suitable haulier (haulage contractor) door-to-door using a ship chartered for this purpose	*(see previous page)*
– insurance	… with full insurance cover … including / excluding … insurance cover			
	… the goods to be insured	against all risks (including particular average and force majeure) warehouse-to-warehouse in transit in accordance with Institute Cargo Clauses A (B,C) with general average (WGA) with particular average (WPA) with general but excluding particular average free of particular average (FPA) free of particular average under 10 % (FPA 10 %) free of all averages		
– charges	… we would charge … our charges would be … the basic charge would be … the costs would amount to	… (amount)	including / excluding	(seaworthy) packing collection from your premises loading and unloading storage charges warehousing all taxes 1 / 2 / 3 etc. lay-day(s) customs clearance documentation legalisation consularisation

	... the total charges would amount to ... excluding demurrage at ... (rate) per day ... our charges would be as follows: ... please refer to the enclosed tariff		
4 Dates – collection	We would need We would require	a week's/2 weeks'/3 weeks' etc. notice of the collection date required	
	Please let us know ... weeks in advance what collection date is required ETS (estimated time of shipment) would be ... (date)		
– raising documentation	The documents specified in your enquiry can be provided at an extra charge (of ...) We are unfortunately unable to obtain the documents you require. Please refer to ... (name of company/organisation) for assistance As you require us to raise all documentation, please allow ... extra weeks/months for processing We will require you to provide us with the following documents needed to export the goods: ... (list, e.g. Test Certificate, Fumigation Certificate etc.) We will be pleased to supply you with 3 originals of the bill of lading, together with 6 (non-negotiable) copies, as requested		
– storage	The goods (specified) can be stored We will make arrangements for the goods to be stored The goods specified would have to be stored	indoors separately from other goods in an open air storage space in a (locked) warehouse in a guarded warehouse (as the goods are (highly) explosive) in a completely dry (air-conditioned) warehouse in a refrigerated warehouse in a heated warehouse on pallets in a warehouse with a rail link in a bonded warehouse	at no extra charge at an extra charge of ... as requested as stipulated
– delivery	ETA (Estimated time of arrival) would be ... (date) You will be notified as soon as the goods have reached • the port of destination • ... Railway Station • ... Airport • ... (location) Please allow ... weeks/months etc. for delivery The goods/load/consignment etc. will/would, in all probability, be shipped on board MS Victoria, which sets sail from ... (port of shipment) on ... (date), calls at ... (name of port) and is due to dock in ... (port of destination) on ... (date)		

5	Reference to enclosure(s)*	Please use the enclosed order form when placing your order Please fill in all sections of the enclosed order form when placing your order to enable us to book cargo space in good time Please refer to the packing instructions enclosed We would request you to follow the enclosed packing instructions carefully to speed up the processing of your order and minimise damage We enclose a copy of the current … (name of publication) for your reference A copy of the export regulations for goods of this nature is enclosed for your reference Before making the goods ready for collection, please ensure the enclosed export regulations have been adhered to
6	Terms of payment	Your order will be dealt with as soon as we have received your remittance for the sum of … (amount) The goods will be collected and forwarded to their destination as soon as we have received your remittance (for … (amount)) On receipt of our invoice please arrange to have the amount in question transferred to our account no. … at … (name of Bank e. g. Deutsche) Bank in … (location) Before we can start processing your order we require an (obligatory) advance payment of … % … % of the charter costs are due when the order is placed. The balance is due when the goods have arrived at the port of destination The charter costs are due in full when placing your order with us. The balance is payable when the goods have reached the port of destination
7	Validity of offer	This offer is / The rates quoted are / The rate quoted is — firm / valid for … + period of time / until … + date / subject to confirmation / without engagement / subject to change without notice As there has been heavy demand for our services recently / In view of the fact that fuel and transport costs are due to rise in the near future / In view of the (potential) political / social / civil unrest in … (location) — we recommend (that) / we suggest (that) — you place your order as soon as possible / you place your order • by … (+ date) • within … (+ period of time)
8	Polite ending	We look forward to receiving your order We hope to receive your order in the near future We hope our offers meet / quotation meets your expectations We look forward to doing business with you (in the near future) We hope that our offer / quotation will prove acceptable to you Please do not hesitate to contact us if you require further details / if you have any queries regarding … Please place your order as soon as possible to enable us to secure the necessary shipping space for you at the lowest rates

		You may rest assured that any order placed will be dealt with promptly and carefully and that our rates are the most competitive available We look forward to receiving your order in the near future and enclose a brochure (catalogue (AE: catalog)) on our entire range of services for your convenience
9	Enclosure(s)	Order form Packing instructions Export regulations Company brochure Catalogue (AE: catalog)

Customer's Enquiry about Freight Forwarding Services

1	**Source of address**	***Quelle der Anschrift***
	We have seen your advertisement in the *Freight Forwarder* of 15 January ..	*Wir haben Ihre Anzeige im* Freight Forwarder *vom 15. Januar .. gesehen*
	We have obtained your company's name from a business associate	*Wir haben den Namen Ihrer Firma von einem Geschäftsfreund erhalten*
2	**Request for quotation***	***Bitte um Angebot****
	– single / regular shipments	***– einzelne/regelmäßige Sendungen (Transporte, Verschiffungen)***
	Please quote us your most favourable rates for a single shipment of machine tools to Durban, South Africa	*Bitte machen Sie uns ein Angebot für Ihre günstigsten Sätze für einen Einzeltransport von Werkzeugmaschinen nach Durban, Südafrika*
	Please quote us your most competitive CIF rates for regular shipments of machine tools to Boston, Massachusetts	*Bitte bieten Sie uns Ihre wettbewerbfähigsten CIF-Sätze für regelmäßige Sendungen von Werkzeugmaschinen nach Boston, Massachusetts an*
	– Incoterm	***– Incoterm***
	... to be transported separately and delivered CIF Boston, Massachusetts	*... zum separaten Transport und Lieferung CIF Boston, Massachusetts*
	– groupage rates	***– Gruppentarife***
	... to be transported as a groupage consignment	*... zum Transport als Sammelladungsgut*
	– insurance	***– Versicherung***
	The goods are to be insured against all risks, including particular average and force majeure	*Die Waren sollen gegen alle Risiken versichert werden, einschließlich besonderer Havarie und höherer Gewalt*
	The consignment is to be insured with general but excluding particular average	*Die Sendung soll mit allgemeiner, aber ausschließlich besonderer Havarie versichert werden*
	– charter rates	***– Chartersätze***
	We wish to charter a ship of approx. 10,000 GRT	*Wir möchten ein Schiff mit ca. 10.000 BRT chartern*
	We would be grateful if you would let us have details of your tariffs to charter a plane with a cargo capacity of 150 tonnes	*Wir wären Ihnen dankbar, wenn Sie uns Einzelheiten Ihrer Tarife zukommen ließen, um ein Flugzeug mit einer Ladekapazität von 150 Tonnen zu chartern*
	Please let us know whether you are able to arrange a time charter for a suitable vessel to ship a consignment of machine tools to Newcastle, UK	*Bitte lassen Sie uns wissen, ob Sie in der Lage sind, eine Zeitcharter für ein geeignetes Schiff zu vermitteln, um eine Sendung Werkzeugmaschinen nach Newcastle, GB, zu versenden*

3	**Details of goods to be transported**	*Einzelheiten von zu transportierenden Waren*
	– quantity	*– Menge*
	We wish to forward one dozen water pumps in foam-lined boxes	*Wir möchten ein Dutzend Wasserpumpen in schaumstoffgepolsterten Kisten verschicken*
	We intend to ship a consignment of 500 bales of cotton to Liverpool, UK	*Wir haben vor, eine Sendung von 500 Ballen Baumwolle nach Liverpool, GB, zu versenden*
	The shipment consists of 1,000 litres of cooking oil in 100-litre carboys	*Die Sendung besteht aus 1.000 Litern Speiseöl in 100-Liter-Glasballons*
	We wish to ship a consignment of livestock consisting of 200 dairy cows by articulated lorry to Birmingham, via the Channel Tunnel	*Wir möchten eine Sendung lebender Tiere versenden, die aus 200 Milchkühen besteht, und zwar mit einem Sattelschlepper durch den Kanaltunnel nach Birmingham*
	– dimensions	*– Abmessungen*
	We would require you to collect, pack and forward an article measuring 1 m × 2.5 m × 2 m (length, width, height)	*Es wäre erforderlich, dass Sie einen Artikel abholen, verpacken und versenden, der die Abmessungen 1 m × 2,5 m × 2 m (Länge, Breite, Höhe) hat*
	… which measures 1 foot in length by 8 foot 6 inches in width by 6 foot in height	*… der 1 Fuß in der Länge, 8 Fuß 6 Zoll in der Breite und 6 Fuß in der Höhe misst*
	– nature	*– Beschaffenheit*
	This consignment is fragile and must be handled accordingly	*Diese Sendung ist zerbrechlich und muss entsprechend gehandhabt werden*
	This substance is highly dangerous and should therefore be handled with appropriate care	*Diese Substanz ist in höchstem Maße gefährlich und sollte deshalb mit der geeigneten Sorgfalt gehandhabt werden*
	Please bear in mind that products of this nature are potentially harmful to human beings and animals and may, under no circumstances, be handled roughly	*Bitte denken Sie daran, dass Produkte dieser Art für Menschen und Tiere schädlich sein können und unter keinen Umständen unsachgemäß behandelt werden dürfen*
4	**Mode of transport required**	*Art des gewünschten Transports*
	We wish to send the goods by road from Würzburg to Edinburgh via London, with delivery to our customer's premises	*Wir möchten die Waren per Straße von Würzburg nach Edinburgh über London mit Auslieferung in den Geschäftsräumen unseres Kunden versenden*
	We require the goods to be shipped by conference ship	*Wir möchten, dass die Waren per Konferenzschiff versandt werden*
	We require transport using a suitable haulage contractor	*Wir benötigen einen Transport durch einen geeigneten Lkw-Spediteur*

5	**Location(s) / Date(s)**	***Standort(e) / Datum (Daten)***
	– collection / delivery	***– Abholung / Lieferung***
	The goods are to be picked up from our premises in Landshut on 15 January .. at 6 am	*Die Waren müssen am 15. Januar .. um 6 Uhr morgens in unseren Geschäftsräumen in Landshut abgeholt werden*
	The consignment would have to be collected from our depot in Mannheim	*Die Sendung müsste von unserem Depot (Lager) in Mannheim abgeholt werden*
	Please let us know the latest dates for shipment of a bulk load of timber from Southampton, UK, to Durban, South Africa	*Bitte lassen Sie uns die spätesten Termine für die Verschiffung einer Großladung Holz von Southampton, GB, nach Durban, Südafrika, wissen*
	Is it necessary to reserve cargo space?	*Ist es notwendig, Laderaum zu buchen?*
	Do ships sailing from Boston, Massachusetts, and docking at Hamburg also call at Liverpool?	*Legen Schiffe, die von Boston, Massachusetts, auslaufen und in Hamburg eindocken, auch in Liverpool an?*
	– storage	***– Lagerung***
	The goods must be kept in a completely dry, air-conditioned warehouse	*Die Waren müssen in einem vollständig trockenen Lagerhaus mit Klimaanlage aufbewahrt werden*
	… in a bonded warehouse	*… in einem Warenzollverschlusslager*
6	**Documentation**	***Dokumentation***
	Do you provide shipping documents?	*Liefern Sie auch die (Versand-) Verschiffungsdokumente?*
	As payment has been agreed by documentary credit, we would require you to provide the necessary documentation	*Da eine Zahlung per Dokumentenakkreditiv vereinbart wurde, wäre es für uns erforderlich, dass Sie die notwendigen Dokumente bereitstellen*
	Are you able to obtain certificates of origin if necessary?	*Sind Sie in der Lage, nötigenfalls Ursprungszeugnisse einzuholen?*
	Does your service include the legalisation and consularisation of documentation?	*Schließt Ihr Service die Legalisierung und konsularische Bescheinigung der Dokumente ein?*
7	**Other formalities**	***Andere Formalitäten***
	– packing	***– Verpackung***
	We would need you to pack the goods on our premises in generously padded, wooden boxes	*Es wäre erforderlich, dass Sie die Waren in unseren Geschäftsräumen in großzügig wattierte Holzkisten packen*
	… in securely sealed, air-tight tins	*… in sicher versiegelte, luftdichte Dosen*
	– customs clearance	***– Verzollung***
	Does your service include customs clearance?	*Schließt Ihr Service die Zollabfertigung ein?*
	Are you able to deal with all the necessary customs formalities for a load of this nature?	*Sind Sie in der Lage, alle nötigen Zollformalitäten für eine Ladung dieser Art zu erledigen?*

	– collection service	*– Abholungsservice*
	Do you also offer a collection service? If so, please send us details of your charges	*Bieten Sie auch einen Abholungsservice an? Wenn ja, schicken Sie uns bitte Einzelheiten Ihrer Gebühren*
8	Polite ending	*Höflicher Schluss*
	We look forward to your reply with interest	*Wir sehen Ihrer Antwort mit Interesse entgegen*
	A prompt reply to this enquiry would be most appreciated	*Eine baldige Antwort auf diese Anfrage würden wir sehr begrüßen*
	Provided you are able to offer us the all-inclusive service we require, we will be pleased to commission you to forward this and other shipments	*Vorausgesetzt, dass Sie uns den alles umfassenden Service anbieten können, den wir brauchen, werden wir Ihnen gern den Auftrag erteilen, diese und andere Sendungen zu transportieren*

Freight Forwarder's Offer

1	Reference to enquiry	*Bezugnahme auf Anfrage*
	Thank you for your fax of 31 August .. enquiring about shipping rates	*Vielen Dank für Ihr Fax vom 31. August .., mit dem Sie (Versand-) Verschiffungstarife anfragen*
	We are pleased to let you have the following quotation	*Wir freuen uns, Ihnen das folgende Angebot zu unterbreiten*
2	Request for further information*	*Bitte um weitere Informationen**
	Before we can send you a detailed quotation, we must ask you to tell us the approximate size and weight of the load	*Bevor wir Ihnen ein detailliertes Angebot senden können, müssen wir Sie bitten, uns die ungefähre Größe und das Gewicht der Ladung mitzuteilen*
3	Mode of transport	*Art des Transports*
	– insurance / charges	*– Versicherung / Gebühren*
	For transporting a consignment of machine tools by road from Ostend to Munich via Cologne, with full insurance cover we would charge ...	*Um eine Sendung Werkzeugmaschinen per Lkw mit voller Versicherungsdeckung von Ostende über Köln nach München zu transportieren, würden wir ... berechnen*
	For shipping printed matter as package freight from Düsseldorf Airport to Oldenburg via Hanover, the goods to be insured warehouse-to-warehouse, our charges would be $1,225, including all taxes	*Um Drucksachen als Paketfracht über Hannover vom Flughafen Düsseldorf nach Oldenburg zu schicken, wobei die Waren von Lager bis Lager zu versichern wären, würden unsere Gebühren 1.225,00 $ einschließlich aller Steuern betragen*
	... the total charges would amount to $3,250, excluding demurrage at $5 per day	*... die Gesamtgebühren würden sich auf 3.250,00 $ belaufen, ausschließlich des Liegegeldes in Höhe von 5 $ pro Tag*

	… please refer to the enclosed tariff	*… entnehmen Sie bitte den beigefügten Tarifen*
4	**Dates**	***Daten***
	– collection	***– Abholung***
	We would need a week's notice of the collection date required	*Wir müssten eine Woche vorher das gewünschte Abholungsdatum erfahren*
	ETS (estimated time of shipment) would be 15 September ..	*Das voraussichtliche Versand(Verschiffungs)datum wäre der 15. September ..*
	– raising documentation	***– Beibringung von Dokumentation***
	The documents specified in your enquiry can be provided at an extra charge of $100	*Die in Ihrer Anfrage aufgelisteten Dokumente können zu einer Extragebühr von 100 $ beigebracht werden*
	We will be pleased to supply you with 3 originals of the bill of lading, together with 6 non-negotiable copies, as requested	*Wir liefern Ihnen gern auf Wunsch 3 Originale des Konnossements, zusammen mit 6 nicht negoziierbaren (begebbaren) Kopien*
	– storage	***– Lagerung***
	The goods specified can be stored indoors at no extra charge	*Die aufgeführten Güter können ohne zusätzliche Kosten drinnen gelagert werden*
	The goods specified would have to be stored in a locked warehouse at an extra charge of $25 per day	*Die aufgelisteten Waren müssten in einem verschlossenen Lagerhaus zu einer Extragebühr von 25 $ pro Tag gelagert werden*
	– delivery	***– Lieferung***
	You will be notified as soon as the goods have reached the port of destination	*Sie werden benachrichtigt, sobald die Güter den Bestimmungshafen erreicht haben*
	Please allow three weeks for delivery	*Bitte geben Sie uns für die Lieferung drei Wochen Zeit*
	The consignment will, in all probability, be shipped on board MS Victoria, which sets sail from Hamburg on 1 September .., calls at Liverpool and is due to dock in Boston, Massachusetts, on 20 September ..	*Die Sendung wird höchstwahrscheinlich an Bord der MS Victoria verschifft, die am 1. September .. Hamburg verlässt, Liverpool anläuft und am 20. September .. in Boston, Massachusetts, eindocken wird*
5	**Reference to enclosure(s)***	***Bezugnahme auf Anlage(n)****
	We would request you to follow the enclosed packing instructions carefully to speed up the processing of your order and minimise damage	*Wir würden Sie bitten, die beigefügten Verpackungsanweisungen genau zu befolgen, um die Abwicklung Ihres Auftrages zu beschleunigen und eventuelle Schäden minimal zu halten*

6	**Terms of payment**	***Zahlungsbedingungen***
	Your order will be dealt with as soon as we have received your remittance for the sum of $4,250	*Ihr Auftrag wird bearbeitet, sobald wir Ihre Überweisung der Summe von 4.250 $ erhalten haben*
	Before we can start processing your order we require an advance payment of 33 %	*Bevor wir mit der Bearbeitung Ihres Auftrages beginnen können, benötigen wir eine Vorauszahlung von 33 %*
	50 % of the charter costs are due when the order is placed. The balance is due when the goods have arrived at the port of destination	*50 % der Charterkosten sind bei Auftragserteilung fällig. Der Rest ist zahlbar, wenn die Waren im Bestimmungshafen angekommen sind.*
7	**Validity of offer**	***Gültigkeit des Angebots***
	This offer is valid for 30 days / until 28 February ..	*Dieses Angebot ist 30 Tage / bis 28. Februar .. gültig*
	The rates quoted are without engagement	*Die angebotenen Sätze sind unverbindlich*
	As there has been heavy demand for our services recently, we recommend that you place your order as soon as possible	*Da in letzter Zeit eine rege Nachfrage nach unseren Dienstleistungen besteht, empfehlen wir Ihnen, Ihren Auftrag so schnell wie möglich zu erteilen*
8	**Polite ending**	***Höflicher Schluss***
	We hope to receive your order in the near future	*Wir hoffen, in Kürze Ihren Auftrag zu erhalten*
	Please do not hesitate to contact us if you have any queries regarding our services	*Bitte zögern Sie nicht, mit uns Verbindung aufzunehmen, falls Sie Fragen bezüglich unseres Service haben*
	You may rest assured that any order placed will be dealt with promptly and carefully and that our rates are the most competitive available	*Sie können versichert sein, dass jeder erteilte Auftrag schnell und sorgfältig ausgeführt wird und dass unsere Tarife die günstigsten sind, die Sie bekommen können*
9	**Enclosure(s)**	***Anlage(n)***
	Order Form	*Auftragsformular*
	Packing Instructions	*Verpackungsanweisungen*
	Export Regulations	*Exportbestimmungen*
	Company Brochure	*Firmenbroschüre*
	Catalogue (AE: catalog)	*Katalog*

Unit 15

Fairs, Exhibitions, Hotel Bookings and Making Arrangements

Enquiry about Trade Fair, Exhibition and Conference Facilities

1 Source of address*	We have been referred to you by We have been given your company's address by	... (name of company) the chamber of commerce in ... (location) a business associate, ... (name of associate)			
	We have seen your advertisement in	this week's/month's/quarter's/the latest edition/current issue	of ... (name of publication, e.g. *Business Weekly*)		
	We saw your advertisement in	last week's/month's/quarter's/the last edition			
	I/We have seen the above-mentioned advertisement I/We have seen your organisation's home page on the Internet	and • am • are	(most) impressed by your interested in your	facilities (range of) service(s) comprehensive service planning organisation	
	I/We recently attended ... (name of trade fair/exhibition, e.g. the D.I.Y. Exhibition)	and • was • were			
	... believe you may be able to offer us ... and think you might be able to help us find ... and feel your organisation may be able to offer us	what we're looking for what we have in mind the venue we need the services we require the facilities we need	to launch our product to advertise our product to present our company to market our goods to get in contact with potential customers for our product/service(s)		
2 Reason for enquiry – conference facilities (seating capacity)	We are looking for We require We wish to hire	conference facilities a conference hall a room for a conference an auditorium a hall	big enough to take ... (number) people with a seating capacity of ... (e.g. 250) able to seat ... (number) people/delegates with enough room for ... (number) people	to host a sales convention for our AGM for the next meeting of the ... (name of event/association/organisation, e.g. European Freight Forwarders' Association)	
– exhibition venue		somewhere the right place suitable facilities a (very) special location	to show to exhibit	... (name of product)	for the first time (this year/season) to the (general) public to our customers to our trading partners to our agents/distributors
			to launch		–

– stand at a trade fair	We wish to My/Our company wishes to		have a hire a rent a put up a be allocated space to put up our	stand	at the next … (name of event) at the … (name of event, e.g. Ideal Home Exhibition)
3 Dates	on … (date) in … (month/year) next … (month/season) … which is due to take place on … (date) from … (date) – … (date) (e.g. from 1–5 May ..) to be held from … (date) – … (date)				
	The dates in question are … (date) – … (date) The dates we have in mind are … (date) – … (date), or … (date) – … (date) We would wish to have these facilities made available to us either from … (date) – … (date), or from … (date) – … (date) We would require these facilities for … (number) days/weeks/months, i.e. from … (date) – … (date)				
4 Request for quotation	Please quote us for … (details) Please let us have your quote for … (details) Please send us your quote for the following: We would therefore be grateful if you would let us have your (most favourable) quotation for a stand/conference facilities/exhibition space incorporating the following features (and services):				
5 General requirements	We would require	the conference facilities the exhibition space the stand	to have to incorporate to be equipped with	the following: the following features: the features listed (below)	
	The	(conference) hall room auditorium conference facilities exhibition area/space stand	must have would need to have would need to incorporate would have to be equipped with		
	We need the following:				
– planning service	A planning service to help us identify our needs A CAD planning service (with 3-dimensional technology) to simulate the exhibition area/stand before we decide how to equip and decorate it				

– size/design of stand	A stand measuring 20 m × 15 m × 4 m (length, width, height) A stand 100' long by 9'6" high by 20' wide		with steps leading up to it with two sets of steps leading up to it	at the front at the side(s) at the front and the back on all sides
			with a counter at the front with a back room with a lockable room or cupboard with an office at the back accessible through a door with a curtained-off back room/side room/kitchenette with a roof over it with a hat and coat stand with a coat rack with a hat rack with coat hooks with a seating area surrounded by a (light) fence and a curtained-off area in the middle for discussions with a reception area (large enough for cafe-style tables and chairs/with space for sofas for people waiting)	
– size of exhibition area	We need We will need We require There must be	at least a minimum of	5,000 sq ft 5,000 m²	of exhibition space of floor space to accommodate our exhibits to exhibit our products
	The exhibition space The exhibition area The floor space	must be (at least) would need to be (at the very least)		in size
– location (on site)	We wish We will need We need We would need We require We would require	the conference hall the auditorium the exhibition area the stand	to be to be located to be situated	at the front of the site at the back of the site in the middle of the site in the main exhibition area near the entrance to the main exhibition area in Hall … (number/letter, e. g. Hall 1, Hall A) in the main building near the main entrance within easy reach of the restaurant near the bar near the car park

				near the lift near the taxi rank close to the … (type of transport, e.g. bus/railway/ underground) station close to the tram stop
6 Fixtures and fittings	We require the following fixtures and fittings: Our requirements as regards fixtures, fittings and other features are listed as follows: Please ensure that the facilities offered include the following: (list) As regards fixtures, fittings and other features of the facilities required, please refer to the following list:			
– stage	The • (conference) hall • room • auditorium • conference facilities • exhibition area/ space	must would need to would have to	have incorporate be equipped with	a (small) stage a full-size stage (with curtains) a fully equipped stage (with a rostrum) a stage able to support heavy objects/a heavy object weighing 5 tonnes a stage able to take a motor vehicle/van/truck/lorry/ tractor etc.
– (electrical) sockets	We need We will need We require There must be Please provide Please supply us with	… (number) electrical sockets … (number) 220–240V sockets … (number) power points	for the counter for the back room for every room	and … (number) outside and … (number) for the rest of the stand
– running water		access to a cold water supply a sink with hot and cold water taps/a cold water tap and sink a fully plumbed sink with hot and cold running water a fully equipped kitchen unit with a sink with hot and cold running water, a draining board and a cutting surface for meat and vegetables		
– lighting		a (strong, fluorescent/halogen) centre light in each room/area (a/2/3 etc.) standard lamp(s) (AE: floor lamp) a halogen lighting system in the reception area and the office fluorescent lighting throughout flood lights (manned) spotlights to pick out the main attractions (full) stage lighting discreet background lighting (everywhere/in the reception/waiting/seating area) lasers for (our) special effects		

– floor covering	*(see previous page)*	lino(leum) a lino(leum) floor non-slip floor covering burn-resistant floor covering carpeting fitted carpet carpet tiles woollen carpeting synthetic carpeting a (woollen/Persian) carpet a rug/rugs (varnished) wooden floor-boards (imitation) parquet flooring	throughout in the office in the back room in the side room in the seating area in the curtained-off area in the middle in the reception area behind the counter at the front	We would like the carpet to be	plain a plain colour striped checked without a pattern	
		a red carpet a tiled path a gravel path a wooden bridge	leading to the stand	we would like it to be	a shade of dark light	red orange yellow green blue indigo violet
	In addition, we would require you to remove and dispose of it/all floor coverings/the carpeting after the event					
– furniture	We need We will need We require There must be Please provide Please supply us with	a counter a bar (for drinks) a dining-room table an occasional table occasional tables a 2 m × 3 m (coffee-) table 2/3 etc. coffee-tables	measuring 2 m × 3 m approx. 5' long by 2'6" wide	made of	wood natural materials water-resistant materials plastic synthetic materials materials which are easy to clean imitation wickerwork	
		a 2 m × 3 m (coffee) table a cane table a rattan table				

		a wickerwork table a glass-topped table a 2 m × 3 m (polished) (wooden) (conference) table and 12 chairs (imitation) cane tables and chairs (imitation) rattan tables and chairs (imitation) wickerwork tables and chairs a polished wooden conference table with leather chairs (with armrests) a(n) (adjustable) swivel chair / adjustable swivel chairs		
		a / 2 / 3 etc. chair(s) a (bar) stool / bar stools a 2-seater / 3-seater (upholstered / leather) settee(s) (a / an / 2 / 3 etc.) (upholstered / leather) armchair(s) a (step-) ladder		
– display panels	The • stand • (conference) hall • room • auditorium • conference facilities • exhibition area	must would need to would have to be	have incorporate be equipped with	a display panel … (number) display panels, measuring (approx.) 2 m × 3 m (width, height) … (number) display panels 6' high by 4'6" wide … (number) display panels 2 m high by 1.5 m wide
– shelves	We need We will need We require There must be Please supply us with Please provide	a shelf shelves a bookshelf bookshelves adjustable shelves sturdy shelves (a set of) (free-standing) shelves / bookshelves (a) (tilted / 45°) display stand(s)	at the side(s) at the back all around in every room under the counter	to take display items for exhibits for (sales) literature
– literature racks		a literature rack literature racks — for our	leaflets brochures catalogues price lists membership forms etc.	by the entrance all around dotted around both inside and outside the stand

7 Audio-visual facilities – audio	*(see previous page)*	a	small portable good-quality high-quality top-quality	(stereo) cassette-recorder (stereo) tape-recorder (stereo) CD-player tape deck	with an external loudspeaker with (external) loudspeakers	and a technician / team of technicians to operate it
		a public-address system with a microphone stand a public-address system wit a / 2 / 3 (portable) (clip-on) (radio) microphone(s) (full) play-back facilities				
– visual		an overhead projector a slide projector an epi(dia)scope		and screen		
		a video-recorder a video-player		with … monitor(s) connected to a giant video screen		
		a flipchart a blackboard slide presentation facilities computer-driven presentation facilities projection facilities for computer graphics multi-media presentation facilities				
– TV		a TV set cable TV satellite TV closed circuit TV with links to national / international / satellite / cable TV channels a giant video screen to relay a picture of the speaker to the audience				
8 (Tele)communication equipment		a telephone (a / 2 / 3 etc.) telephone line(s) (a / 2 / 3 etc.) mobile phone(s) (a / 2 / 3 etc.) cordless phone(s) (a / 2 / 3 etc.) fax machine(s) (an / 2 / 3 etc.) ISDN line(s) an Internet link e-mail a photocopier / photocopying facilities a colour copying machine a laser colour copier desktop publishing facilities				

9 Advertising	Are you able to Will you be able to Is your organisation in a position to	arrange for posters to be put up advertising this event? provide a full advertising campaign in the local/national media? advertise this event • on the radio? • on TV? • on the Internet? • in the local/national newspapers? recommend an advertising agency to organise an advertising campaign for us? arrange for TV and radio commercials to be made for this event? design and set up a web site for us on the Internet?	
	You'll have to We want you to We need you to We would need you to We will need you to We will require you to	start advertising get the ball rolling advertise this event publicise this event	a month/2 months in advance well in advance on a major scale both locally, nationally and internationally
	Are you able to arrange for Please arrange for Would it be possible to get We will be inviting We have arranged for	a celebrity a local dignitary a prominent politician a prominent person a film star a pop star a famous model	to open the stand(?) to appear on the first day(?) to put in an appearance(?) to make a guest appearance(?) to say a few words on stage(?) to come for a photo session with us(?) to be photographed with our board of directors(?) to have his/her photo taken on the stand/at the conference/on the stage(?) to hold a press conference on the stand/at the conference/on the stage(?)
10 Catering	We need We will need We require There must be Please supply us with Please arrange for there to be	a/2/3 etc. drinks machine(s) a/2/3 etc. hot drinks machine(s) a/2/3 etc. cold drinks machine(s) a/2/3 etc. soft drinks machine(s) a/2/3 etc. tea machine(s) a/2/3 etc. coffee machine(s) a/2/3 etc. sandwich machine(s)	

	(see previous page)	a catering service a catering and waiter service	for because we wish to serve because our guests will expect as we intend to provide because we wish to give our • guests • visitors • delegates • guest speakers		(a champagne) breakfast morning coffee lunch afternoon tea dinner drinks and snacks on-stand hospitality morning coffee and biscuits a (two-course) buffet luncheon afternoon tea and biscuits a three-course waiter service dinner
11 Security	We need We will need We require We will also require	supervised car-parking a security guard to be on duty security guards to be at hand/on call an attendant/attendants video surveillance closed-circuit camera surveillance security cameras a security alarm/security alarms	at all times day and night during opening hours for the duration of the event whilst the • site • fair • exhibition • conference is open	as since in view of the fact that	we anticipate a large crowd our exhibits are (extremely) valuable … (name of celebrity) will be appearing a number of prominent people will be coming we expect to draw a crowd of at least … (number) people
	There must be We will need Please arrange for there to be	video surveillance closed-circuit camera surveillance security cameras a security alarm/security alarms			
12 Transport	Please let us have details of When sending us your quotation please include details of all		(public) transport links to the site road, rail and air links to the site		

	Is there	a shuttle a taxi a rail a tram an underground train	service	to to and from	the site? the hotel? the airport? the town centre? the city centre?	If so, how frequent is it? If so, how often does it run?
	Can you provide Are you able to lay on Can you arrange for there to be Please let us have your quotation for		(a)/2/3/enough car(s) (a)/2/3/enough minibus(es) (a)/2/3/enough chauffeur-driven limousine(s)		to pick up … (number) people from the station/airport to ferry our guests/models/important visitors from … (location, e.g. exhibit) to … (location)	
13 Accommodation	We need We'll be needing We require We will require We would also be most grateful if you would help us to find		accommodation hotel rooms		for … (number) people for a party of … (number) people/delegates/company employees	
	Do you offer assistance with finding Are you able to help us find Does your planning service include help with finding		suitable accommodation		near in the vicinity of within easy reach of	the exhibition centre? the trade fair? the conference hall/building/centre?
14 Polite ending	Hoping to hear from you soon We hope to hear from you shortly Many thanks in advance for your attention to our enquiry We look forward to your early reply A prompt reply to this enquiry would be most appreciated If you are unable to supply any or all of the facilities requested we would be grateful if you would recommend a suitable contractor/suitable contractors or pass this enquiry on to them					

Hotel Bookings

1 Source of address*	We have been referred to you by … (name) We have been given your company's address by … (name of company/person/institution) Your hotel has been (warmly) recommended to us by … (name of company/person/institution) The accommodation service at … (name of exhibition centre etc., e.g. the National Exhibition Centre in Birmingham) has given us the address of your hotel The Tourist Information Office in … (location) has given us the address of your hotel	
	We saw your advertisement in | last week's/month's/quarter's/the last edition of | … (name of publication, e.g. *The Sunday Times*)	
	We have seen your home page on the Internet As employees of our company have already stayed at your hotel in the past/on several occasions …	
2 Request for information*	Please send us written information on the facilities your hotel has to offer We would (therefore) be grateful if you would send us details of the facilities at your hotel	, including details of its size and location
– location	Is your hotel near Is the hotel within easy reach of Is the hotel located in the vicinity of	the airport? the railway station? the motorway (AE: Interstate)? the town/city centre? the shops? the exhibition centre? the trade fair site? the conference hall/building/centre?

– facilities	Before we can make a booking Before making a reservation	we would like to know we need to know	if whether	you have there is/are your hotel has	parking facilities a lift a bar a restaurant a(n) indoor/outdoor swimming pool a sauna a tennis court a golf course a fitness room a solarium a jacuzzi (24-hour) room service	Do the rooms have Are the rooms equipped with	a mini-bar? radio and TV? colour TV? satellite TV? cable TV? en-suite facilities?

			a safe for valuables a dance floor a floor show entertainment facilities for a dinner and dance
	Are the rooms en suite? Do the rooms all have a private bathroom and shower?		
– size of the hotel	How big is the hotel? How many rooms does the hotel have?/How many beds does the hotel have? How many people can your hotel accommodate?		
3 Type of accommodation required – rooms/number of beds	We would like to book We wish to reserve Please reserve We/I require	bed and breakfast … (number) (en-suite) single room(s) … (number) (en-suite) double room(s) … (number) (en-suite) twin-bedded room(s) … (number) (en-suite) doubled-bedded room(s) … (number) (en- suite) double room(s) with single beds/(a) double bed(s) … (number) (en- suite) 3-bed room(s) with single beds … (number) (en-suite) family room(s) with two double beds (and a folding bed) … (number) (en-suite) king-size room(s) with (a) double bed(s) … (number) luxury suite with all facilities	for … (name of person, e.g. Herr Landgreber, our Managing Director) for one gentleman/lady for two gentlemen/ladies for a married couple (with one child/two/three etc. children) for a party of … (number) people (, comprising 10 ladies and 5 gentlemen)
		… (number) single/double/twin-bedded/doubled-bedded/ 3-bed room(s)	
	… the/each room to be en suite … (the room(s) should/must be) with en-suite facilities … (each room must be) with a private bathroom (and shower)		(and) on the same floor (and) on different floors (and) next to each other (and) with a communicating door
– smokers/ non-smokers	… for a non-smoker/for non-smokers All rooms are for smokers/non-smokers We require non-smoking rooms (only) We require … (number) non-smoking rooms and … (number) rooms for smokers Our party consists of … (number) smokers and … (number) non-smokers		

– meals	… with / without	breakfast			
	… with	breakfast and an evening meal / half board all meals / full board			
	He / She / They / Our guest(s) / We	want(s) to have will want to have wish(es) to have will wish to have will require	breakfast in the hotel breakfast and a buffet lunch breakfast and lunch (half board) breakfast and an evening meal (half board) breakfast, lunch and dinner (full board)		
		wish(es) to give	a private dinner party a special dinner party with entertainment and dancing		
4 Dates	… for The booking is for We wish to book for Please reserve the room(s) for We require the room(s) to be reserved for	… (number) nights	from … (date, e.g. 2 March ..) to … (date) He / She wishes / They / Our guest(s) / We wish to arrive at … (time, e.g. 2 pm) on … (date) and depart on … (date)		
	We need We wish to have We must have We will be needing	the room(s) the accommodation	in the first / second / third / last week of January / February etc. this (coming) January next January this year next year		
5 Special requests – location of room	Please make sure that Please ensure that Please confirm that	the room each room the rooms all rooms	has have	a balcony a balcony facing south a sunny balcony a view of the sea / harbour / beach / river	
			is are	near the	reception area foyer (AE: lobby) main entrance lift (AE: elevator) car park (AE: parking lot) restaurant
				quiet away from the (main) road in a quiet part of the hotel	

			face overlook look out over	the sea the harbour the beach the river	
– food	Mr/Mrs/Ms … (name) … (number) of our party … (number) member(s) of our group		will require	vegetarian food vegetarian meals kosher meals	
			is a (strict) are (strict)	vegetarian(s)	and does/do not eat eggs or fish but eat(s) eggs and fish
			is are	diabetic allergic to … (details, e. g. milk products)	
			does/do not eat pork (or sea food) does/do not eat beef		
	Please send us a choice of menus, including a vegetarian dish, for dinner on … (date) We would be grateful if you would let us have a choice of menus for (a 3-course) dinner on … (date). Please offer at least 3 main courses, including a vegetarian dish, and a choice of desserts				
– disabled	Mr/Mrs/Ms … (name) … (number) of our party … (number) member(s) of our group	is/are disabled is/are in wheelchairs	and must therefore have		a room on the ground floor rooms near the lift rooms accessible by wheelchair
		is/are	deaf hard of hearing dumb blind partially sighted	Please take this into consideration when allocating him/her/them his/her/their room(s) Please bear this in mind when reserving his/her/their room(s)	
6 Prices	Please quote us your best rate for the above-mentioned accommodation including all taxes We look forward to receiving your quotation for the rooms and dates stated. Please include all taxes and details of your telephone charges in your quotation We would be grateful if you would let us have your quotation for the accommodation as described including details of all taxes and your telephone charges				
– corporate rates	Please indicate whether the prices quoted are regular or corporate rates We would point out that we are only prepared to make bookings on a regular basis/on this occasion if you are able to offer us corporate rates (including all extras including taxes) Please let us have details of your corporate rates for the accommodation requested				

	We trust you will be able to offer us corporate rates for the accommodation required We would like you to quote us your corporate rates for the accommodation described. We anticipate using facilities in your area quite frequently in the near future We regularly require accommodation for our employees in your area and would therefore be pleased to receive details of your corporate rates	
– block bookings	Please let us have details of your rates for (regular) block bookings In view of the size of our party we would request you to treat this as a block booking and quote us appropriate rates As this would be a block booking for … (number) people please indicate the discount granted for groups of this size As our company frequently sends (large) parties of employees / delegates / salesmen / saleswomen / sales staff to events in your area, we would be grateful if you would let us have details of your rates for block bookings	
7 Payment	The bill will be settled by us All bills will be settled by us All bills will be paid by us Please forward all bills to us for payment Please send all bills to our company for payment Mr / Mrs / Ms … (name) will settle his / her own bill All bills will be settled by each guest individually (by credit card) Each member of the party is responsible for settling his / her bill in full Our company will pay for board and lodging. Any extras, including mini-bar and telephone charges, are to be paid for by the guest(s) himself / herself / themselves Please let us know if a deposit is payable We enclose a deposit of … (amount) and would request you to confirm receipt of it Please let us know if you accept … (name of credit card)	
8 Polite ending	We would be grateful if you would confirm this booking Please let us know if you are able to make these reservations We need to know if the reservations are possible as listed	at your earliest convenience by return as soon as possible by … + date within … + period of time
	Please let us have your confirmation of this booking by letter / fax (on … (fax number) / e-mail (address: … , e. g. dtyd@aol.com) / telephone (on … telephone number)	
	Your prompt attention to this enquiry would be very much appreciated If the accommodation and services requested are available and your rates are competitive, we will consider making use of your facilities again in the future We look forward to receiving your offer and will consider making use of your services again in the future, if the accommodation requested is available and your rates are reasonable	

Making Arrangements

1 Reference to previous correspondence*	We just got We have just received Many thanks for With reference to	your letter/fax/e-mail/ message	about … in connection with …		
	We are writing to you				
2 Reference to arrangement(s)*	… my … our representative's … our Sales Director's … (our) Ms Pervical's	appointment breakfast/lunch/ dinner appointment meeting discussion talks	with	(your) Mr/Mrs/Miss/Ms … (name) your representative you yourself yourself and your colleague(s) Ms … (name) and Mr … (name)	
	… the	… fair (e.g. Home and Garden Fair) … exhibition (e.g. Ideal Home Exhibition) conference convention open day	which	I (our) Mr/Mrs/Miss/Ms … (name) our representative(s), Ms … (name) and Mr … (name)	wish/wishes to attend … would like to attend … hopes to attend … am/is/are planning to attend … will be attending … am/is/are invited to attend
		presentation of … (e.g. our/your new machine/product/equipment/ garments)			due to take place … scheduled to take place … which is due to take place … which will be taking place … which we will be giving … to which you are invited … to which I am/we are/he/she is invited you have invited me/us/him/her (our) … (name) to which we would very much like you to attend
		working breakfast business lunch lunch appointment afternoon tea appointment dinner appointment	with … (name of person(s), e.g. Mr Ramsbottom) with your representative(s)		

	(see previous page)	cocktail sherry cheese and wine garden	party		to be held … due to take place …	
		reception buffet				
		ceremony	in honour of … (name of person) to commemorate … (e. g. the death of …) on the occasion of … (details, e. g. the 25th anniversary of the company)			
	my our Ms … 's (name, e. g. Ms Mey's)		visit to	your	company company's site company's factory company's warehouse company's distribution centre Head Office	
3 Time and place	on … (date, e. g. Monday 24 May)	at … (time, e. g. 3.45 pm)	in … (city/town, e. g. in Frankfurt)		at the Frankfurt Hilton in the Morgenstern Room at the Hamburg Hilton in conference hall no. 49 at Earls Court Olympia in London	
4 Confirmation of arrangement(s)*	I am We are … (name) is … (names) are	able to pleased to delighted to	confirm that	I we … (name) he/she they	will be coming will be attending will be taking part	as planned as arranged as agreed as requested
					wish(es) to accept the invitation will be pleased to accept your invitation	
– mode of transport	I We … (name)	will be arriving will be travelling	on flight no. BA 8195 landing at London Heathrow at … (time) on the Eurostar to London. After that I'll/we'll/he'll be taking a train to … (location, e. g. Birmingham)			
		am/are/is taking the train to … (location) and will then take a taxi to … (location) am/are/is taking the ferry to … (name of port) and will then be travelling by train to … (location) am/are/is flying to London Gatwick, after which I'll/we'll he'll/she'll be going the rest of the way to … (destination) by train				

– estimated time of arrival	I/We/… (name) should be at Manchester Piccadilly (Station) by … (time) (at the latest) I/we/he/she/… (name) expect(s) to be there at about … (time) I/we/he/she/… (name) expect(s) to arrive at approximately … (time) Please expect me/us/… (name) at about … (time)					
5 Change in arrangements*	Unfortunately, owing to … (reason, e.g. an air traffic controllers' strike), Due to unforeseen circumstances, I'm/I am/We're/we are sorry to say that I/We regret to inform you that			I we he/she they	won't be able to will not be able to can't cannot	make it at the time agreed on … (date) make it before … (time, e.g. 2 pm) make it by … (time, e.g. 2 o' clock) keep the appointment come at the time arranged attend the meeting/conference/convention/presentation (after all)
				the time agreed will not be convenient for … (person, e.g. Frau Meyer)		
	I We They	therefore	suggest	that	we	meet at … (time) in … (location) instead look for an alternative time/place to meet look for an alternative location for us to meet/for the appointment try to find a more convenient time/place to meet agree on a suitable time the next day/week/after 3 pm etc.
	He/she … (name)		suggests		you they	
	I suggest	we phone to arrange a new appointment we look for a suitable date, week beginning … (date, e.g. 10 July)/in week 42 we meet at the Hotel Seemöwe in Lübeck instead we book a room at the airport/near the station/at your/my hotel we try to find somewhere more convenient	• for both of us • for all of us • for all the participants • for all concerned • for everyone			
	Could you perhaps	call me (BE) give me a ring fax me get in touch	some time today some time this week in the next few days by 4 o'clock this afternoon	to in order to so we can to enable us to	arrange a new appointment? agree on a new time/place to meet?	
		drop me a line in the near future				
	Would a meeting/an appointment on … (new date) instead of … (old date) be all right for you? Might I/we suggest we meet on … (new date) instead of … (old date)?					

– apologise*	We're very sorry about this but there wasn't much we could do about it					
	We apologise for the change in plan. Please accept our apologies for this.		We would point out, however, that		we had no alternative there was nothing else we could do this was due to circumstances beyond our control the matter is not in our hands	
6 Cancellation of arrangement(s)*	I'm sorry but Unfortunately, owing to … (reason, e.g. a rail strike), Due to unforeseen circumstances, I'm/I am/We're/we are sorry to say that I/We regret to inform you that		I we … (name)	won't be able to will not be able to can't cannot	come attend the meeting/ conference/ presentation/ convention take part in the talks	this time on this occasion
			I/we have/… (name) has to cancel this time because … (reason, e.g. because Ms Balster has been taken ill)			
– apologise*	I We	apologise wish to apologise	for any inconvenience caused for the change in plan for not letting you know earlier for not having been able to let you know earlier		and will be in touch and will be contacting you again	shortly in the near future in due course as soon as possible
	He/She … (name)	apologises wishes to apologise				
	We're very sorry about this but there wasn't much we could do about it					
	We apologise for having to cancel. Please accept our apologies for this.		We would, however, point out that		we had no alternative there was nothing else we could do this was due to circumstances beyond our control the matter is not in our hands	
7 Request for confirmation*	Please Perhaps you'd like to		call me (BE) give me a ring drop me a line fax me send me an e-mail e-mail me	to let me know	if this is all right if this suits you if this is convenient/acceptable	

	I We … (name)	would be most grateful would (very much) appreciate it	if you would	let us know if this is all right confirm the new arrangement(s)
	Please let us know if this is all right Please confirm that this will be convenient for you Please let us have your confirmation of the new arrangements so we can book the room/hall/accommodation/ facilities etc.			
8 Polite ending	I'm I am We're We are	(very much) looking forward to meeting you (again) pleased to have the opportunity of meeting you personally		
	… (name) is			
	I/We look forward to	hearing from you in the near future meeting you … (time, e. g. next Monday, next week, in June) (having) the opportunity of getting to know you personally		
	We feel sure that this meeting/visit will be of great value to all concerned I'm very much looking forward to taking part in the meeting We are very much looking forward to the meeting I/We look forward to seeing you on … (date) Many thanks once again for your kind invitation. I/We/… (name) will most certainly take the earliest opportunity to reciprocate We're sorry it didn't work out this time Please accept my/our apologies for any inconvenience caused			
9 Enclosure(s)*	Directions Map Brochure Photograph(s)			

Fairs, Exhibitions, Hotel Bookings and Making Arrangements

Fairs and Exhibitions

1	Source of address*	*Quelle der Anschrift**
	We have been referred to you by The Metal Box Company Ltd	*Wir sind von The Metal Box Company Ltd. an Sie verwiesen worden*
	We have been given your company's address by a business associate, Mr Thomas van Ahlen	*Wir erhielten die Adresse Ihrer Firma von einem Geschäftsfreund, Herrn Thomas van Ahlen*
	We have seen the above-mentioned advertisement and are interested in your comprehensive service	*Wir haben die oben erwähnte Anzeige gesehen und sind an Ihrem umfassenden Service interessiert*
	I recently attended the D.I.Y. Exhibition and was impressed by your range of services	*Ich habe kürzlich die D.I.Y. (Do it yourself) Ausstellung besucht und war beeindruckt von der Palette Ihrer Dienstleistungen*
	We believe you may be able to offer us the venue we need to market our goods	*Wir glauben, dass Sie uns vielleicht den Veranstaltungsort bieten können, den wir brauchen, um unsere Waren zu vermarkten*
2	Reason for enquiry	*Grund für Anfrage*
	– conference facilities (seating capacity)	*– Konferenzräumlichkeiten (Sitzplatzkapazität)*
	We are looking for conference facilities big enough to take 250 people to host a sales convention	*Wir suchen Konferenzräume, die groß genug sind, um 250 Leute für eine Vertretertagung aufzunehmen*
	We wish to hire suitable facilities to show our new collection of fashion garments for the first time this season	*Wir möchten geeignete Räume mieten, um zum ersten Mal in dieser Saison unsere neue Modekollektion von Kleidungsstücken vorzuführen*
	– stand at a trade fair	*– Stand auf einer Fachmesse*
	Our company wishes to put up a stand at the Ideal Home Exhibition	*Unsere Firma möchte einen Stand auf der Ideal Home Exhibition aufstellen*
3	Dates	*Daten*
	… which is due to take place on June 30 ..	*… die am 30. Juni .. stattfinden soll*
	The dates in question are June 30 – July 5 ..	*Die infrage kommenden Daten sind der 30. Juni .. – 5. Juli ..*
	We would require these facilities for 5 days i.e. from July 1–5 ..	*Wir würden diese Räumlichkeiten für 5 Tage brauchen, d.h. vom 1.–5. Juli ..*
4	Request for quotation	*Bitte um Angebot*
	Please let us have your quote for a stand as follows:	*Bitte lassen Sie uns Ihr Angebot für einen Stand zukommen, der wie folgt aussieht:*

	We would therefore be grateful if you would let us have your most favourable quotation for a stand / conference facilities / exhibition space incorporating the following features and services:	*Wir wären Ihnen daher dankbar, wenn Sie uns Ihr günstigstes Angebot für einen Stand / für Konferenzräumlichkeiten / für eine Ausstellungsfläche zukommen ließen, der (die) folgende Merkmale und Dienstleistungen beinhaltet (beinhalten):*
5	**General requirements**	***Allgemeine Erfordernisse***
	We would require the conference facilities / exhibition space / stand to have the following features:	*Die Konferenzräumlichkeiten / Ausstellungsfläche / der Stand müsste(n) folgende Merkmale aufweisen:*
	– planning service	***– Planungsservice***
	... a planning service to help us identify our needs	*... einen Planungsservice, der uns hilft, unseren Bedarf festzustellen*
	... a CAD planning service with 3-dimensional technology to simulate the exhibition area / stand before we decide how to equip and decorate it	*... einen CAD-Planungsservice mit dreidimensionaler Technik, um die Ausstellungsfläche / den Stand zu simulieren, bevor wir uns entschließen, wie wir sie (ihn) ausrüsten und gestalten*
	– size / design of stand	***– Größe / Design des Standes***
	A stand measuring 20 m × 15 m × 4 m (length, width, height) with steps leading up to it at the front	*Ein Stand mit den Abmessungen 20 m × 15 m × 4 m (Länge, Breite, Höhe) mit Stufen, die von vorne zu ihm hinaufführen*
	... with a counter at the front	*... mit vorne einem Schalter*
	... with an office at the back, accessible through a door	*... mit einem Büro im hinteren Teil, das durch eine Tür zugänglich ist*
	... with a seating area, surrounded by a light fence and a curtained-off area in the middle for discussions	*... mit einer Sitzfläche, die von einem leichten Zaun umgeben ist, und in der Mitte einer durch einen Vorhang abgetrennten Fläche für Besprechungen*
	– size of exhibition area	***– Größe der Ausstellungsfläche***
	We need at least 5,000 sq ft of exhibition space	*Wir benötigen mindestens 5.000 Quadratfuß Ausstellungsfläche*
	The exhibition space must be 5,000 m² in size	*Die Ausstellungsfläche muß eine Größe von 5.000 m² haben*
	– location (on site)	***– Lage (vor Ort)***
	We will need the auditorium to be located at the front of the site	*Das Auditorium muss sich auf der Vorderseite des Geländes befinden*
	We require the stand to be in the main building	*Der Stand muss sich im Hauptgebäude befinden*
6	**Fixtures and fittings**	***Einbauten und Zubehör***
	Our requirements as regards fixtures, fittings and other features are listed as follows:	*Unser Bedarf an Einbauten und Zubehör sowie anderen Besonderheiten ist wie folgt:*

– stage	– *Bühne*
The auditorium must be equipped with a full-size stage with curtains	*Das Auditorium muss mit einer Bühne in voller Größe mit Vorhängen ausgestattet sein*
– (electrical) sockets	– *(elektrische) Steckdosen*
We require two electrical sockets for the back room and six for the rest of the stand	*Wir benötigen zwei Elektrosteckdosen für den hinteren Raum und sechs für den übrigen Stand*
– running water	– *fließendes Wasser*
Please provide a fully plumbed sink with hot and cold running water	*Bitte liefern Sie ein voll angeschlossenes Becken mit fließend warmem und kaltem Wasser*
– lighting	– *Beleuchtung*
There must be a strong, fluorescent centre light in each room	*Jeder Raum muss mit einer starken, fluoreszierenden Beleuchtung in der Mitte ausgestattet sein*
Please supply us with discreet background lighting everywhere	*Bitte liefern Sie uns überall diskrete Hintergrundbeleuchtung*
– floor covering	– *Bodenbeläge*
We need carpeting in the office. We would like the carpet to be a plain colour	*Wir brauchen im Büro Teppichboden und hätten gerne einen einfarbigen Teppich*
– furniture	– *Möbel*
There must be occasional tables approx. 5' long by 2'6" wide, made of wood	*Wir benötigen Beistelltische aus Holz, die ungefähr 5' lang und 2'6" breit sind*
Please provide wickerwork tables and chairs	*Bitte liefern Sie uns Korbtische und -stühle*
Please supply us with a polished wooden conference table with leather chairs	*Bitte liefern Sie uns einen Konferenztisch aus poliertem Holz mit Lederstühlen*
We will need a 2-seater leather settee	*Wir brauchen ein 2-sitziges Ledersofa*
– display panels	– *Display-Tafeln*
The stand must be equipped with four display panels, measuring approx. 2 m × 3 m (width, height)	*Der Stand muss mit vier Display-Tafeln ausgerüstet sein, die ca. 2 m × 3 m (Breite, Höhe) messen*
– shelves	– *Regale*
We require adjustable shelves all around to take display items	*Wir benötigen verstellbare Regale ringsum, um die Ausstellungsstücke zu zeigen*
– literature racks	– *Prospektgestelle*
Please provide literature racks for our leaflets both inside and outside the stand	*Bitte liefern Sie uns Prospektgestelle für unsere Broschüren, sowohl innerhalb als auch außerhalb des Standes*

7	**Audio-visual facilities**	*Audiovisuelle Einrichtungen*
	– audio	*– audio*
	There must be a good-quality tape deck with external loudspeakers and a technician to operate it	*Wir benötigen ein Tapedeck guter Qualität mit Außen-Lautsprechern und einen Techniker, der es bedient*
	We need a public-address system with a microphone stand	*Wir brauchen eine Lautsprecheranlage mit einem dazugehörigen Mikrofon (plus Ständer)*
	– visual	*– visuell*
	There must be an overhead projector and screen	*Wir brauchen einen Overheadprojektor und eine Leinwand*
	We require a flipchart	*Wir benötigen ein Flipchart*
	We need projection facilities for computer graphics	*Wir brauchen Projektionsmöglichkeiten für Computer-Grafiken*
	– TV	*– Fernsehen*
	Please supply us with a giant video screen to relay a picture of the speaker to the audience	*Bitte liefern Sie uns einen Großbildschirm, um ein Bild des Sprechers für das Publikum zu übertragen*
8	**(Tele)communication equipment**	*(Tele)kommunikationsausrüstung*
	We require three ISDN lines, an Internet link and e-mail	*Wir benötigen drei ISDN-Leitungen, eine Internet-Verbindung und einen E-Mail-Anschluss*
9	**Advertising**	*Werbung*
	Will you be able to arrange for posters to be put up advertising this event?	*Sind Sie in der Lage, dafür zu sorgen, dass Plakate angebracht werden, um diese Veranstaltung anzukündigen?*
	Are you able to design and set up a web site for us on the Internet?	*Können Sie uns eine Website im Internet entwerfen und einrichten?*
	We want you to start advertising two months in advance	*Wir möchten, dass Sie zwei Monate im Voraus mit der Werbung beginnen*
	We will need you to publicise this event both locally and nationally	*Wir wollen, dass Sie für diese Veranstaltung sowohl lokal als auch national werben*
	Are you able to arrange for a celebrity to open the stand?	*Sind Sie in der Lage, eine bekannte Persönlichkeit für die Eröffnung des Standes zu gewinnen?*
10	**Catering**	*Lieferung von Speisen und Getränken*
	We need a drinks machine	*Wir benötigen einen Getränkeautomaten*
	We will need a catering and waiter service, as we intend to serve a champagne breakfast	*Wir brauchen einen Catering-Service, da wir ein Sektfrühstück servieren wollen*
11	**Security**	*Sicherheit*
	We will need security guards to be on duty at all times, as Zsa-Zsa Laroche will be appearing	*Wir brauchen Sicherheitskräfte, die jederzeit im Dienst sind, da Zsa-Zsa Laroche auftreten wird*

	We will also require security cameras for the duration of the event, in view of the fact that a number of prominent people will be coming	*Wir brauchen auch Sicherheitskameras für die Dauer der Veranstaltung angesichts der Tatsache, dass eine Anzahl prominenter Leute kommen wird*
	We will need closed-circuit camera surveillance	*Wir benötigen Überwachungskameras, die den ganzen Raum erfassen*
12	**Transport**	***Transport***
	When sending us your quotation, please include details of all transport links to the site	*Wenn Sie uns Ihr Angebot schicken, fügen Sie bitte Einzelheiten aller Transportverbindungen zum Gelände bei*
	Is there a shuttle service to the site? If so, how frequent is it?	*Gibt es einen Shuttle-Service zum Gelände? Wenn ja, wie häufig verkehrt er?*
	Can you provide enough chauffeur-driven limousines to ferry our models from the changing-rooms to the stage?	*Können Sie genug Wagen mit Chauffeur für den Transport unserer Models von den Umkleideräumen zur Bühne bereitstellen?*
13	**Accommodation**	***Unterbringung***
	We need accommodation for 12 people	*Wir benötigen Unterbringung für 12 Personen*
	Are you able to help us find suitable accommodation in the vicinity of the trade fair?	*Können Sie uns helfen, geeignete Unterkünfte in der Nähe der Fachmesse zu finden?*
14	**Polite ending**	***Höflicher Schluss***
	Many thanks in advance for your attention to our enquiry	*Vielen Dank im Voraus für die unserer Anfrage gewidmete Aufmerksamkeit*
	If you are unable to supply any or all of the facilities requested, we would be grateful if you would recommend suitable contractors, or pass this enquiry on to them	*Wenn Sie nicht in der Lage sind, eine oder mehrere der gewünschten Einrichtungen zu liefern, wären wir Ihnen dankbar, wenn Sie uns geeignete Lieferanten empfehlen oder diese Anfrage an sie weiterleiten könnten*

Hotel Bookings

1	**Source of address***	***Quelle der Anschrift****
	We have been given your company's address by the Tourist Information Office in Birmingham	*Wir erhielten die Adresse Ihrer Firma vom Fremdenverkehrsamt in Birmingham*
	The accommodation service at the National Exhibition Centre in Birmingham has given us the address of your hotel	*Der Übernachtungsservice im National Exhibition Centre in Birmingham hat uns die Adresse Ihres Hotels gegeben*

2	**Request for information***	***Bitte um Information(en)****
	Please send us written information on the facilities your hotel has to offer	*Bitte schicken Sie uns schriftliche Informationen über die Einrichtungen, die Ihr Hotel anzubieten hat*
	– location	***– Lage***
	Is the hotel located in the vicinity of the trade fair site?	*Liegt das Hotel in der Nähe des Messegeländes?*
	– facilities	***– Einrichtungen***
	Before we can make a booking, we would like to know if you have a restaurant	*Bevor wir eine Buchung vornehmen können, möchten wir gern wissen, ob Sie ein Restaurant haben*
	Are the rooms equipped with radio and TV?	*Sind die Zimmer mit Radio und Fernseher ausgestattet?*
	Are the rooms en suite?	*Haben die Zimmer ein eigenes Bad?*
	– size of the hotel	***– Größe des Hotels***
	How many beds does the hotel have?	*Wie viele Betten hat das Hotel?*
3	**Type of accommodation required**	***Art der gewünschten Unterkunft***
	We would like to book bed and breakfast for Herr Landgreber, our Managing Director	*Wir möchten für Herrn Landgreber, unseren geschäftsführenden Direktor, ein Zimmer mit Frühstück reservieren*
	– rooms / number of beds	***– Zimmer / Anzahl der Betten***
	We wish to reserve 10 double rooms with single beds for a party of 20 people, comprising 14 ladies and 6 gentlemen	*Wir möchten 10 Doppelzimmer mit Einzelbetten für eine Gruppe von 20 Personen, 14 Damen und 6 Herren, reservieren*
	… each room to be en suite and on the same floor	*… jedes Zimmer mit Bad; alle Zimmer auf dem gleichen Stockwerk*
	smokers / non-smokers	***Raucher / Nichtraucher***
	We require eight non-smoking rooms and two rooms for smokers	*Wir benötigen acht Nichtraucher-Zimmer und zwei Zimmer für Raucher*
	– meals	***– Mahlzeiten***
	… with / without breakfast	*… mit / ohne Frühstück*
	… with breakfast and an evening meal / with half board	*… mit Frühstück und Abendessen / mit Halbpension*
	We will wish to have breakfast and an evening meal (half board)	*Wir wünschen Frühstück und eine Abendmahlzeit (Halbpension)*
	We require full board	*Wir benötigen Vollpension*
4	**Dates**	***Daten***
	The booking is for five nights from 2–6 March ..	*Die Reservierung gilt für fünf Nächte vom 2.–6. März ..*
	We must have the accommodation in the first week of January	*Wir benötigen die Unterkunft für die erste Woche im Januar*
5	**Special requests**	***Besondere Wünsche***
	– location of room	***– Lage des Zimmers***
	Please make sure that the room has a balcony	*Bitte stellen Sie sicher, dass das Zimmer einen Balkon hat*

	Please confirm that all rooms are in a quiet part of the hotel	*Bitte bestätigen Sie, dass alle Zimmer in einem ruhigen Teil des Hotels liegen*
	– food	***– Essen***
	Herr Langreber will require vegetarian food	*Herr Langreber wünscht vegetarische Küche*
	Please send us a choice of menus, including a vegetarian dish, for dinner on 5 March ..	*Bitte senden Sie uns eine Auswahl von Menus, einschließlich eines vegetarischen Gerichts, für ein Abendessen am 5. März ..*
	– disabled	***– behindertengerecht***
	Five of our party are disabled and must therefore have rooms on the ground floor	*Fünf Mitglieder unserer Gruppe sind behindert und benötigen daher Zimmer im Erdgeschoss*
6	**Prices**	***Preise***
	Please quote us your best rate for the above-mentioned accommodation, including all taxes	*Bitte bieten Sie uns Ihren besten Tarif für die oben beschriebene Unterkunft einschließlich aller Steuern an*
	We would be grateful if you would let us have your quotation for the accommodation as described, including details of all taxes and your telephone charges	*Wir wären Ihnen dankbar, wenn Sie uns Ihr Angebot für die Unterkunft wie beschrieben zukommen ließen, einschließlich der Einzelheiten aller Steuern und Ihrer Telefongebühren*
	– corporate rates	***– Firmentarife***
	Please let us have details of your corporate rates for the accommodation requested	*Bitte schicken Sie uns Einzelheiten Ihrer Firmentarife für die gewünschte Unterbringung*
	We would like you to quote us your corporate rates for the accommodation described. We anticipate using facilities in your area quite frequently in the near future	*Wir bitten Sie, uns Ihre Firmentarife für die beschriebene Unterbringung anzubieten. Wir weisen schon jetzt darauf hin, dass wir in naher Zukunft recht häufig Räumlichkeiten in Ihrer Gegend benutzen werden*
	– block bookings	***– Gruppenbuchungen***
	As this would be a block booking for 100 people, please indicate the discount granted for groups of this size	*Da dies eine Gruppenbuchung für 100 Personen wäre, geben Sie uns bitte den Nachlass an, den Sie für Gruppen dieser Größenordnung gewähren*
7	**Payment**	***Zahlung***
	Please forward all bills to us for payment	*Bitte schicken Sie uns alle Rechnungen zwecks Zahlung zu*
	All bills will be settled by each guest individually (by credit card)	*Alle Rechnungen werden von jedem Gast einzeln (per Kreditkarte) bezahlt*
	Our company will pay for board and lodging. Any extras, including mini-bar and telephone charges, are to be paid for by the guests themselves	*Unsere Gesellschaft wird für die Unterbringung und Verpflegung aufkommen. Alle Zusatzkosten, einschließlich Minibar und Telefongebühren, müssen von den Gästen selbst bezahlt werden*

	Please let us know if a deposit is payable	*Bitte teilen Sie uns mit, ob eine Anzahlung nötig ist*
8	Polite ending	*Höflicher Schluss*
	We would be grateful if you would confirm this booking at your earliest convenience	*Wir wären Ihnen dankbar, wenn Sie diese Reservierung sobald wie möglich bestätigen würden*
	If the accommodation and services requested are available and your rates are competitive, we will consider making use of your facilities again in the future	*Wenn die gewünschte Unterkunft und die Dienstleistungen erhältlich und Ihre Tarife wettbewerbsfähig sind, werden wir die Benutzung ihrer Einrichtungen auch in Zukunft wieder in Betracht ziehen*

Making Arrangements

1	Reference to previous correspondence*	*Bezug auf vorangegangene Korrespondenz**
	We have just received your message in connection with …	*Wir haben soeben Ihre Nachricht bezüglich … erhalten*
	We are writing to you about …	*Wir schreiben Ihnen bezüglich …*
2	Reference to arrangement(s)*	*Bezug auf Vereinbarung(en)**
	… my appointment with (your) Mr Gardener	*… mein Treffen mit (Ihrem) Herrn Gardener*
	… the open day which our Mrs Hülshoff is invited to attend	*… der Tag der offenen Tür, zu dem Frau Hülshoff aus unserem Hause eingeladen ist*
	… the presentation of your new machine, due to take place on …	*… die Präsentation Ihrer neuen Maschine, die am … stattfinden soll*
	… the business lunch with your representative(s)	*… das Geschäftsessen mit Ihren Vertretern / Vertreterinnen*
	… my visit to your company	*… mein Besuch in Ihrer Firma*
3	Time and place	*Ort und Zeit*
	… on Monday 24 May at 3.45 pm in the Morgenstern Room at the Hamburg Hilton	*… Montag, den 24. Mai, um 3.45 Uhr im Raum Morgenstern im Hilton-Hotel Hamburg*
4	Confirmation of arrangement(s)*	*Bestätigung der Vereinbarung(en)**
	I am pleased to confirm that Dr Haverkamp will be attending as planned	*Ich freue mich Ihnen zu bestätigen, dass Dr. Haverkamp wie geplant teilnehmen wird*
	– mode of transport	*– Transportmittel*
	He will be arriving on flight no. BA 8195 landing at London Heathrow at 6 pm on 10 June	*Er wird am 10. Juni um 18.00 Uhr in London Heathrow ankommen, Flug Nummer BA 8195*

	We're taking the Eurostar to London. After that we'll be taking a train to Birmingham	*Wir werden den Eurostar bis London nehmen, danach den Zug nach Birmingham*
	– estimated time of arrival	*– geschätzte Ankunftszeit*
	Please expect me at about 10 am	*Sie können mich gegen 10.00 Uhr erwarten*
	Dr Haverkamp should be at Manchester Piccadilly (Station) by 3 o' clock at the latest	*Dr. Haverkamp sollte bis spätestens 3 Uhr nachmittags in Manchester Piccadilly (Station) sein*
5	Change in arrangements*	*Änderungen der Vereinbarungen**
	Due to unforeseen circumstances, he won't be able to keep the appointment	*Aufgrund unvorhergesehener Ereignisse wird er nicht in der Lage sein, die Verabredung einzuhalten*
	Unfortunately, the time agreed will not be convenient for Frau Meyer	*Leider passt die vereinbarte Zeit Frau Meyer nicht*
	I therefore suggest that you meet at 3.30 pm in Edinburgh instead	*Ich schlage daher vor, dass Sie sich statt dessen um 15.30 Uhr in Edinburgh treffen*
	I suggest we look for a suitable date, week beginning 10 July	*Ich schlage vor, wir suchen einen passenden Termin in der Woche des 10. Juli*
	Could you perhaps call me in the next few days so we can arrange a new appointment?	*Könnten Sie mich eventuell in den nächsten Tagen anrufen, damit wir einen neuen Termin ausmachen können?*
	Might I / we suggest we meet on the Tuesday instead of the Monday?	*Dürfte ich / Dürften wir vorschlagen, dass wir uns Dienstag statt Montag treffen?*
	– apologise*	*– entschuldigen Sie sich**
	We apologise for the change in plan, would, however, point out that we had no alternative	*Wir entschuldigen uns für die Änderung, möchten aber darauf hinweisen, dass wir keine andere Wahl hatten*
6	Cancellation of arrangement(s)*	*Stornierung der Vereinbarung(en)**
	We're sorry to say that Frau Winkelmann will not be able to attend the meeting this time	*Wir müssen Ihnen leider mitteilen, dass Frau Winkelmann dieses Mal an dem Treffen nicht teilnehmen kann*
	I regret to inform you that I have to cancel this time because Ms Balster has been taken ill	*Leider muss ich Sie darüber informieren, dass ich den Termin diesmal absagen muss, da Frau Balster erkrankt ist*
	– apologise*	*– entschuldigen Sie sich**
	We wish to apologise for any inconvenience caused and will be contacting you again shortly	*Wir möchten uns für etwaige Unannehmlichkeiten entschuldigen und werden uns in Kürze wieder mit Ihnen in Verbindung setzen*
	We apologise for having to cancel. We would point out, however, that the matter is not in our hands	*Wir entschuldigen uns für die Stornierung. Wir möchten aber darauf hinweisen, dass diese Angelegenheit nicht in unseren Händen liegt*

7	**Request for confirmation***	***Bitte um Bestätigung****
	Perhaps you'd like to fax me to let me know if this is all right	*Vielleicht könnten Sie mir per Fax mitteilen, ob dies in Ordnung ist*
	I would very much appreciate it if you would confirm the new arrangement(s)	*Ich würde es sehr schätzen, wenn Sie die neue(n) Vereinbarung(en) bestätigen würden*
	Please confirm that this will be convenient for you	*Bitte bestätigen Sie, dass Ihnen dies passt*
8	**Polite ending**	***Höflicher Schluss***
	Frau Langhorn is very much looking forward to meeting you again	*Frau Langhorn freut sich sehr darauf, Sie wieder zu treffen*
	We look forward to hearing from you in the near future	*Wir freuen uns darauf, bald wieder von Ihnen zu hören*
	We feel sure that this visit will be of great value to all concerned	*Wir sind sicher, dass dieses Treffen für alle Beteiligten von großem Wert sein wird*
	I look forward to seeing you on 10 July	*Ich freue mich darauf, Sie am 10. Juli zu treffen*
	Many thanks once again for your your kind invitation. I will most certainly take the earliest opportunity to reciprocate	*Nochmals vielen Dank für die nette Einladung. Ich werde mich ganz sicher bei der nächsten Gelegenheit dafür revanchieren / erkenntlich zeigen*
	Please accept my apologies for any inconvenience caused	*Bitte nehmen Sie meine Entschuldigung für etwaige Unannehmlichkeiten entgegen*
9	**Enclosure(s)***	***Anlage(n)****
	Directions	*Wegbeschreibung*
	Map	*Stadtplan*
	Brochure	*Broschüre*
	Photograph(s)	*Fotografie(n)*

Layouts

- Business Letters
- Private Letter

Business Letters

British Layout

Block form / open punctuation. This is the most common form of layout.

Green Wrap Ltd

21 Fullwell Rd
Preston PN2 5AJ
England
Tel. +44 (0)17 72 5 62 23
Fax +44 (0)17 72 5 62 25
E-mail: Johnson@greenwrap.co.uk
http://www.greenwrap.co.uk

• *(One free line – optional)*
MB/TT
10 September ..
• *(one free line)*
URGENT
•
Messrs Smith & Co
12604 Prince Street
Buda, TX 78610
USA
•
For the attention of Mr Lewis, Despatch Section
•
Dear Mr Lewis
•
<u>Your Order of 3 September .. for Packaging Material</u>
•
Many thanks for the above-mentioned order, which will be processed by our Despatch Department within the next ten days.
•
We trust the goods will arrive punctually and in good condition and look forward to the pleasure of serving you again in the near future.
•
Yours sincerely
GreenWrap Ltd
•
Margaret Brown
•
Margaret Brown (Ms)
Managing Director
•
•
Enc
•
•
cc: T. Johnson, Sales Manager

1. Letterhead with logo, postcode (UK), telephone, fax and e-mail numbers and Internet address
2. Reference initials
3. Date
4. Special marking
5. Inside address. "TX" stands for "Texas" and 78610 is the ZIP code.
6. Attention line
7. Salutation
8. Subject line
9. Body of the letter. The first word has a capital letter.
10. Complimentary close with the signature, name (followed by preferred title in brackets in the case of a woman) and position of the signatory clearly written
11. Enclosure
12. Carbon copy for Mr T. Johnson

American Layout

Block form / open punctuation.

Green Wrap Ltd

488 East Prince Street
Reno, NV 89509
U.S.A.
Tel. +(9 16) 2 72-8 94 99
Fax +(9 16) 2 72-9 14 88
E-mail: gwinc@greenwrap.com
http://www.greenwrap.com

• *(one free line)*

September 20, ..

•

Carl T. Lewis, Vice-President
Smith Shipping Corp.
12604 Prince Street
Buda, TX 78610
U.S.A.

•

Re: Your Order of September 3, ..

•

Dear Mr. Lewis:

•

Many thanks for the above-mentioned order, which will be processed by our Despatch Department within the next ten days.

•

We trust the goods will arrive punctually and in good condition and look forward to the pleasure of serving you again in the near future.

•

Sincerely,

•

Michael Brown

•

Michael Brown
President
MB:tt

•

Enclosure: Catalog

•

•

Copies: Trent Johnson, Sales Manager
Alicia Montara, Export Division

1. Letterhead with logo, ZIP code (Nevada), telephone, fax and e-mail numbers and Internet address
2. Date (month-day-year)
3. Inside address. with ZIP code.
4. Subject line before the salutation
5. Salutation followed by a colon
6. Body of the letter
7. Complimentary close (AE: complimentary closing) followed by a comma, the signature and the name and position of the signatory clearly written
8. Signatory's and typist's initials, separated by a colon
9. Enclosure(s)
10. Copies for Trent Johnson and Alicia Montara

Private Letter

Heinrich-Gustav-Str. 99
69121 Heidelberg
Germany

Your ref. ESC/kw 20 January ..

Ms Kate Williams
Human Resources Officer
PowerGen Plc
90–100 Coronation Street
LANCASTER
LA1 4GH
England

Dear Ms Williams

<u>Your Advertisement on the Internet for the Post of European Sales Clerk</u>

I am writing with reference to the above-mentioned advertisement and am most interested in applying for the post you offer.

I am currently employed as a business administrati-on clerk at Neckarstahl AG in Heidelberg and have held this post for five years. Even though I am successful in my current position I would like to work for a firm at which I would be able to put my knowledge of English to good use.

I enclose my CV and copies of my qualifications. Should you require a reference Frau Wiebke Pütz, who teaches business administration theory and English at Heidelberg Vocational Training College, will be pleased to provide you with any information you may need.

I look forward to hearing from you at your earliest convenience.

Yours sincerely

Rita Räumschüssel

Rita Räumschüssel (Ms)

<u>Encs:</u>
CV
Certificates

Notes:

1. The sender's address is written in the top right-hand corner. The sender's name is *not* normally written at the top of the page.
2. The date can be written under the sender's address or above the inside address
3. "Your ref." can be included above the inside address on the same level as the date.
4. The sender's name (Rita Räumschüssel) is clearly written after the signature. A woman can add how she wishes to be addressed by adding (Miss), (Mrs) or (Ms) after her name.